*At 5:00 p.m. Allan Legere finally took his seat. His ankle chain was bolted to the courtroom floor. Two guards sat on each side, another sat by the door. Legere glanced around the room, his face blank.*

*The jurors — six women and five men — looked tired as they entered the courtroom, their shoulders slumped, their faces slack. Not one looked at Legere.*

*Gerald Pugh, the court clerk, called out the jurors' names, then asked: "Have you reached a verdict?"*

*"Yes, we have," said foreman Letitia Lancaster. Everyone in the courtroom leaned forward. Everyone, that is, except Allan Joseph Legere ...*

**Terror's End** offers the fullest, definitive account of the sensational, ground-breaking trial of convicted murderer Allan Legere and the events leading up to it. Here's the story that shocked a nation and terrified a province — from Legere's daring daylight escape from police custody in May 1989 to his re-capture seven months later; from the savage slayings — including the death of an elderly Catholic priest — that marked Legere's escape to the desperate police search and Legere's eventual conviction on four counts of first-degree murder in November 1991.

Paced like a novel, packed with information, **Terror's End** moves the reader from the dark woods of New Brunswick to the panicked townsites along the Miramichi River, from crowded courtooms to sophisticated forensic laboratories. Written by three veteran New Brunswick journalists, it's sure to stand as a classic of Canadian true crime writing.

RICK MACLEAN  ANDRÉ VENIOT

SHAUN WATERS

# Terror's End
## *Allan Legere on Trial*

M&S

An M&S Paperback Original from
McClelland & Stewart Inc.
*The Canadian Publishers*

An M&S Paperback Original from
McClelland & Stewart Inc.

First printing July 1992

**Canadian Cataloguing in Publication Data**

MacLean, Rick, 1957–
Terror's end: Allan Legere on trial

"An M&S paperback"
ISBN 0-7710-5595-1

1. Legere, Allan, 1948–     2. Murder – New
Brunswick – Miramichi River Region.  3.  Trials (Murder)
– New Brunswick.  I.  Veniot, André, 1950–
II.  Waters, Shaun, 1959–     III.  Title.

HV6535.C32N32 1992   364.1′523 ′0971521   C92-094761-1

Front cover photo: Canapress/Andrew Vaughan
Typesetting by M&S, Toronto
Printed and bound in Canada

McClelland & Stewart Inc.
*The Canadian Publishers*
481 University Avenue
Toronto, Ontario
M5G 2E9

To our wives and families, with love.

While portions of the dialogue in this book are taken directly from court transcripts, there are instances in which it has been reconstructed on the basis of the authors' interviews with relevant individuals or published/broadcast media reports. In addition, some scenes have been recreated using interviews, media stories and reports from police and legal authorities as the basis.

# Contents

Acknowledgements 9

Prologue 11

PART ONE

1. Escalating Violence 19
2. Murder 35
3. On Trial 53
4. On the Stand 67
5. Plotting Escape 84
6. Back Home 95

PART TWO

7. The First Attack 99
8. The Second Attack 115
9. Keeping Secrets 130
10. The Third Attack 146
11. Where Is He? 158
12. Profile of a Serial Killer 174
13. Hostages to Fear 182
14. Capture 188
15. In Custody 211

PART THREE

16. A Sense of Theatre                        233
17. Pieces of the Jigsaw                       260
18. DNA on Trial                               292
19. The Verdict                                313
20. An Interview with Allan Legere             328
21. Postscripts                                346

# Acknowledgements

This book could not have been written without the help of many people, especially those who spoke with us on the condition of anonymity.

Help provided by Newcastle librarian Catherine Martin and Moncton *Times and Transcript* librarian Nola O'Brien made this work much easier.

A number of people were kind enough to read parts of the manuscript and offer their comments. Editor James Adams of McClelland & Stewart did a splendid job of helping us whip the work into shape.

A number of books were helpful in preparing this work: *Serial Murderers and their Victims* by Eric W. Hickey (Brooks/Cole, 1991); *Women Who Love Men Who Kill* by Sheila Isenberg (Simon and Schuster, 1991); *The Serial Killers: A Study of the Psychology of Violence* by Colin Wilson and Donald Seaman (Carol Publishing Group); *Hunting Humans: The Rise of the Modern Multiple Murderer* by Elliott Leyton (McClelland & Stewart, 1986); *Why They Killed: The Secret Motivations of America's Most Notorious Killers* by Jean F. Blashfield (Popular Library, 1990), *The Confessions of Henry Lee Lucas: The True Story of America's Most Notorious Serial Murderer* by Mike Cox, (Pocket Star Books, 1991); *The Blooding: The True Story of the Narborough Village Murders* by Joseph Wambaugh (Perigold

Press, 1989); *Mass Murder: America's Growing Menace* by Jack Levin and James Alan Fox (Berkeley Book, 1991); *Buried Dreams: Inside the Mind of a Serial Killer* by Tim Cahill with Russ Ewing, (Bantam Books, 1986); *Jack the Ripper: The Complete Casebook* by Donald Rumbelow (Berkley Books, 1990); *Ted Bundy: Conversations with a Killer* by Stephen G. Michaud and Hugh Aynesworth (Signet, 1989); *Written in Blood: A History of Forensic Detection* by Colin Wilson (Grafton, 1990).

Any errors or omissions in this work are, of course, solely the responsibility of the authors.

# Prologue

THE evening of November 3, 1991. It was unusually warm. Fog rising off the Saint John River worked its way up the bank towards the small courthouse on the hill in Burton, New Brunswick.

The door to Courtroom 1 rattled, then swung open. "Okay, put'em through the machine," deputy sheriff Les Sears told the guards. "We're going back in shortly." He motioned the crowd in the waiting area toward the airport style metal detector. He paused to kick a wooden wedge in place under the door to keep it open.

After thirteen hours of deliberations spread over two days, the jury had reached its verdict in the murder case against 43-year-old Allan Joseph Legere, charged with killing four people in his native Miramichi area after he escaped from prison where he was serving a life sentence for murder.

The seven-month hunt in 1989 to capture the man dubbed the "Madman of the Miramichi" had created headlines across Canada, the United States and as far away as Paris. The hunt had involved more than one hundred police officers, tracking dogs, a helicopter using heat-seeking equipment, and a special team of officers equipped with scopes designed to enhance night vision. Ten weeks of riveting, sometimes heart-rending courtroom testimony

had been a sensation as the Crown tried to prove that
Legere was a serial killer intent on terrorizing the region
where he had grown up.

The jurors had spent months looking at dozens of exhibits and listening to close to 250 witnesses describe the killings: May 28, 1989 – elderly shopkeeper Annie Flam
beaten, her charred body found half-clothed in the burning
remains of her downtown Chatham home, her jaw shattered by a blow to the face; October 13, 1989 – sisters Linda
and Donna Daughney of Newcastle beaten beyond recogni-
tion and sexually assaulted in their home, then left to die in
the ensuing fire; November 15, 1989 – Father James Smith,
tortured for hours in his rectory, beaten so viciously half his
ribs were broken.

The senior Crown prosecutor in the case, Tony Allman,
was in the washroom when he heard the commotion. He
shoved open the door and headed down the hall to the small
modern courtroom. Inside that windowless room were
eight benches, four to a side, capable of holding a total of
about seventy people. Red carpeting covered the floor. The
jury box to the judge's right contained a dozen padded gray
chairs. The prisoner's dock on the judge's left was a box
with a long bench.

Outside, reporters from around the country awaiting the
verdict had jammed the long, narrow waiting room with its
uncomfortable, straight-backed pine benches. The journalists jumped to their feet, scrambled to pack up blankets,
board games, playing cards and lap-top computers.

"I was wondering what was going to come first, our turn
or the verdict," joked veteran bailiff George Melvin, looking at the trivia game he had been on the verge of losing.
Quickly, he reverted to official form, shooing reporters and
spectators alike into an impatient line-up behind the metal
detector. "Handbags on the table please. Change out of
your pockets."

RCMP officers with walkie-talkies in their hands worked
their way down the corridor towards the courtroom, test-

ing doors on each side of the hallway to ensure they were locked.

Reporters with cellular phones pulled them from bags and carrying cases. Those without made a mental note to grab seats near the back of the courtroom so they could dash to the lone pay phone once the verdict was announced. A cameraman stood off to one side, celebrating quietly: he'd won $80 in a pool set up by police officers, court officials and reporters who had bet on when the jury would return.

The courtroom filled quickly with police and spectators sitting on the benches on the right side of the aisle. Sitting in the first three rows of benches on the left, reporters draped microphones and tape recorders over the five-foot high wood-and-glass partition separating them from the Crown prosecutors and jury.

The three prosecutors entered, wearing their long, black robes and starched white shirts with winged collars. Allman took his customary seat at the prosecution table, which faced the judge. On the other side of the aisle was the table reserved for defence lawyer Weldon Furlotte, in front of the benches taken up by police officers and spectators.

Allman's mind seemed blank, which surprised him, but he knew he had done everything possible. A pianist and lover of Mozart who tried to make time to play his music for a half-hour each evening when at home, Allman had managed to stay calm throughout the trial. At times he'd had to restrain his more emotional colleagues, grabbing the backs of their gowns to prevent them from jumping up to protest Furlotte's tactics.

Beside Allman, in the middle, sat Graham Sleeth, his chair pulled back slightly from the table. His square, wire-rimmed glasses slid down his nose yet again. At 44, born in Montreal and fluently bilingual, he was known for his encyclopedic knowledge of the law and a dry wit capable of deflating opponents. A brilliant student who learned to read at age three and to write before he started school, he

had earned his first university degree, in arts, at age 16 from
Stanstead College in Quebéc. He graduated from the University of New Brunswick law school in 1968 at age 20. An
aviation enthusiast who enjoys building model war planes
in his spare time, he had devoted countless hours to prepare
this case.

Jack Walsh, assigned to convince the jury to accept the
new technology called DNA fingerprinting, took his seat
nearest the jury. In the weeks previous Walsh's scowls and
smiles had often given away the emotions he'd fought to
control. For this Miramichi native, anything less than four
convictions for first-degree murder would be considered a
defeat. Fidgeting, still replaying parts of the trial, the prosecutor wondered if he should have done anything differently. He stared at the vacant prisoner's box and wished
desperately for a plug of chewing tobacco, a habit picked up
during the trial.

Weldon Furlotte rushed into the courtroom, his long,
gray hair combed forward in a cut reminiscent of The Bea-
tles in their heyday. An electrician for twenty-two years
and a lawyer for seven, he had taken on a client shunned by
every other criminal lawyer in the province. He'd just had
yet another stormy meeting with his client, and he was
angry.

"All rise," said court clerk Gerald Pugh.

Mr. Justice David Dickson of the Court of Queen's
Bench entered the courtroom. The 72-year-old judge looked
fresh despite the ordeal of overseeing one of the longest,
most expensive, and most closely followed legal jousts in
New Brunswick history. He nodded to the lawyers and took
his seat overlooking the rest of the court. He turned and
stared at the side door through which Allan Legere was
expected to enter.

The court stenographer sat in her place at the table
below the judge, checking and rechecking her machine.
Deputy sheriff Sears stood to the judge's right, half-turned
toward the door through which the jury would enter once

Legere was in his seat. Gerald Pugh stood beside the stenographer, silently rehearsing the legal preamble he would recite to the jury. The judge had it written down for him. "Read each one out clearly and don't stop whatever you do," Dickson had warned him that afternoon.

Five minutes passed. Ten minutes. Still no Legere. The courtroom was silent. Everyone stared at the door. Where was he? Dickson knew, so did Furlotte: Allan Legere was refusing to leave the holding cell across the hall.

Minutes earlier, Legere had backed into a corner and snapped at Furlotte. "Tell the judge I'm not going in there. You won't take me against my will."

Faced with lack of co-operation from his client, Furlotte had hurried into Dickson's chambers to parley. "There's going to be trouble, M'Lord," Furlotte warned. "I can't change his mind." Legere preferred to watch the proceedings on the closed-circuit television set up outside the cell. Would that be all right?

Furious, the six-foot-two-inch judge looked down at the lawyer. "There's no bargaining, Mr. Furlotte. He's coming in. We'll give him ten minutes." Dickson then turned to Pugh, who had arrived for some last-minute instructions, and ordered him to reinforce Legere's guards. Pugh rounded up four officers: the biggest Mountie in the building, a deputy sheriff built like a linebacker, and a pair of tough francophone cops.

"He's coming one way or the other," Dickson had warned before returning to the courtroom. "Put chains on his hands and feet. If we have to, I want him carried out of that cell. Chain him to the floor in the court and if he starts yelling, we'll let him do it for a few minutes and take him out again. We'll keep doing it and I think he'll probably get tired."

Meanwhile, outside the holding cell, police officers were relaying Dickson's decision. "Judge says you have to come in, Allan."

Legere looked up and grinned. "Well," he finally said,

"you guys have been pretty good to me all along in this trial. This is how it has to be, I guess. I don't think it would be right for you to go into court with your shirts ripped and blood all over you."

"We have to put the handcuffs on you, Allan."

This upset Legere. They had chained his ankles to the floor during the trial, but had never forced him to wear handcuffs in front of the jury. He insisted they let him wear his blue sports coat so he could tug the sleeves down, hiding the cuffs.

"Please don't put the belt on me," he pleaded as an officer approached him, the waist chain in his hands. The officers relented.

At 5:00 p.m. Legere finally took his seat. His ankle chain was bolted to the courtroom floor. Two guards sat on each side, another sat by the door. Legere glanced around the room, his face blank.

The jurors – six women and five men – looked tired as they entered the courtroom, their shoulders slumped, their faces slack. Not one looked at Legere.

Pugh called out their names, then asked: "Have you reached a verdict?"

"Yes, we have," said foreman Patricia Lancaster. Everyone in the courtroom leaned forward. Everyone, that is, except Allan Joseph Legere.

# PART ONE

# ONE

# Escalating Violence

Aʟʟᴀɴ Legere's journey to the Burton courthouse began more than forty years earlier. He was born at home on February 13, 1948 – Friday the 13th – in Chatham Head, next to the Miramichi River. Years later, fascinated by numbers and their significance, Legere would embellish the story, telling people he weighed thirteen pounds at birth. The youngest of four children, he had an older brother Freddy and two sisters.

Chatham Head was a difficult place for children growing up in the 1940s and 1950s. Although it was just across the Morrissy Bridge from Newcastle, it was considered a ghetto by other Miramichiers. People from Chatham Head were looked down on as rough and poor, socially inferior. The section of Chatham Head called Verdun was considered the bottom of the barrel. A ramshackle collection of houses jammed onto a square of land next to the bridge, the tiny community had a reputation for being a dangerous place at night. Children from there were taunted by their classmates, who pronounced the word *Vurd-n* and as if it was unclean.

"We were at the bottom and yet there were places poorer than us," recalled a woman who went to school with Legere. "We knew some of the teachers wanted to leave as fast as they could. The kids from Chatham Head were looked down upon and I always thought it was discrimination."

Legere's family life didn't make it any easier. His mother, Louise, had married Vince Legere in the 1930s. She described her husband as "the most twisted, vicious person I knew." She claims she sent him packing to his sister and mother in Minto in 1945 so he could find work. He never came back. A domineering woman, unafraid to speak her mind, and struggling to make ends meet, Louise took in boarders to supplement her income. One of them, Leonard Comeau, moved in and fathered Legere before moving on.

A photograph of Legere from September, 1955 shows the seven-year-old standing with his classmates. A cute boy with a pixie-like face, he stood out. He was the only one in the photo not standing prim and erect, not looking straight ahead or trying to smile for the camera. Neatly dressed in a long-sleeved shirt and wearing suspenders, he has his head turned slightly to the right and down. His distinctively pale blue eyes eyes peek at the camera from beneath a shock of dark hair falling forward over his face. Instead of a smile, there is an engaging smirk.

Tragedy struck the family when Allan was just nine. His older brother Freddy, a soldier, was run down while he and two friends were walking three abreast one night. They'd just crossed the bridge when a car roared up from behind and hit them, killing Freddy and one of the others. Years later, the family would continue to insist the case was covered up because they didn't have the money to push for justice. To this day, Legere puts quotation marks around the word "accident" when he refers to the episode.

Descriptions of Allan Legere from the period vary. A childhood acquaintance remembers him as a bright student. "Allan should have been sitting in Parliament today, not running away." A former teacher thought of him as a good boy, never saucy. She once gave him $2 to permit him to take the high school entrance exam in nearby Newcastle after discovering him alone at school because he didn't have the money. He ran all the way to Newcastle, more than a mile away, and scored 75 per cent.

A friend remembers him as a boy who was unfailingly polite. "He had the cutest fleck of black hair and he was so shy and polite, always yes ma'am, yes sir. Oh, sometimes he could be a bully, pulling girls' hats off and throwing them and stuff. But all the little boys were like that."

Another friend never forgot his ability to draw. "He was so good, he could draw anything."

When he picked up the mail for his mother, he used to tease the woman working at a local store, saying he could steal anything in the store if he wanted and she would never know. "He never did though," she added.

Others have less fond memories. "He was a bad little bastard," said a woman who grew up with him. "He was always throwing stones. You'd be out on the street, he'd wave and smile at you and as soon as your back was turned, he'd throw stones at you."

Whatever his behavior, he was a difficult youngster to miss, the way he like to walk around with his chest stuck out like a bantam rooster. He was training to be a boxer, he explained. Legere began a life-long passion for pumping iron while at Harkins Junior High in Newcastle. He worked out at least three times a week prior to class, rising early and walking to school to arrive at 7:45. Since there was no one to show him what to do, he devised a training system on his own, using whatever books he could find as guidance. "He was always alone, but he didn't mind asking for help," a teacher recalls.

Legere first ran into trouble in the early 1960s. He became a Peeping Tom – a habit he blamed on the crowded conditions of the house, which had him sleeping with his sisters until he was 12. The sight of them undressing for bed had started him masturbating. When he was 16, he said a neighbourhood girl began giving him voluntary undressing exhibitions through the window and encouraged him and other boys to watch. Soon after, he attempted to have sex with a girl he'd known for years, but when he found he couldn't get an erection, she made fun of him. Legere said he wasn't able to achieve an orgasm for a year afterwards.

His grades deteriorated and he failed Grade 9. A classmate, though, remembers him as a bright student, especially in mathematics. Good looking, he had piercing blue eyes and a foul mouth. He avoided talking about his family, preferring instead to try to shock fellow students with remarks like "What a set on her!" when talking about girls in his class. Another classmate remembered him pulling the blouse off one girl and saying, "You want to show it, show it!"

Occasionally, he would take his shirt off at school to show off the scars he claimed he got from fighting. His classmates doubted his braggadocio. "We always wondered if they were self-inflicted," said one. Other times he'd arrive with the skin torn off his knuckles, the result of punching a board wrapped in rope, he'd say.

He left home and eventually was convicted of theft, fined $15 and jailed for fifteen days. His mother blamed it on his desire to be perfect. He always tried too hard to be everything, wanted too much to be like everyone else, she said. Two years later, he was convicted of theft over $50 and given an eighteen month sentence. He bounced from job to job, working as a lumberjack for a while, later finding work as a longshoreman. He loved fast cars and at one point owned a 429 Ford Torino capable of doing wheelies when he hit the gas going up a hill.

At 18, he moved to North Bay, Ontario where he became a machinist. He lived there for four years, marrying a psychiatric attendant when he was 20. It was an unhappy marriage. Even though they eventually had two children, a girl, Natasha, and a boy, Dean, Legere seemed unable to settle down.

He moved back to the Miramichi in the early 1970s and found work at the pulp mill in Nelson-Miramichi, but he soon ran into trouble with the law. In the fall of 1972 he was convicted of three counts of possession of stolen property and sentenced to fourteen months in jail.

His restlessness made it difficult for him to adapt to life in jail. His personality deteriorated. Although he remained polite and co-operative, he complained about being stupid and unable to do simple things. He admitted he had emotional problems, but claimed he had no control over them. He was depressed much of the time and seemed to spend most of his waking hours concocting a rich fantasy life.

At the same time, his ability to read and react to the feelings of others was heightened, as were his collection of obsessions and phobias. He was preoccupied by religion and the idea of good and evil. According to one psychology expert, he displayed all the signs of a sociopath – someone who lacks a conscience and cares only about what makes him feel good.

After Legere was paroled in July 1973, a union official managed to get him back his job at the mill. Rather than being grateful, Legere was furious at the way he felt he was treated and quit. "The dogs gave me labour work and a greenhorn took my machinist position," he would later charge.

Out of work, his compulsion for watching women undress deepened. In fact, he preferred watching women undress to the actual act of sexual intercourse. Not content with watching through windows, he began to break into houses to look at women asleep in their beds. He always stole something to ensure people would think it was a "normal" burglary.

Still married at this time, Legere and his wife wanted a second child but he was convinced his wife Marilyn's inability to conceive was the result of sterility on his part. He began sleeping with other women and masturbating often. He found achieving an orgasm with a woman difficult: it required about ten minutes of intense concentration and the woman had to remain very quiet. (Legere and his

wife did eventually have another child, born in the
mid-1970s.)

His pride in his body, sculpted by years of weightlifting,
became obsessive. In 1972, when RCMP Constable Vince
Poissonnier managed to stop him following a car chase,
Legere yelled, "Don't touch my body! Don't touch my
body! Do you think my body is beautiful?"

He managed to find work as a longshoreman, but it
didn't last. George (not his real name) was working with
Legere the day he got into a fight with another man working
the boats. They were evenly matched until Legere knocked
the man down and grabbed a peavey, the long wooden pole
with a heavy metal tip and hook that loggers then used to
snare logs. "Allan was going to drive that peavey into him
when three of us jumped him. He would've killed that fellow for sure." The incident resulted in Legere being thrown
out of the union.

His mind polarized. He ignored his thefts and dwelled
instead on every wrong, imagined or real, done to him. "Me
pay for anything?" he would later sneer, "I've been paying
all my life." His mother blamed his wife, accusing her of
being too demanding.

By the mid-1970s, his behaviour grew increasingly
bizarre. He would attempt to dominate any conversation,
talking incessantly, changing the subject constantly. He
liked to be a "good man," he said. "I do not like to hurt anybody." He was deeply interested in the Bible and spent
hours reading it, along with books on satanism and
demonology. He claimed he wasn't a smoker or drinker, but
admitted taking drugs so he could feel happy and save the
world.

Once he walked into a Baptist church during Sunday service wearing nothing but cutoff jeans. He told the stunned
worshippers they were all going to hell because he was
Jesus Christ and they could not get to heaven but through
him.

Drugs and alcohol fueled his temper. When his mother's home burned down and arson was cited as a possible cause, he decided to exact revenge on the man he suspected of doing it. Wearing a mask, Legere jumped the man one night in Chatham Head and beat him so badly that after, when the man staggered to a nearby house for help, the neighbour didn't recognize him. Shortly afterwards, when Legere discovered the man truly wasn't responsible, he apologized to him.

A friend of Legere's said that when Legere was straight, he was a different person. "He had a good heart in him. If you were stuck on the side of the road and your car broke down and it was raining, he'd stop and help you out, even if he didn't know you. He wouldn't leave anybody stuck."

For all the violence that seemed to surround Legere, he was never suspected of murder – until, that is, police found the mutilated body of 56-year-old Beatrice Redmond outside the door of her Chatham Head home on March 24, 1974. She had been stabbed more than eighty times, yet there was no sign of blood. Police believed she had been killed after attending evening mass at the Blessed Virgin Mary Roman Catholic Church just around the corner, then dragged to her home. Her coat, purse and hat had disappeared. Neither her mother, who lived with her, nor the family living downstairs, had heard anything. Her husband was visiting relatives.

Legere was one of the first people picked up for questioning. Police interrogated him for eighteen hours. The questioning was so long and detailed that one police officer looking through a one-way window said later *he* was ready to confess to the murder just to get it over with. Stymied by Legere's ability to talk non-stop without incriminating himself, police let him go and the case was never solved.

Legere was also suspected of being involved in the decapitation of a corpse in a crypt at a cemetery. The head was dropped on a man's doorstep. Later an acquaintance of

Legere's, Owen Swain, was found guilty of the crime and sentenced to three years.

In the meantime, Legere became the manager of the Zodiac Club in Chatham, a place notorious for fights, even shootings in the parking lot. His reputation as a fighter preceded him. "I seen him fighting a few times," recalls a friend. "When he fights, he fights seriously. He'd tear a guy's eye out if he had to. He doesn't care. He believes in surviving. When it comes to fighting, he's a vicious fighter. He doesn't like to lose. He fought with a lot of people and he could fight, but he was dirty. He'd hit you from behind, hit you whichever way he could. He believes in winning. He didn't like to lose."

Legere lost his job at the Zodiac Club in April 1978 after he forced his way into the sound booth of the disco and forcibly kissed the young woman working as disc jockey. When she resisted, he grabbed her between her legs with one hand while ripping her sweater and tearing at her bra with the other. He was sentenced to thirty days in jail. He wrote the woman a letter of apology, saying he'd been taking drugs.

On another occasion when another woman refused to dance with him, he spit in her face. In a third incident, he ordered a woman to dance with him. When she refused, he pulled her onto the floor, grabbed her by the crotch, twirled her around and said, "Dance when I say dance."

Legere wrote a letter to a local paper in Chatham. He talked about the world as he saw it. It is composed of two kinds of people, he said, the pirates and the sheep. The sheep live inside the law and do what they're told, enjoying the safety they feel that brings. The pirates understand what's happening and refuse to go along. They live outside the law, on the risky edge of society. Most people are sheep. Few are destined to be pirates. Legere said he preferred piracy to dutiful obedience.

Drugs released those pent-up feelings. A friend recalled:

"He'd dream he was a superpower with the attitude that 'I can do what I want to do.' Once he got into the drugs he didn't care what he done. He'd break-and-enter more, just got crazy."

He would brag about his illegal exploits, according to an acquaintance. "He used to break into the Morada Motel (in Chatham) especially. He used to go in through a window and feel women up while they were sleeping beside their husbands. 'That's how slick I am,' he said. 'I can do it.'"

A friend woke up one night to find him standing next to his bed, a knife in his hand. Asked what he was doing there, Legere just laughed at how easy it had been to break in through a basement window and creep past the people sleeping in the other rooms. Satisfied that he'd made his point, he left.

By this time Legere's previous mental problems – his propensity to be depressed, his incipient paranoid schizophrenia – seemed to have disappeared. Yet he was unquestionably a dangerous man. Unable, or unwilling, to consider the effects of his actions, he would make up his own versions of history to explain away his crimes. His lying became more accomplished and when he got caught for an assault or a break-and-enter, he seemed genuinely surprised.

Legere's marriage finally broke up in 1978. Marilyn moved to Ottawa, taking with her their children, Dean and Natasha. He described the marriage as suffocating. "The biggest mistake of my life. I will never get married again." He later broke that vow and married Donna Clouston O'Toole. His mother liked her even less than Marilyn, calling her a mixed-up girl who had already been married a couple of times.

His name was attached to murder for a second time in 1979 when Nicholas Duguay of Chatham Head was found murdered in his shack. In an attack reminiscent of the Redmond killing, Duguay had been hacked to death, struck sixty-seven times with an axe. Police soon arrested a teenager, Robbie Cunningham, and charged him with the murder. Just hours before the killing, Cunningham had been picked up by police on another charge, photographed and released. Bloody clothing found near the Duguay home matched the clothing Cunningham wore in the police photo. He was convicted of murder, but won a new trial. In 1981, he was convicted of the lesser charge of manslaughter and sentenced to twelve years after the jury decided he had been too stoned on LSD at the time of the attack to realize what he had been doing. Cunningham always maintained his innocence and said Allan Legere was the killer. In turn, Legere claimed Cunningham had killed Redmond.

Legere had his own problems with the law in 1979. That fall, he nearly cut off a man's cheek during a fight after he drove a broken beer bottle into the man's face and twisted it. Legere had been drinking in a Chatham club, the RCAF 254 Wing, and grabbed a beer belonging to another man at the bar. The man snatched it back. Legere broke a glass and charged. An off-duty policeman grabbed a pool cue and smashed it across Legere's face, breaking his jaw. Later, at the police station, Legere pulled a knife on one of the officers.

Convicted of possessing a weapon dangerous to the public peace, Legere spoke on his own behalf at his appeal. In a brilliant, forty-five minute presentation, he described how the system had abused him, how the community blamed him for all the crimes on the Miramichi, how they hated him and were out to get him. The court sentenced Legere to twenty-four months, far less than what the Crown wanted.

Fred Ferguson was the Crown prosecutor handling the case. When the court recessed that day, the clerk of the court – who had the ear of the judges – came up to him. "You know, that guy gave some kind of speech. It was very effective, because I understand the sentence the court handed out was not the one they had in mind when they came in here this morning."

Chatham police chief Dan Allen knew Legere's reputation for violence and burglary – and his ability to avoid a long prison term. "A lone man is hard to get. Nobody to talk on him. Nobody to tell stories, and only himself knows what he's achieved and what he hasn't. He was good. I hate to give him credit for anything. But to give the devil his due, he was the best I ever run up against, and I've run up against a lot of criminals."

Legere didn't return to the Miramichi when he got out of jail. Instead, he moved south to Moncton. Sporting a ponytail, he went to auctions in the city's East End to get furniture for the modest apartment he shared with his wife, Donna. Yet even in Moncton, trouble was never far away: one night, while he was standing by a canteen at the back of a hall, some local toughs moved in front of him to block his view. He politely asked them to move. "They thought he was an easy punching bag," recalled an eyewitness. "One of the toughs gave Allan a sucker punch in the nose. Worst mistake he made. Next thing you know, Allan knocked him out cold."

Eventually, the Legeres moved out of the apartment. He and Donna bought a mobile home in the city's West End. As with his first marriage, it was not a happy union. Legere would beat Donna, blackening her eyes and on one occasion breaking her ribs.

During the summer of 1982, there were a series of break-and-enters in the city. In one case, a man crept into the home of a United Church minister. He walked into a bedroom and started to cut off the underwear of a still-sleeping woman who, as it turned out, was to be married the next day. The woman awoke and screamed. Her attacker crashed through a closed window and disappeared. The break-ins, in the meantime, continued all summer. Police tried to track the assailant, but he always managed to elude their dogs.

Finally, early on the morning of August 19, police got a break. Dr. Marcel Charlebois was awakened by a noise in his house. He walked into the hallway and saw a man standing there. As Charlebois turned to call police, the man crashed through a second-storey window, landing on the ground fifteen feet below, still clutching some stolen jewelry.

A police dog picked up a trail leading from the back yard into woods, but it couldn't run the man down. About two hours later in another part of the city, police spotted a man who turned out to be Allan Legere coming out of the woods. He bolted when told to stop. In the ensuing chase, two officers spotted Legere throwing something away.

A few minutes later, Corporal Ross Hickey and Constable Robert Hart knocked on the door of Legere's trailer. Nearby police had found a wallet stolen during a burglary hours earlier. Legere denied having anything to do with the thefts and refused to go to the police station to talk about it.

Ordered to come out, or face tear gas, Legere crawled out a small rear window and fled. Police charged after him. A shot rang out and Legere fell wounded, shot in the left shoulder. Later, a search of Legere's trailer turned up more stolen property. Legere, then 34, faced two counts of break-and-enter.

In August 1983, during his jury trial, two witnesses couldn't be there to testify. As a result, the Crown wanted to read into the court record the witnesses' evidence from the preliminary hearing. Legere didn't want that. At the same time, he also opposed an adjournment to allow the witnesses an opportunity to show up.

The judge had barely announced a four-day adjournment when Legere arose, pulled out a hidden fragment of razor and raked it across his left wrist. "That's what I think of this," shouted Legere at the judge and jury, waving his arm in the air, sending blood flying across the courtroom. The judge pounded on his desk with his gavel. Jurors screamed. The court stenographer bolted from the room.

Legere was taken to nearby Dr. Georges L. Dumont Hospital where a doctor found the cuts were only deep enough to draw blood. As a result, Legere did not have to stay in hospital. Two days later, Legere was back in court, his wrists bandaged. He soon realized he'd made a mistake in blocking use of evidence from the preliminary hearing. Had he allowed that testimony, the court would have heard from just Dr. Charlebois' wife. The delay allowed the husband to take the stand.

When Doctor Charlebois testified he was asked how he could be so certain that it was Legere in his house that night.

"I'll never forget those eyes," he replied.

When Legere took the stand in his own defence, he denied having anything to do with the Charlebois break-in. In fact, he had been jogging in the woods near his home earlier that day and noticed some "junk jewelry." He picked it up and continued running, but panicked when an "unfamiliar" car pulled up. Fearful that he might be suspected of theft, he ran, stopping only long enough to throw away the jewelry.

He accused the police and provincial justice department of cooking up the theft charges as part of a conspiracy to get him. They had also blocked his efforts to hire a local lawyer, he declared. "It's just about like Russia," he testified. "Now I know how Lech Walesa feels."

He concluded by warning that the case was not over because he intended to sue the city over the shooting.

In his summation, Crown prosecutor Tony Allman mocked Legere's story, calling it a "remarkable coincidence" that two athletic men happened to run past the Charlebois home that day. Legere's story was a "tissue of lies and falsehoods."

The jury found him guilty in the Charlebois case, but not guilty in a second break. Legere pleaded guilty to two other charges of possession of stolen goods.

There was a chance the accused might straighten out, the judge said when he sentenced Legere to three years imprisonment. He noted that despite his long record,

Legere had never spent any time in a federal prison. With that, he sent Legere to the imposing maximum-security prison in the nearby village of Dorchester.

Later, Legere was moved to the medium-security institution in Springhill, Nova Scotia. There he fought with black inmates and tried to force them to pay him protection money. After two months, he was moved back to Dorchester.

In 1985, Legere wrote to the parole board asking to be released: "Since crime does not pay, the main plan is to live honestly with my daughter and wife. As of yet, we have no steady job, but since we have a car will seek work of any type. I've approximately $2400 in my savings, and I may purchase with permission a few old vehicles to repair, and resell since I can do autobody repair. I sold cars for a General Motors firm in Ottawa, 1979. I never plan to return to any jails ever again. I'm 36 years old, much too wise in age to be wasting anymore years in these places, terrible places. I do not smoke or drink. Haven't even a beer since July 1979. And as my wife can verify not only this, but I don't bother with drugs. Therefore any restrictions placed upon will be no burden at all since I've learned my lesson. Wife and I have own mobile home. Later move it out of the country. My mother is always by my side in case of need. My word is good and I don't lie."

No one else shared his opinion. The parole board considered him dangerous and a likely recidivist. Police, for their part, considered Legere a psychopath who would inevitably seriously hurt or kill someone. His wife wrote a letter to the board saying, "I do not have any idea if he has been approved for parole in the near future. I would appreciate if I can be advised. As I've said before it would be very risky for me not to know he is free." Although Louise Legere said her son could stay in her small apartment until he got on his feet, she nonetheless considered him too old to change his ways.

Despite the warnings, the board had no legal choice.

Mandatory supervision regulations required that Legere be released on parole after serving two-thirds of his sentence. Upon Legere's parole, a frightened Donna Legere fled Moncton after selling his car and the mobile home. This infuriated Legere and he vowed to sue her.

The day of his release, Legere returned to the Miramichi and visited Chatham police chief Dan Allen at his home. Things would be different this time, he vowed. "I want to go straight and I'll never bother your town again," he told Allen. The chief, however, dismissed Legere's promises. "No matter where you do something," he warned Legere, "I'll let police know."

Out of work, Legere started spending time at a gym in downtown Newcastle. Called the Fitness Warehouse, it was used by locals who found the site on the second floor of an old, red brick building overlooking the town square convenient for lunch-time workouts.

Among the customers were Donna Daughney and her sister Linda. Donna was in her early forties, Linda her late thirties. The gym was just a five-minute walk from their downtown Newcastle home, so they decided to join.

There was talk that Allan Legere was more than a little interested in the sisters, both of whom were single. Considered good-looking, with dark hair and distinctive blue eyes, he'd built a powerful torso through years of bodybuilding in and out of prison. He worked out now in the afternoons, often coming to the Fitness Warehouse four or five times a week.

If the Daughney sisters were at the gym when Legere was there, he would sometimes offer to help them with their weight training. Legere made no secret of his interest in Donna. "Legere used to help Donna Daughney with exercises," said gym employee Ken Black. "He was fantasizing about her, used to say, 'Take a look at her ass. She's built for comfort.'"

Gym member Joseph Hawkes also heard Legere talk about the sisters. "Legere showed quite an interest in

Donna, had the hots for her. She'd be on the exercise bench with her legs up and Legere would say, 'Wouldn't you like to chew the ass off that? Boy, wouldn't you like to bury your face in that?' He told me he'd like to fuck Donna, but first he'd have to get the little one out of the way."

## TWO

# Murder

JUNE 21, 1986. 9:30 p.m.

In Black River Bridge, a rural area about twenty miles east of Chatham, John and Mary Glendenning were closing the small general store they'd opened in 1953. As always, they tidied up and filled the pop machine before locking the door and walking across the yard to their home. It was a square, two-storey house with an enclosed verandah overlooking the front yard, and sat, with the store, in a field with woods on one side, houses on the other.

John, 66, was a big man, bald, just under six feet tall, and muscular with a barrel chest. Mary, 61, kept the house meticulously clean. The cleaning lady had been in just the day before to tidy up.

Mary sat in her rocking chair in the kitchen. John came in a few minutes later. "We decided to have a lunch. We had jam, crackers and cookies. We talked for a few minutes and John called his brother in Napan, Kenneth Glendenning. He also made a call to a cousin in Bathurst. By then, it was after ten o'clock."

Neighbour Harry Watling was home watching a baseball game on television when the telephone rang. It was his wife. She was in nearby St. Margaret's and wanted a drive home. Watling left the house around 10:30. As he walked to his car he noticed the four, square tail lights of a vehicle parked about 200 feet down a woods road directly across from his house. He thought it was odd, but it was Saturday night and high school graduation time. Probably a teenager parking with his girlfriend. He drove off.

Less than a mile from the Glendenning home, Bud Somers and his wife were celebrating a wedding anniversary with a party at the Black River Recreation Centre. About ten minutes after Watling left to pick up his wife, Adrienne Johnston left the Somers' party to drive to work at the senior citizens' home in Chatham. As she passed Watling's driveway, a car started to pull onto the highway from the dirt road leading into the woods. The car, big and red, stopped abruptly, forcing her to brake and pull around it. Thinking nothing of it, Johnston didn't look in her rearview mirror to see where it was going.

Inside the Glendenning home, Mary and John continued to relax. "I was sitting in my rocking chair finishing my tea," Mary remembered. "The dishes were still on the table. John was inside. He was on the phone, the phone in the dining room. After the last call, he went in and turned on the television in the living room. I was still in the kitchen and going in to tell him something when I hear this desperate crash."

"What the hell is going on?" John yelled.

Three men burst through the front door. One wore a tight-fitting nylon stocking that distorted his face. The second wore a cap pulled over his eyes. The third, clearly older and heavier, hung back at first, staying by the door. The one with the hat clubbed John, using a rock from the flower garden just outside.

"John was bleeding something awful hard," Mary said. "He kind of staggered back and sat on the rug by the couch."

"What do you want?" John cried out. "I'll get it for you. You don't have to beat us around."

The man wearing the nylon came at Mary, shoving her

into the kitchen. "He was very young, not over 20. He pushed me in the chair, put my face down and tied me there." He shoved her from behind as he ran into the dining room and tore the phone off the wall.

Discovering her knots were poorly tied, Mary wriggled free, her eyes fixed on the older man standing in the doorway. He said nothing. She started to walk towards him, but one of the other two men rushed up. "He picked up a rag and tried to gag me and tried to throw me in the closet in the front room. The younger guy, he took my clothes down, took my panties down. He put his hands all over me. John was still bleeding. John was on the floor with the other guy standing over him. The guy hit him. The third guy was still on the porch."

"Leave us alone," John said, begging for their lives. "I'll give you whatever you want." The men didn't want what was in the store. There was a safe in the house and they wanted the money inside. Now.

Mary Glendenning tried to speak, but one of the younger men shouted: "Shut up or I'll cut your ear off." He spoke to the man on the porch, but Mary couldn't make out what he said.

"The safe, where's the safe?" the young guy demanded.

"I'll take you upstairs and open the safe if that's what you want," Mary pleaded. She was untied, but since her glasses were gone, she could barely see. One of the younger men and the man on the porch shoved her up the stairs, leaving the third man still standing over John.

"I went right to the safe to see if I could open it. It was right in our bedroom. When I got hold of the dial I got severely hit on the head with something."

"If you leave me alone, I'll open it for you," she pleaded, glancing at her attacker, then turned back to the safe. "I just touched the dial when I got a more severe smack on the head. I never knew anything after that." Mary Glendenning lost consciousness. When she recovered, "I was in the toilet bowl. I don't know. Then it dawned on me, I had to call

Margaret." Her daughter, Margaret Gibson, lived nearby.

Somehow, Mary managed to get to the upstairs phone. Miraculously, it worked. While the line for the downstairs phone had been cut, her attackers didn't know the upstairs phone was a separate line. At 12.14 a.m. an operator took the call, knew immediately something was horribly wrong, and patched the call through to Rachelle Desroches, who was working at the RCMP's central dispatch in Moncton. Desroches had been with the RCMP just fifteen months. She answered as she always did. "RCMP, GRC."

"Okay," the operator explained, "I have this lady on the line there. Someone broke into her house."

"Oh," Mary groaned, "they near killed us. Come quick."

"They left? You just got home then?" Desroches asked.

"No, I didn't. We've been here, they just about killed us. I bet they killed my husband, get somebody quick."

"Just stay on the line, just a moment."

"Yeah, we're both hurt. I don't know where John is. I'm upstairs, I can't get down."

Using a second line, Desroches called the RCMP detachment in Newcastle. She knew there wasn't much time. Mary seemed to be fading, she could feel it.

"Oh, I'm going to die," Glendenning groaned.

"Just hang on. Did they hurt you?"

"Yeah."

"Did, what did they do to you?"

"They beat me around. They tried to rape me and everything."

Desroches talked to officers in Newcastle a second time. Mary moaned.

"We got three cars going down to help you out," Rachelle said.

Somehow, Mary managed to give Desroches her daughter's number. In the meantime, the dispatcher tried to keep Mary talking.

"Oh, they hurt me awful bad," Mary cried out.

"Oh, I know they did. And we're gonna get them for doing that to you too."

Margaret Gibson was in bed reading when Desroches called. Margaret's husband, Aubrey, had been asleep. The call sent both of them scambling into their truck, and rushing to the Glendenning home.

Aubrey Gibson burst into the house first. Margaret, who used a cane, followed. "It was a mess. Everything was everywhere," Margaret said. The verandah door was closed, but the main door leading inside was shattered, pieces of it everywhere. "We could see blood, or what appeared to be blood, on the floor and walls." There was even blood dripping from the ceiling. Mosquitos buzzed in the warm summer air.

"John! Mary! Where are you?" they shouted. A faint sound came from upstairs. Aubrey bolted up the stairs, Margaret following as best as she could.

"Upstairs it was the same," Margaret said. "Everything was everywhere. There was glass all over the floor. The light had been broken out in the hall. The lighting was not all that good. I put on a light in the bedroom to the left, almost across from where she was sitting."

Aubrey found his mother-in-law slumped in the doorway of the first bedroom on the right.

Margaret was stunned. "If I hadn't known I was going to find my mother there, I wouldn't know it was her. She was badly bruised and swollen. She still had the phone in her hand. She was sitting on the floor."

Margaret gently took the phone out of her mother's hand. Rachelle Desroches was still on the other end. Unable to speak, Margaret handed the phone to her husband.

"Listen," Desroches said, "we've got about six cars headed down there. Is your father okay?"

"We don't know anything yet," Aubrey replied. "We can't find Mr. Glendenning." He hung up.

Margaret tried to comfort her mother. "I pushed back

her hair. It was wet. She colours her hair and I could smell
the colouring on her. We got something and washed her
face and Aubrey got her a drink of water."

Mary Glendenning was bleeding from the nose and
mouth. She was trying to talk, but because she didn't have
her dentures in, it was difficult to understand her. There
also was a scarf tied tightly around her neck. Aubrey Gibson couldn't undo it, so he turned it slightly to loosen its
grip.

At this point, RCMP Constable Gilles Turgeon came
through the door, a .12 gauge shotgun in his hands. He
heard voices and ran up the stairs, where he found Aubrey
and Margaret Gibson with Mary Glendenning. He cut the
scarf from Mary's neck with the jackknife he always carried, then called to ensure the ambulance was coming. He
didn't hold out much hope for Mary. She's dying, he
thought to himself.

They still hadn't found John Glendenning. Turgeon
thought he might have been kidnapped. A few minutes
later, however, Aubrey shouted that he'd found John
upstairs on the floor behind the door in the master bedroom. He was dead, slumped on his left side, covered in
blood. Even the soles of his socks were soaked in it. His
hands had been tied with the electric cord from a digital
clock and his feet were tied with his braces. A light brown
shirt was around his neck, tied at the back.

The imprint of a boot was clearly visible on the right side
of his head. A blood-stained rock the size of a grapefruit lay
partly hidden underneath his head. His face was cut and
scraped from the beating. His nose was broken, as were a
cheek, the right side of his jaw, some toes and fingers. The
shirt around his neck had been tied so tightly it had broken
his Adam's apple, strangling him.

Margaret Gibson went downstairs where a police officer
gave her a sweater. She went outside and sat down on the
step to wait for the ambulance. She looked down, spotted

something on the ground. "I know they were store keys and a knife and rule my father always carries in his pocket."

Dr. Bill MacGillivary met the ambulance at Hôtel Dieu Hospital in Chatham when Mary Glendenning arrived. "I couldn't believe a person could be as badly beaten and still be alive. The whole scalp area was bruised and swollen, everywhere I looked, every part of the body."

A blow had broken her forehead. Her eyes were blackened and puffy, the right eye swollen shut. When MacGillvary managed to gently pry it open, he found a pool of blood.

The doctor examined Glendenning for other injuries. He found a broken nose; a badly scraped right cheek; a three-inch slash below the left ear; a rectangular bruise nearly four inches long by the right ear; severe bruises to the left side of the neck and right shoulder; a bruised third rib; more bruises, some two inches in diameter, on her left hand. The right hand was swollen, and the right arm was swelling as blood seeped from an internal injury. There was a six-inch-long bruise on her chest. One lung was damaged. Both legs were battered. And her attackers had sexually assaulted her using a gun.

"I have never seen anything like it," a stunned MacGillvary would recall. "When I went home I couldn't sleep – and I've seen some pretty bad ones through the years."

Crown prosecutor Fred Ferguson had been at a wedding that day. When he returned to his home from the party late that night, he paused to look at the full moon over the Miramichi River shining through the windows. The senior prosecutor for the area, he'd been called "Frantic Freddy" by his law-school classmates because he was always on the move, always talking.

The sound of the phone ringing broke the silence at 2:00 a.m. It was the RCMP. There's been a murder, the officer

said. A few hours later, Ferguson was on his way to the
RCMP station in Newcastle for a briefing. As he drove past
the McDonald's restaurant in Douglastown, near Newcastle, he spotted Allan Legere pulling out of the parking lot in
a 240Z Datsun. The two men knew each other from previous court appearances.

"I can remember our eyes met, an icy stare from him to
me. I remember thinking, 'That's not a good look.'"

Later that day, Norman Savage, a resident of the Black
River area, dropped into Ted's Grocery, a corner store in
Chatham. Everyone there was talking about the Glendenning murder. Allan Legere walked in, bare-chested, with
several gold chains around his neck and rings on his fingers.
He hadn't seen the 26-year-old Savage in eight or nine years,
but he remembered him instantly.

"I didn't recognize you there, Norman," he said. "I see
you're still growing." He asked Savage what he was doing
and where he was living.

"Black River."

Legere's eyes narrowed. "Black River. What's it like living there, quiet?"

"Real quiet until last night," Savage replied.

"Why? What happened last night in Black River?"
Legere asked.

Savage started to describe the murder. As he did, Legere
blushed a bright red, then broke into a laugh and slapped his
hand on his knee. Stunned and frightened, Savage glanced
at Legere's bare upper body, thinking that if he had been
involved, there might be tell-tale scratches. He saw none.
He glanced down at Legere's hands, noting how powerful
they looked, then he turned and left the store as quickly as
he could.

At a few minutes after seven o'clock that Sunday evening, an unidentified woman called police and said three
Newcastle men – Todd Matchett, Scott Curtis and Allan
Legere – had left the Miramichi after ripping open a safe and
stealing about $5000. She hung up before police could ask

any questions. Two hours later, there was a second call. The same woman said the men had dumped $50 and $100 bills into the river. They had then driven to Saint John in a red car owned by Dorothy Matchett, Todd's mother, and planned to flee to Toronto. There was a gun in the car, she warned. (The caller didn't know that the police had just installed tracing equipment and were managing to trace the call. The woman caller's name was never revealed.) A quick check showed that Dorothy Matchett did own a red car.

The hunt was on.

Before the day was out, there was a second break when a local couple biking along the Kelly Road area on the out-skirts of Chatham found the Glendenning's green safe. It had been flipped upside down and the bottom ripped open. Coins, personal papers and bonds were scattered on the ground.

Like Legere, the other two suspects were well known to local police. Todd Matchett, who had just turned 18 in March, and Scott Curtis, who would be 20 in October, had a history of getting into trouble when together. Over a six-year period, they had snatched purses, gone on vandalism sprees and broken into homes and stores. Just five months earlier they had broken into a convenience store in Doug-lastown. Matchett was convicted in the case in May, sen-tenced to one year probation, and ordered not to associate with Curtis, who was still awaiting trial when John Glen-denning was murdered.

Curtis was the bigger of the two, about six feet tall, his brown hair parted in the middle. Matchett was blonde. About average in size, he was considered good looking by teenage girls who knew him. The second of three children, he had two sisters, and he came from a broken home. He had a bad temper and was known for throwing tantrums.

Tuesday morning, the informant called police again to say Dorothy Matchett was preparing to leave town for Toronto, where her son was waiting for her to bring him some money. Two RCMP officers were assigned to watch her.

In the meantime, two other police officers visited the caller. The informant said that Matchett, Curtis and Legere had disappeared in a red car after the killing. They had taken a large amount of money from a safe. While Matchett and Curtis denied hurting anyone, they did admit to beating and tying up Mary Glendenning before dumping her in a closet. Curtis, the informant said, wanted nothing to do with the money and left it in boxes in his mother's basement because he wasn't willing to take it to Toronto. A gun had been used in the robbery. A fourth man whose first name was Donnie was involved too – he was in his 20s and had reddish hair.

Police arrived to search the Curtis home. When an RCMP officer appeared at the door, Scott's mother exclaimed, "I'm pretty sure Scott hid some money downstairs in a box." Inside a sealed box, police found a plastic bag containing money, coins and other items from the Glendenning home.

Later that same day a caller told police that Allan Legere had been spotted parked along the King George Highway in Newcastle. Minutes later, RCMP Sgt. Mason Johnston pulled in front of a blue Datsun 240Z sitting on the side of that road and cautiously approached the driver.

"Mason Johnston?" the driver asked.

"Yes. Allan Legere?"

"Yes."

"I'm arresting you for the murder of John Glendenning. It is my duty to inform you that you have the right to retain and instruct counsel without delay. Do you understand?"

"Yes, but what is this all about?"

Johnston pressed on, reading the standard police caution. "You need not say anything. You have nothing to hope from any promise or favour, and nothing to fear from any threat, whether or not you say anything. Anything you do say may be used as evidence."

"What's this about?" Legere demanded again. Instead of

a response, he was handcuffed by a second officer and driven to the RCMP station in Newcastle. Legere remembered Johnston from an incident in the mid-1960s. Johnston, who had been with the RMCP for about a year, had chased Legere after spotting him fleeing a burning roadblock that had been set up by a group of teenagers as a Halloween prank. Legere managed to escape, but Johnston picked him up the next day. "It was the one and only time he manipulated me," Johnston would later recall. Legere convinced the officer that he must have seen someone else and was let go. "He has this amazing power, I don't know what it is. He sort of mesmerizes you. You get caught up with what he has to say. You have to give your head a goddamn shake to bring yourself back to reality."

Now under arrest for murder, Legere talked to Johnston as if they were old friends, using his first name and joking with him. Legere insisted he be allowed to show off his strength, Johnston remembers. "He picked me up under the arms and lifted me right over his head. I weighed quite a bit then, about 180 pounds."

RCMP officer Kevin Mole was one of two file coordinators in the case, which meant he kept notes on the investigation, helped prepare the police case, and collated the evidence to prepare for court. He was involved in following up leads on Curtis and Matchett on the day of Legere's arrest. Mole knew hair samples had been found at the Glendenning house and he was eager to see if they might match samples from Legere.

His chief concern was a 1985 decision of the Ontario Court of Appeal. Known as the *Alderton* case, it set limits on when and how police can obtain hair samples from a suspect. Samples, for instance, could not be taken through use of violence, threat or intimidation. However, samples were admissible in court as long as they were collected in good faith and didn't bring the administration of justice into disrepute.

RCMP in Newcastle knew they had to follow the rules

strictly. Earlier, they had asked Legere to give a sample voluntarily. When he refused, a call was made to Graham Sleeth, a special Crown prosecutor based in Fredericton, to try to find out what options were left open. When Sleeth returned their call, an officer flicked on the speaker phone to permit everyone to hear. Sections of the *Alderton* decision were read to them. They were told they had to take the hair as part of the arrest.

Satisfied, Sergeant Johnston and three other officers went to the cell at about 1:55 a.m. on Wednesday and demanded the hair samples from Legere. When he refused, they began to remove hair from his head anyway. Legere did not resist. At one point, he waved the officer away and pulled out the hairs himself.

Later that day, Mole talked with experts in the hair and fibre section of the RCMP's crime laboratory in Sackville, New Brunswick. They confirmed what Mole had feared – a scalp hair found at the crime scene could only be compared to a scalp hair from a suspect, and the same was true of pubic hair.

At the same time, police were told the red car reportedly used in the Glendenning attack – a 1976 Pontiac Parisenne – had been taken to Saint John and painted black. Dents that had apparently been made while wedging the 350-pound safe into the trunk had been repaired and the tires replaced. RCMP in Saint John checked mall parking lots, the airport terminal and the train and bus stations, but failed to find the car or Matchett and Curtis. The Chatham apartment of Legere's girlfriend, Christine Searle, was searched and some clothing seized. A search of the Newcastle apartment of his mother, Louise, turned up nothing. Louise did have $2000 in $50 bills in her purse, but police were unable to connect them to the robbery.

At the same time, Louise Legere told an RCMP officer her son had mentioned the attack on the Glendennings when he visited her Sunday. "They probably didn't mean to do it. There were three of them and they took a safe," he had told his mother. Louise said her son then turned as if he'd made a mistake and just said, "Oh." The officer make a note in his pad – at that time police had no idea how many people were involved in the attack and had not recovered the safe.

Another tip led police to McKnight Motors in Saint John where an $800 repair-and-paint job was just being started on a Pontiac Parisenne. The car, identified as belonging to Dorothy Matchett, was seized and police issued Canada-wide warrants for the arrest of the Matchett and Curtis.

Meanwhile, the RCMP and Crown prosecutor Ferguson continued to worry about the lack of a pubic hair sample. They realized a sexual assault had been committed during the attack, but they weren't sure the hair they'd recovered from the scene was from an attacker's head or pubic area. Finally, on June 30, police got a search warrant, went to Dorchester Penitentiary and took a second set of hair samples from Legere.

By July, police had determined that Todd Matchett and Scott Curtis were hiding in a Toronto motel and talking about slipping across the border into the United States. They changed their minds, however, and through a friend, told police they would turn themselves in. On July 3, three RCMP officers from New Brunswick flew to Toronto, met the teenagers in a restaurant, and arrested them. The teenagers were held in neighbouring cells while awaiting their first court appearance in Newcastle. Apparently unaware that guards were listening to them, they talked freely about rumours swirling around the amount of money in the Glendenning safe.

Curtis: "The taxi driver said he seen us with $75,000."

Matchett: "No! The woman said she was missing $75,000? Ha. If they ask me about $75,000, I'll say I never won the Lotto. You know, Legere is a big boy. Keith (Keith Curtis, Scott's brother) told them everything – we were supposed to be meeting with Legere."

Curtis: "I think we are up shit creek without a paddle. I wish we were still up on that arson charge."

Matchett: "Scott, you always wanted to be a movie star."

Curtis: "Yeah, but not this way."

They discussed their chances of having a closed trial because they didn't want anyone to hear their testimony. They talked about the length of sentence they could expect to serve – ten years. They wondered aloud if Legere had buried his share of the money. They worried about making bail.

Curtis: "If the bail is high, is your father going to put up bail money?"

Matchett: "He'll put up the house for bail money for both of us. If both of us make bail, it would be better."

Curtis: "Todd, that's all I needed to boost up my career was a murder charge."

Two weeks after the murder of John Glendenning, Scott Curtis and Todd Matchett appeared in Newcastle court and were charged with second-degree murder and attempted murder. Allan Joseph Legere was charged the next day. Both court appearances were a sensation, especially that of Legere. Hundreds waited outside to catch a glimpse of him. "You should be hanged," someone shouted as he walked up the stone steps into the courthouse – an imposing two-storey stone building on the busiest corner in town.

Security inside was tight. The second-floor courtroom was packed, with the crowd spilling into the hallway and down the stairs. People in the courtroom balcony leaned forward, straining to see Legere. The judge, Drew Stymiest, told them to sit down. The hearing went quickly, with Legere's second court date set for the next week. Legere stood up, paused briefly to stare at the crowd in the balcony, then followed his escort out of the room.

Outside, police had a tough time keeping drivers eager to see Legere from slamming into each other as they ignored the traffic lights. A parking lot across the street – normally less than half full – was jammed with cars and people. It was the same at a service station across the street from the courthouse. Police had to force a path through the crowd before escorting Legere to a car waiting at the bottom of the courthouse stairs.

Across the Miramichi River in downtown Chatham, a customer at a corner store on Water Street was talking with the 72-year-old owner about the arrests. Annie Flam said she couldn't believe Allan Legere was involved.

"He's been in my store," she said. "He was always a gentleman."

The death of John Glendenning marked the start a bloody summer for the Miramichi.

On August 12, after an all-night search, family members found two young girls who had earlier been reported missing. Tara Prokosh, 13, was dead, while her 14-year-old friend was barely alive. They had been stabbed, sexually assaulted, then left for dead next to a fishing camp built beside the Bartibogue River, about twelve miles north of Chatham. The camp, a small wooden building, was at the end of a dirt road, minutes from Tara's home in the rural community of Russellville.

Newcastle town council approved a $1,000 reward for information leading to the arrest and conviction of Prokosh's killer. A reward fund was set up at a local bank by two men from nearby Tracadie. Police were flooded with hundreds of calls from people who thought they knew something. More than a hundred people responded to a write-in poll in the *Miramichi Leader*, with all but four or five demanding the return of capital punishment.

Meanwhile, on September 9, the preliminary hearing in the Glendenning case began. The courtroom was filled. Again, crowds waited outside to see who came and went. The downstairs of the courtroom was packed, but not with spectators, as only reporters, witnesses and family members were allowed in. There was no room left after that. The next day, Legere, Matchett and Curtis were ordered to stand trial.

Three weeks later, the body of a 19-year-old single mother, Theresa MacLaughlin, was found in a gravel pit near her home in the village of Neguac, a short drive north of where Tara Prokosh's body had been found. MacLaughlin had been bludgeoned to death.

Within days, police arrested Kenneth Esson, a Neguac-area resident who worked at the pulp mill in Nelson-Miramichi, and charged him with two counts of murder and one count of attempted murder. Eight policemen escorted the slightly built, five foot six inch man into the courthouse, protecting him from an angry crowd. "Electrocute him," someone shouted. "Hang him by his toes from the courthouse. Why bring him here? Why not just slaughter him and get it over with."

Still, the killing was not over. At 10:00 a.m. on October 14, the body of Patrick Murphy, 39, of Chatham was found by the river near the downtown. He had been stabbed to death. Earl Lewis, 42, of Chatham, a convicted killer out on mandatory supervision, was quickly arrested and charged with the murder.

Esson pleaded guilty and was sentenced to life with no chance of parole for twenty-five years. Lewis was convicted and jailed for life. He died of cancer five years later.

The bloody summer of 1986 added a violent chapter to what was already a long history of fascinating murder trials on the Miramichi.

In 1963, 62-year-old Joe Mercure was arrested after police discovered Patrick Martin, 91, murdered in the kitchen of his home. Mercure was charged with clubbing him to death. The key evidence was a hair from a bumble-bee's leg embedded on a dollar bill in the remains of Martin's partially burned wallet. Bits of the same bee's leg put Mercure at the scene. He was found guilty and sentenced to hang, a sentence later commuted to life imprisonment. Mercure, at the time Canada's oldest living inmate, died in 1986 still protesting his innocence.

In 1977, retired boxer Yvon Durelle, known as the "Fighting Fisherman," was charged with murder. A world famous light-heavyweight who'd lost a controversial bout to American fighter Archie Moore in the 1950s, Durelle had opened a tavern in his native Baie Ste. Anne, a fishing village about thirty miles east of Chatham. One of his customers, Albin Poirier, was giving him problems – bothering other customers, forcing Durelle to throw him out on occasion. On the evening of May 20, after Durelle had escorted him to his car, Poirier twice tried to run him over. Durelle pulled out a gun and fired five times, killing Poirier. Lawyer Frank McKenna, who would become premier of New Brunswick ten years later, convinced the jury that Durelle had shot in self-defense and he was acquitted.

"The Miramichi" is actually a collection of small towns, villages and rural communities scattered for more than one hundred miles along the picturesque Miramichi River and its tributaries. Its 50,000 people stretch from the tiny English-speaking lumbering community of Boiestown in the middle of New Brunswick, past Newcastle and nearby Chatham downstream to such French fishing villages as Neguac and Escuminac where the river enters the Gulf of St. Lawrence.

It has been home to some famous businessmen: a member of the Cunard family, best known for building the *Queen Elizabeth II* passenger ship, for one; and Max Aitken, later Lord Beaverbrook. Beaverbrook grew up in Newcastle, became a leading newspaper publisher in England, and was a member of Prime Minister Winston Churchill's war cabinet.

The forests, dark and vast, have been and remain the key to the region's economy. A mill producing magazine paper is the biggest industry, employing more than two thousand

directly and thousands more who sell raw wood and sup-
plies to the plant. A military base in Chatham, a mine north
of Newcastle and a maximum security prison in the small
community of Renous, about 20 miles south of Newcastle,
are also important to the local economy.

Situated in the northern part of the province, isolated by
miles of woods, the area has developed a culture of its own.
Its tradition of folk music tells of the rivers, of fishing
Atlantic salmon, and the woods. Among the songs pre-
served from the days when lumberjacks used horses and
axes is one about a camp cook murdered in the forest. His
shrieking ghost – known to local people as the Dungarvon
Whooper – was silenced only when a priest finally performed an exorcism. Or so the story goes.

# THREE

# On Trial

As the Miramichi struggled to come to grips with the bloodiest summer and fall its residents could remember, the Glendenning case slowly worked its way to trial, but not without a few final twists.

While Todd Matchett denied having anything to do with the Glendenning murder, Allan Legere blamed Scott Curtis for the killing and claimed to have a letter from Curtis clearing him. In this letter, Curtis allegedly described how he, Matchett and an unidentified Saint John man had robbed the Glendennings. Legere's involvement was limited to loaning Curtis a jacket and accepting part of the loot. "We told Allan we had to slap them around a bit he wanted to call the ambulance but we did [not] think that they where hert that bad. People think Allan was there but he was not there," the letter said.

At 11:00 p.m. on November 7, Legere was playing cards with three other inmates in the Dorchester Penitentiary. Someone rushed up from behind and stabbed him with a sharpened bread knife, driving the blade six inches deep in the back, narrowly missing the heart. Legere leaped to his feet and bolted after Scott Curtis, the knife still sticking out of his shoulder.

Frightened, Curtis dashed into the pool room, grabbed a cue, and ran around a table. Legere, who had pulled the knife out of his shoulder and jammed it into a back pocket, also grabbed a cue and, screaming obscenities, slashed at Curtis, who swung back. Frustrated he couldn't hit Curtis, Legere grabbed balls off the table and threw them at him. Curtis ducked behind a steel post.

A guard shoved his .12-gauge shotgun through a porthole facing the pool room and yelled at the two men to stop fighting. When the guard yelled a second time Legere turned and walked toward the television lounge. Curtis lowered his pool cue, grabbed a ball and retreated outside to the exercise yard.

A blood stain spread across the front of Legere's white T-shirt as two inmates – one of them black, something Legere always remembered – helped him to the door. "You'll get yours, you red-haired cocksucker," one of them yelled at Curtis.

The knife had punctured Legere's left lung. Blood was flooding into his chest, sending him into shock. He was perspiring heavily and his colour ashen. His blood pressure was only ninety over sixty. He was coughing and having trouble breathing. With his lips turning blue, he was given oxygen and rushed to nearby Moncton Hospital. He recovered quickly and returned to Dorchester about a week later. In the meantime, Curtis was charged with assault, but no one, not even Legere, would testify.

Determined to blame the Glendenning killing on Curtis and Matchett, Legere wrote to RCMP Sgt. Mason Johnston offering a deal: "Hi Mason, it's me ... 'Breakout', and the guy who can hoist your scrawny body up over my head (Re: June, 1986 – Newcastle R.C.M.P.) Surely an old owl like you heard of my recent stabbing at Dorchester on Friday, November 7 ... A punk of this caliber will kill anybody at a whim. Just before he struck me, I offered him half a salmon sandwich, and he just played a hand of cards while I got hot water for tea. A really sick bastard, and a fucking murderer – positively. If we can strike up some kind of deal, Mason, I would be a Crown witness for his stabbing of me, plus I would give a play by play of what I know he has done to others – hint – hint."

He went on to intimate that he knew where $25,000 from the Glendenning safe was hidden and more: "I can be an expert and unlying witness concerning those two guys, against the mad stabber, which will make him look like the murderer he really is. P.S. Please do come and talk to me as quickly as possible, and do come alone, no tapes or bugs, just to see what, if any arrangement, we can come up with to save 1000's and 1000's on trials, trials, expenses. And I am not a murderer, and it would be nice to be banished from Canada, a new name, etc. I'm fed up with killers, liars, jails, just give me some peace other than death. I'm a changed person. You can help clear up a lot of loose ends, and I could use a break. Important to get here this week. Contact me this week at Prison Hospital, pretend it's concerning the stabbing, okay?"

Johnston didn't show up that week but another meeting was arranged for early in the new year.

In court in Moncton on December 17, Matchett said he wanted his case heard separately. He feared some of the evidence against Legere might hurt his chances. David Hughes, Legere's lawyer, agreed, saying some evidence against the teenagers might hurt *his* client's chances. Then Hughes dropped his bombshell – the Curtis letter.

Curtis' lawyer was caught off guard and instantly suspicious. Struggling to control his anger, Henrik Tonning glared through his horn-rimmed glasses and stalled for time. He accused Legere of forging the confession. "It was not made by my client, Mr. Curtis. In fact, it was made by Mr. Legere as a further effort to extricate himself from his involvement in the very matter which is going to trial."

Tonning made a snap decision: he now wanted the three men tried together.

Fred Ferguson, the lead prosecutor in the case, couldn't believe his luck. He'd wanted a single trial all along, convinced it was his best chance to convict all three men. He argued that the web of circumstantial evidence demanded one trial. Determined not to let his opportunity slip away, Ferguson proceeded to cite case after case backing his argument – *Regina v. Agawa and Mallet, Regina v. McLeod, Pinnock and Farquharson, Regina v. McCaw* …

"Just a second, just a second," Judge Paul Godin cut in. "You're going way too fast. Not only can I not write that fast, Mr. Ferguson, I can't even think that fast."

After a few minutes, the judge sided with Ferguson and Tonning. There would be one trial.

Legere piped up, defending the Curtis letter. "I never wrote it," he declared, then launched into a description of an alleged meeting with Curtis and Hughes where they discussed the letter.

Godin: "Yes, Mr. Legere, I – "

Curtis interrupted. "I never said that. I said – I said that I *didn't* write it."

Godin cut them off. Hughes suggested the court give Legere a few minutes to gather himself because he was taking medication for pain associated with the stabbing.

"I got to watch out for these back stabbers, eh," Legere said.

Godin ignored him and responded to Hughes request. "*That* motion I can grant."

Fifteen minutes later, Hughes asked that the trial be moved from Newcastle because of the publicity surrounding the case. William Fenton, Matchett's counsel, said he didn't care where it was held. Tonning, still angry, insisted the case be held on the Miramichi.

Hughes called Dan Allen of the Chatham Police to the stand to talk about Legere's notoriety. Allen said Legere was well known to police officers and others he'd dealt with on the Miramichi and in Moncton, but the officer was unsure how widespread his reputation was among members of the public. Under cross-examination, Allen said he believed Legere could get a fair trial on the Miramichi. "If I was charged with a serious criminal offence, I'll take my chances in Northumberland County ahead of any other county in this province."

In his decision, Godin refused the request to move the trial, saying the murder had received publicity across New Brunswick, not just the Miramichi. The trial would be held in Newcastle and it would begin early in the new year.

Thursday. January 7, 1987.

The Crown had spent much of the first three days of the trial wading through technical evidence.

Todd Matchett and Scott Curtis seemed loose and relaxed. Matchett returned to the courthouse after lunch one day and made some dancing motions with his shackled feet. It was a shuffle, as if he were pretending the leg irons forced him to walk that way. He smiled to a sister and talked to her and other family members. Back inside, Curtis lit a cigarette. "They won't let *me* smoke," Matchett joked. A guard told Curtis to put it out.

Midway through the morning, Matchett's lawyer stood up. His client wanted to plead guilty. When asked, Matchett calmly told Judge Paul Godin he understood he was facing a life sentence with no chance of parole for at least ten years. The judge then ordered Matchett remanded in jail until he could be sentenced after the trial.

Margaret Gibson took the stand and described finding her mother, Mary Glendenning. Her parents owned a safe, she said, and kept it upstairs in their bedroom. Her father always kept a fair amount of cash on him -- between $300 and $500 -- but she said she knew of no one who had heard about the safe. Still, she worried about her parents with the money in the house.

When, after the lunch break, court resumed at 2:15, the jury was not present. Lawyer Henrik Tonning stood up to address the judge: "As I advised my learned friends and yourself a short time ago with respect to my client, Scott Michael Curtis, I'd like to, at this time, make a motion, that he be allowed to change his plea from the earlier one of not guilty." With Curtis pleading guilty, only Allan Joseph Legere would be left to proclaim his innocence.

The judge then called a brief recess. Lawyer David Hughes walked into the holding cell to talk to Legere. One of the top criminal lawyers in the province, the son of the former chief justice of New Brunswick, Hughes was known for never giving up so long as there was any hope for a client. This time, however, he was convinced his client's only chance for a lighter sentence was to plead guilty.

Hughes knew it would be a tough sell. Hired by Legere seven months earlier, he'd learned how his client thought. "My first impression of Allan was that he was very suspicious of me, as he was of all lawyers. He was not going to tell me anything more than what he thought I should know. He could be very charming at times when it suited his purposes, but was always very insistent that he was going to take a very active role in his own defence. Allan always wants to control the direction of the trial. He refuses to plead guilty to anything, and insists he be found guilty by either a judge or a jury."

Minutes after meeting Legere, Hughes stormed out of the holding cell. Red-faced, he headed back into the courtroom. Ferguson crossed the room to talk to him.

"What's it going to be, Dunc?" he asked, using Hughes' nickname.

"I can't talk to him. You talk to him," Hughes replied.

"Is that all right?"

"Go ahead."

As he walked to the cell, Ferguson met Legere's mother, Louise, coming out. "Grow up, Allan," she ordered her son. "For once, be a man."

Ferguson walked into the cell and closed the door.

"I've got Mary Glendenning waiting in the judge's chambers. What's it going to be, Allan?"

"You're putting too much pressure on me," Legere said. "I need more time. Give me 'til Monday."

"You've had eight months to make up your mind. It's

time to fish or cut bait." Ferguson turned and walked out.

Just eight minutes after the recess began, Ferguson had his answer. Legere took his seat. The trial would continue.

Struggling to hold back tears, Mary Glendenning took the stand and proceeded to describe the attack of June 21, 1986. In a soft voice, she told of her futile attempts to give the killers what they wanted and of the call to her daughter.

There had been a warning of sorts prior to the attack. About eight days earlier, on a Friday night, a car had stopped in their yard and backed right up to the garage. "I told John there was a reddish coloured car backed up to our garage. I looked out the window and saw it. By the time I called John, it had moved and he just saw it going through the laneway."

Later that same night she'd heard a car drive up to the front door, but by the time they got out of bed to look, it was heading slowly down the road. The next day she noticed her downstairs phone wasn't working. A repairman came to fix it. "He asked me if I had cut the wires ... to get him down there. He was joking, but the wires looked as if they had been cut."

Mary said she still couldn't sleep with the back of her head on a pillow because of a blow received during the attack.

There was no cross-examination.

By this point in the trial, not only were people standing in line to get into court, they were standing in line read about the trial. The *Miramichi Leader* provided pages of coverage, delaying publication by a couple of hours each publishing day to ensure it could include the latest testimony. One night, about 125 people waited at a downtown service station to get a copy.

Early in the second week of the trial, Donald Langan took the stand. The 21-year-old friend of Matchett's said the robbery was Allan Legere's idea and that it was Legere who recruited the others to help him steal money.

Legere, Langan said, met with them several times the week before the attack, promising them an easy $15,000 each. He would drive them to the Glendenning house, they would steal the money. They drove past the house one time to check it out, convincing Curtis to help them.

All four men met in Chatham on Wednesday, June 18 and headed toward the Glendenning home. "Allan was driving," Langan said. "Todd was in the front. Me and Scott laid down in the back." They put on gloves and nylon masks. Matchett had a sawed-off shotgun. Curtis had a knife. Legere dropped them off roughly two hundred feet from the house and drove away.

After working their way through brush a couple of hundred feet from the house, the trio found themselves in the Glendenning's back yard. There was a light on upstairs. Too risky, they decided, and turned back, dumping clothing and the gun along the way. "We were all scared of Allan because we knew he wanted it done. Todd did the talking. He said he didn't feel right about it, there was a light on, probably someone was home and he didn't want to go through with it."

An enraged Legere shouted at them all the way back to Chatham about how the job had to be done, that there was big money in it.

Langan said the next time he saw Legere was four days later, on June 22, the morning after the murder. Legere pulled into the garage where he worked, pointed his index finger as if it was a gun barrel, and moved his thumb up and down. Langan took it as a warning – he would be killed if he said anything.

Hughes tried to discredit Langan, probing for inconsistencies in his testimony, forcing him to admit he had committed two break-and-enters. He also challenged the claim that Legere had threatened him. "I've checked the preliminary hearing over and I didn't see it in there," Hughes said. He quoted from Langan's earlier testimony – "Once I knew about it, I felt maybe if I tried to back out or something like that, that he would maybe harm me or something like that."

Hughes stared at Langan. "You don't mention anything about him threatening you. You said you felt intimidated by him."

"Well," Langan responded, "maybe I forgot to say it."

RCMP Sgt. Mason Johnston took the stand at the end of the second week. He told the court that on January 2 he had met with Allan Legere for more than an hour at Dorchester Penitentiary. During that meeting Legere had, he said, inadvertently admitted to taking part in the attack on the Glendennings.

Legere wanted a deal, according to Johnston. He would testify against Matchett and Curtis in return for a ten year sentence for manslaughter. Matchett, Curtis and a mysterious third guy from Saint John, he said, had killed John Glendenning.

"This third person stayed outside and only came inside after a big fuckup," Legere told Johnston. "But this third person only stayed in the background. Scott had problems with the old man. He got away and went outside or stumbled."

Curtis hit the old man with the gun, then they dragged him back inside. "He was staggering and this time Curtis told the old man they would rape his wife if he didn't open the safe." Neither John nor his wife, however, could open it.

"Curtis hit the old man and tied him up in the same room as the safe. Curtis told this third person that the old man was not breathing."

As his excitement grew, Johnston recalled, Legere started to slip into the first person, rather than third. "I parked behind the rec centre," he told Johnston. "I took a garbage can and I put water on his face," he said, describing his attempt to revive John Glendenning. "Curtis and Matchett were so much in a frenzy I had to holler, I had to scream at them twice so they would stop hitting the old woman."

At this point, Legere regained self-control. The third man told them to take the safe. Curtis screamed at Mary, "You old bag. We're going to burn the house down with you in it." The third man told him to cool it, then went for the car.

Curtis had sexually assaulted Mary using the barrel of his shotgun, Legere said. If police wanted the kit bag containing the gun and clothing the men had used, search the river near the Morrissy Bridge in Newcastle.

"Allan said again that if he could get ten years, he'd be out in seven," Johnston told the court. "He would have to serve this time in solitary as he would testify. He said he would do hard time in the pen and after seven years he would go to Afghanistan to live the rest of his life there."

Legere, who had been glaring across the courtroom at Johnston, shouted and swore at him.

Johnston pressed on. Legere had vowed he was innocent. "I didn't kill anybody, but I feel partly responsible for the death of the old man. I still feel responsible. I was sick to my stomach after I learned that he was dead. Those fucking idiots, Curtis and Matchett. I'm no killer. It was supposed to be a safe attack."

Johnston said during their January 2 meeting he had suggested that Legere talk to Ferguson. Legere was dubious, certain public opinion would prevent him from getting a fair trial. "You know fuckin' well, Mason, fuck, they wanted to hang me because of my name. I was involved, but no one was supposed to get killed."

In his cross-examination, Hughes asked Johnston why he hadn't arranged for a tape recording of the interview. Legere had insisted there be no tape recording, Johnston replied. Besides, wearing a bug meant risking discovery.

Hughes next wanted to know why the officer hadn't sat down immediately after the meeting and written up his notes, instead of waiting more than an hour. Well, Johnston explained, there was a snowstorm coming and he had to get home.

Hughes: "You didn't think that time dulls the memory a little bit?"

Johnston: "Well, I have written notes upon notes as an undercover officer, first in drug – in the RCMP and sometimes I don't get to make my notes for two hours or three hours afterwards."

Hughes suggested Johnston had misunderstood Legere's use of the word *I*, citing the example of a meeting Legere claimed he'd had with Todd Matchett's father, Billy, right after the murder.

Hughes: "You said that Mr. Legere said, 'Billy didn't see the third person, but I saw him.' Were those your words?"

Johnston: "Yes. 'But to tell the truth, I saw him.' Yes."

Hughes: "Isn't it possible what he meant there, Sergeant Johnston, is that '*I, I, Allan Legere, saw the third person?*'"

Johnston: "It's possible."

Hughes turned to Legere's detailed knowledge about what had happened inside the Glendenning house – things like seeing the two men going into a frenzy and beating John Glendenning.

Hughes: "Any information that he gave you on that particular date, isn't it possible that he could've obtained information from some other party?"

Johnston: "No. I don't think he could have."

Hughes: "I'm asking you if it's possible?"

Johnston: "No."

The third week began with testimony from Legere's ex-girl friend, Christine Searle. She arrived wearing hot pink pants, white ankle boots and a white pullover. Her bleached blonde hair was swept back from her face, her eyes hidden behind large sunglasses.

Theirs had been a stormy relationship, she said. They fought most of the time. True, Legere had talked about getting married, but Searle insisted she would never have married him. She and Legere spent much of June 21, 1986 together. He left early in the evening, however, and didn't return to her Chatham apartment until about 4:00 a.m. on June 22. She woke up and heard him in the bathroom. A few minutes later, he walked into her bedroom.

"He had nothing on and he said something like, 'We have it made now' and threw some money on my bed," Searle testified. "He told me to count it. I asked him where he got it. Again he told me to count it, so I counted it and it counted $14,000. It was all in $100 Canadian bills and one $1,000 Canadian bill."

Legere took the money, bundled it up with an elastic and jammed it in the pocket of a pair of jogging pants.

"I asked him where he got the money again. Mr. Legere told me that him and some friends had planned a robbery, but that his friends had done it, that he was not there, nor was he near the property when this happened. I asked him who his friends were. He told me it was Scott Curtis, Todd Matchett and another man from Saint John, but he wouldn't tell me who it was. And he told me Curtis and Matchett beat the people very badly, that they were an elderly couple. He said he told them to call an ambulance for them and they refused – and they gave him a share of the money because he knew about the robbery and when it was going to happen. Legere told me that there was $45,000 in the safe and they split it three ways." (Slightly more than $20,000 was eventually recovered.)

Eventually, Legere and Searle fell asleep. Sunday morning, Searle asked him if the old woman had been raped. Legere said no, but Curtis had sexually assaulted her with a weapon. Legere took a dishcloth from the sink and began to wipe his leather jacket, which was on the back of a chair. It was an old habit. He took good care of the jacket, keeping it in the back seat of his car if he wasn't wearing it.

Christine asked a boy from downstairs to come up. She wanted him to run and buy her a pack of cigarettes. "I asked Allan for a dollar. He gave it to me, then he threw the little boy out of the apartment and grabbed the dollar from me. There were dark red-brown stains on it and Allan turned the burner on my stove and burned it. He said it didn't look good."

Legere was spooked by the death of John Glendenning, Searle recalled. He threatened her if she said anything, warning that Todd Matchett and Scott Curtis had friends who would hurt her, or her son.

To discredit this testimony, David Hughes read from a letter Searle wrote to Legere eight days before she testified against him at his preliminary hearing.

"I want you back in my arms, in my bed, in my life," the letter read. "God I really do miss you. I feel empty inside. I know I'll never find anyone in my lifetime to take the place of Big Al."

Searle tried to explain that when she wrote that letter "[she] was on so many pills."

Hughes pressed his advantage. "You're saying that you didn't really mean it? You were lying to him, are you?"

"Well, no. I didn't really mean it. I never did love him," Searle replied.

Hughes resumed reading the letter: "I know it's hard on you, but it's a lot harder on me. We'll just have to wait and hear all the rats say their testimonies. But let them – you weren't there, so they can all go fuck themselves. I'll fix them, Allan. You wait and see."

He looked at Searle. "Were you lying to him or what?"

"I'm not sure at the time," Searle answered. "I was on a lot of nerve pills after he was arrested. I cared about him, but I didn't love him."

Hughes began reading yet again. "No one talks to me now, not a goddamn soul, unless it's getting information about you. By the way, the hitchhiker you picked up has been interested in your well being. She isn't the only one, but I won't go on about that slut you have been fucking behind my back. Whatever you were getting, I was probably getting more than you."

Legere burst out laughing at this. But Judge Godin was not amused. "This is difficult enough as it is," he said. "This is not being done for entertainment."

Searle's testimony ended a few minutes later. She left the building through the judge's chambers with an RCMP escort as court recessed for lunch. Searle had worn a strong perfume. As Godin entered his chambers, he sniffed the air. "Ahh," he said, "Eau de Christine."

# FOUR

# On the Stand

THAT afternoon, after Christine Searle had completed her testimony, the prosecution faced a crucial test. In a session with the jury temporarily absent, called a *voir dire*, the prosecutors strived to convince the judge to let them use as evidence the hair samples police had taken from Allan Legere.

Yes, the Crown had found witnesses linking Legere to the plot to steal the safe. Yes, Mason Johnston's testimony suggested Legere was the third man involved in the attack. What was required now was physical evidence putting Legere inside the Glendenning house, and they needed his hair to do it.

The legal argument centred on sections of the Canadian Charter of Rights and Freedoms protecting a person against unreasonable search and limiting what police can do to get evidence.

The Crown argued the first hair sample – taken just hours after Legere was arrested – met the Charter's legal standard because it was seized as part of the arrest. They admitted the search warrant used to get the second sample on June 30 was illegal under the charter. However, police had *thought* they were within the law and, in fact, had asked for legal advice. David Hughes argued the samples should be excluded from the trial because the way the police got them violated the Charter. "What it does is encourage the police in the future to assault prisoners in order to obtain samples of hair."

In the end, the judge sided with the Crown, and on Tuesday morning, the Crown called its final witness. Duff Evers of the RCMP laboratory in Sackville, New Brunswick told the court that a hair found on the face of John Glendenning matched Legere's. As well, hair from Mary Glendenning was found in the zipper of Legere's leather jacket.

That afternoon, Allan Legere, overruling the advice of his lawyer, took the stand. Hughes, although angered by Legere's decision, began his questioning by asking his client about his lengthy criminal record. It was a standard legal tactic used by lawyers representing a client with a criminal past to show the client has nothing to hide.

Hughes asked Legere if he'd been fined in 1964 for theft. Yes.

What about a 1966 sentence of eighteen months for another theft?

"Shoplifting really," Legere replied. "I stole some rings at Eastertime for my girlfriend. Couldn't afford any."

Could he remember any details of the 1977 assault case where he was jailed for three months?

"Yes. I was working at a Fina Station in Chatham and I had – her husband was accusing me of running around with her, so I got in a fight with him down at the Chatham mall and I hit him a punch in the face and he kicked me."

Did he receive a total of three months for a case involving assault causing bodily harm and common assault on April 16, 1978?

"Yes, I was working at the club in Chatham, a night club, and I got pretty drunk one night. I went in and I shoved the disc jockey out of the way and I got a common assault charge for that. I went back to my room and I got in a fight with my roommate and I punched him in the face and I got three months for that."

Hughes' tactic was backfiring. Instead of answering simply and concisely, Legere was offering excuses and rationalizations that were unlikely to sit well with the jury.

Still, Hughes pressed on. What about a string of convictions in September 1979 involving resisting arrest, possession of a weapon for a purpose dangerous to the public, and creating a disturbance?

"I had come from Ontario and I'd bought a trailer. I was living by myself and I was drinking. That was the last time I drank. A young fellow in Chatham gave me two lock-blade knives and I got into a little argument in a couple of clubs. They jumped me and I pulled it out. I said to back off and whey they did I put the knife back on the table and I fought with them again. But just for threatening I did about twenty months in jail. And one of the policemen had broke my jaw with a pool stick, both sides."

Finishing the list with Legere's 1983 conviction for break and enter, Hughes was able to turn to the murder. Legere said the first he'd heard of the Glendennings was in April 1986 when a local businessman approached him. "He just asked me if I was interested in making $15,000 to $30,000 – about a safe. I said I was too old for that crap."

He remembered Billy Matchett mentioning it in passing a few days later, then being approached again in early June by someone who planned to leave town and wanted some quick money.

"I never planned nothing about taking any safe," he was quick to add. "I just divulged something that was told to me – just how guys talk when they sit around – about whether it's rich people or what. I never got there and sat down with no bunch of guys and planned what I'm going to do. Because if I'm going to do that, I sure wouldn't pick a bunch like was involved."

He admitted driving two unnnamed individuals and Donald Langan to the Glendenning home not once, as Langan testified, but twice – on June 11 and again two days later.

He swore that on the first trip he'd warned Langan to be careful, saying, "Don't go around the goddamn place if anybody is home. Make sure there's no lights on." He dropped them off, waited for them, and eventually found them hitchhiking back towards Chatham. "What in the name of Jesus took you so long?" he said he'd demanded. "Does it take you all night to find out if the light's on?"

Legere refused to name Todd Matchett or Scott Curtis, even though he claimed he had a letter from Curtis in his back pocket describing what had happened that night.

"As far as taking a chance of being found guilty because I don't tell names," Legere explained, "I'd rather do a hundred years than point somebody out. I don't mind this Langan because he's a Crown witness."

He said Donald Langan asked him to drive the three men there the second time because they couldn't leave the car on the side of the road. "Holy Jesus Christ man," Legere had replied, "what's going on? I told you I didn't want anything to do with this shit."

"Well," Langan said, "if there's nobody home, we'll steal the safe."

Legere said he'd insisted there be no violence. He figured the plan might work because he'd been told the elderly couple were often away visiting friends. Against his better judgement, he drove the men to Black River Bridge and dropped them off near the store, then parked behind a nearby community centre to wait. When, after an hour, they had not returned, he angrily drove to the house, backed into the driveway and yelled for the three men to come out. That was probably the car Mary Glendenning saw at her house. Unwilling to risk waiting any longer, he drove back to Chatham, picked up his own car and went to Newcastle. The three men made it back on their own.

"Would it be fair to say," Hughes asked, "that the same people that went the second time were the same people that went the first time?"

"Basically."

Legere said on the night of June 21 he was having trouble with his car and spent much of the night in a downtown parking lot trying to fix it. Eventually giving up, he walked to Christine Searle's nearby apartment and played a game of Scrabble before returning to the car, which he managed to start around one o'clock in the morning. He then returned to Searle's. Around 2:30, he heard a noise outside the apartment. He looked out and saw a red car parked under the window.

"I went out in the yard and I talked to the guys. I recognized two of the fellows, but there's one guy whom I later found out was from Saint John."

No, he didn't know the third man, but "he was about my size." It was too dark and the light inside the car was broken. They had to use a flashlight.

"I jumped in the back seat. In the front seat I noticed there was a couple of bags of money on the floor, plastic bags filled with money. In the back seat there was coveralls. The light shone on the coveralls and they were loaded with blood, what I thought was blood anyway."

Legere recalled their conversation:

"What in the fuck happened?" he demanded. They told him about the robbery and beating the elderly couple.

"Are they – like, they're not dead or anything, are they?"

"No, no, they're just slapped around. The old guy was knocked out or something. I poured some water on his head and he came around."

"Listen, how about if I go upstairs and phone the ambulance and I'll just tell the ambulance that somebody had a heart attack?"

"No! Don't call the ambulance, because if you do, they'll set up a roadblock and we'll get caught," one of the men in the car said.

They talked for about twenty minutes before they handed him a bundle of money – his share, they told him. Legere noticed his black leather jacket was in the car, so he took it with him. The three men left.

"I didn't know what the Jesus to do," Legere told the jury. "I knew it was more than a nose bleed from what I seen on the clothes. I went upstairs, I woke up Christine, in fact, I had to shake her. And on the bed was a stack of money, and I'm telling you, I didn't have to tell her to count it because she crossed her legs and counted." The next morning, she peeled off $500 for clothes and shoved the rest in a plastic bag saying she would hide it behind her mother's home.

Yes, he talked to Langan the day after the murder, but he only stopped after Langan waved to him from the gas bar where he worked. There were never any threats.

Langan, he said, asked if he knew about the robbery. "I said, 'As far as I'm concerned, Donnie, I don't know nothing about it. A fellow wouldn't be wise to know anything about it.'"

Next, Hughes turned to the meeting between Legere and Johnston. Legere said it was *Johnston* who wanted a meeting. It was Johnston who had hinted at a deal if the money was returned.

Sure, they met on January 2, but he hadn't implicated himself. It was *Johnston* who kept steering the conversation towards the mysterious third person. Johnston suggested he plead guilty. It would look better and he might get a lighter sentence. Legere said he had refused, because he wasn't there.

Hughes was ready to ask his final few questions, but Legere had been talking for about an hour and his throat was dry.

"Can I have some water before I die here?" he demanded. Spotting the water glass the judge had been using for the two and a half weeks of the trial, Legere calmly reached over and picked it up, catching Godin off guard.

"Just a moment," the judge started to say, but by then Legere was drinking from the glass. "You might as well keep it," Godin added.

"Okay?" asked Hughes when Legere finished drinking.

"All right."

"Now, were you in Black River Bridge on either June 21 or June 22, 1986?"

"Nowhere near there."

"And did you murder John Glendenning?"

"No sir, I didn't."

Crown prosecutor Fred Ferguson couldn't believe Legere's testimony. "He was asking the jurors to buy the story that he'd gotten $15,000 from the robbery and murder of John Glendenning because he knew about it, because he'd participated in the planning of a routine break-and-enter, as he called it. That the people who'd perpetrated the crime all of a sudden had come to his door and given him one-third of the money that was allegedly taken in the robbery-murder." It made no sense.

No, the facts were clear as far as Ferguson was concerned. Legere was guilty. The three men went to the Glendenning home with murder on their minds. "Our position right through this was there was *absolutely* no question what the intention was here. All you had to do was go back and look at the photographs, the brutality, listen to the medical evidence from the doctors, the pathologists and the way they beat these people. No one in their right mind can imagine that there was anything less than the intention to kill here. The brutality was that monstrous."

Allan Legere had attacked the credibility of three witnesses crucial to Ferguson's case – Langan, Searle and Johnston. Langan portrayed Legere as the mastermind. Searle put him in the house. Johnston had his confession. It was up to Ferguson to bolster their credibility and convince the jury that Allan Joseph Legere was a liar.

In his cross-examination, the Crown prosecutor pressed Legere about what happened after the three men showed up outside Christine Searle's apartment on June 22 and handed him a bundle of bills totalling about $15,000. Legere said he barely looked at, left it to Searle to count it. Ferguson, his face taut with the strain of keeping his anger under control, allowed a mixture of disbelief and sarcasm to seep into his voice. "You must be a man of considerable means, Mr. Legere."

"Mr. Ferguson, I've had up to $26,000 in my hand at one time. It doesn't bother me too much."

"It doesn't, eh."

"No. And I think that week before that, I think I had about $1,500 on me."

"What? Do you carry that kind of money on you all the time?"

"Well, when the police arrested me in Moncton back in '83 I had $5,800 in my pocket in thousand –"

"Did you have that $1,500 for quite a bit of time?"

"Well, I usually carry $7,000, $8,000 sometimes."

"No, that time there, did you have the $1,500 for quite a bit of time?"

"Well, I sold a few cars, plus Christine's brother run in the side of me and I got – I'm with the Co-operators Insurance and I got $1,500 for the damage he did on the side of my car. And I don't drink and I don't smoke, so I always got money on me."

"So, in any event, she counts the money, takes a bunch out for herself, and you tell her to get what? Get rid of it? Go hide it somewhere?"

"I never told – very little – I never told her of too much. She counted the money. She was all happy about the money. I –"

"I suppose she would be," said Ferguson.

"I didn't care too much about the money. Like I said, it thrilled her more than it did me."

"It was just money."

"It was just money," Legere agreed.

"Sure."

Ferguson asked Legere about the fate of the money. "Where did you hide it?"

"I was to going to say, wouldn't you like to know."

"There's 150 people in this courtroom who want to know."

"Pardon?"

"Do you know where the money is right now?"

"I've got an idea, yes."

"You have an idea?"

"Yes, if Christine never took it."

"Oh, if she didn't take it."

"I know she got some of it."

"And I'm sure you're prepared to take the authorities to it just as soon as court is over today?"

"You never know, as long – "

"No, I want to know."

"Well, you never know, as long as you don't take me to the cleaners."

"I want to know right now, are you going to take me to it, or not?"

"I don't know exactly if I could find it, to tell you the truth."

"Yes?"

"And that's the God's truth. I don't know exactly if I could find it, especially in wintertime."

"I bet you could take me within one hundred feet of it."

"I wouldn't say that either."

Ferguson asked Legere about his meeting with Johnston. Hadn't he written the RCMP officer a letter in November asking him to visit him in the Dorchester Penitentiary?

No.

What about the meeting on January 2? "Your position here today is that you sat back and he did all the talking?"

"I never said that."

"No? Most of the talking?"

"He talked and I would answer some things, but he was hoping to get me as being a third person and I denied it. He wanted me to be number three."

"And you weren't going to have any part of that."

"No sir, because it wasn't true."

"So then, after this meeting on Friday that he so detailedly talked about last Friday, he went back to Moncton and fabricated the complete case against you?"

"Well, I can tell you, he did a lot of lying for a policeman on the stand."

"Twenty-one years on the force."

"That's right. That's what I said to him. I said he must want me some bad. Because if they would have had a tape recorder ..."

Crown co-counsel, Bill Corby, caught Ferguson's eye. *You 've got what you wanted. It's time to quit*, the look said. Ferguson nodded. He turned to Legere one last time. Johnston lied. Langan lied too?

"Only about not being there any more than once."

"But he's lying about that Wednesday night, three nights before?"

"Yes, he is."

"He's lying about big things. Christine, she's lying about some stuff, right?"

"Well he – they never – they never got charged, did they?"

"Right? Is Christine lying?"

"About what?"

"Different things – the money, what happened to the money?"

"Well, she helped hide it."

The next morning, David Hughes presented his closing arguments. He had tried to create enough reasonable doubt to let Legere avoid a murder conviction. "This matter comes down to your decision on two issues," he told the jury. "The first one is: did Mr. Legere abandon his intention to rob and beat the Glendennings the week before this robbery took place? He's testified that he had. The second one is: was Mr. Legere the third person in that house? He has testified that he wasn't."

He argued that the Crown had failed to discredit Legere's version of what happened. They had only Langan's word for it, and he couldn't be trusted. Nothing in Christine Searle's testimony disproved the third man theory. Sergeant Johnston may have misunderstood Legere's use of the third person. As for the hair from the Glendennings found on his jacket, well, Legere said he had loaned the jacket to someone.

"Mr. Legere didn't have to take the stand in this matter, but insisted on it," Hughes said in closing. "He got on the stand, he told you about his record. He doesn't pretend to be any angel. But what he's saying is that he wasn't guilty of this crime. He's admitted by his evidence, that fine, he may be guilty of conspiracy to commit robbery. He's testified that's what he did. Or he may be guilty of receiving stolen goods. He's admitted to it. But he says, 'I am not guilty of killing that man. I wasn't there.'"

Fred Ferguson, for his part, had two objectives: leave the jury with a clear picture of the events surrounding the attack; and destroy Legere's credibility while heightening that of Langan, Searle and Johnston.

He mocked the third man theory. No one had every seen him. Langan had never met him. Legere had lied to Searle, inventing the story about the man because he didn't trust her. He attacked Legere's suggestion that the three men in the car handed him thousands of dollars to ensure his silence, suggesting it made no sense. Why would anyone pay him off to keep quiet when, on the stand, Legere had refused to say that Matchett and Curtis were the two men involved in the killing, even though they had already pleaded guilty to the crime? "You only knew Allan Legere for a couple of hours yesterday afternoon in the box," he told the jury. "God knows how long Todd Matchett knew him for. Did he strike you as the kind of man who you'd pay $14,000 to to buy his silence? No. This is the man who knows the honour code of the penitentiary. You wouldn't have to pay him five cents."

Referring to the meeting between Johnston and Legere, the prosecutor told the jury they had to make a choice. "This is not a case where one guy thought it went this way and one guy says, 'No, it went the other way.' It's one or the other. Either you believe him, that is Mr. Legere, or you believe Mr. Johnston about what happened in that room in Dorchester. I put it to you that if you believe Mason Johnston, Mr. Legere is guilty beyond a reasonable doubt of murder – regardless of whether you believe he struck a blow or not."

As part of his lengthy charge to the jury, Judge Godin explained the law on murder. He was particularly concerned with two sections of the Criminal Code of Canada – 213(d) and 21(2). He took the unusual step of supplying each juror with a copy of the sections.

Normally, to be convicted of murder, the Crown had to prove the accused had intended to kill the victim – either by planning it, or by recklessly injuring the person in a way likely to cause death.

Section 213(d), however, was an oddity. It allowed for a murder conviction under much less stringent grounds. Called *constructive murder*, all the Crown had to show was that the accused killed someone while, in the Legere case, committing a robbery. It didn't matter if the accused intended to kill the victim or not.

Section 21(2) allowed for a murder conviction if the accused helped or encouraged someone else to do the killing. Coming upon a murder and doing nothing was not sufficient for a conviction. Acting as a look-out was. It required that there be a plot. If, as Legere claimed, he'd dropped out of the plot, he couldn't be convicted under 21(2).

The judge completed his review the evidence late in the afternoon. He told the jury they had three choices – not guilty, guilty, or guilty of manslaughter. "In considering your verdict, please do not concern yourselves with the consequences of it."

The next morning, the jury filed back into the courtroom. Jury foreman Gary Williston carried the sheet of paper containing the verdict in his left hand. The two-storey courtroom with the ornate balcony that extended halfway across the room was packed. More people stood in the corridor, straining through the open door to hear what was going on inside. Behind them, through a window overlooking the town, more people could be seen milling around in the parking lot across the street from the sandstone building.

Legere stood silently, his back to the crowd, his body unmoving as he stared at the jury. Court clerk George Martin turned to the jurors.

"Members of the jury, have you agreed upon your verdict and who shall speak for you?" he demanded.

Williston rose from his seat in the front row nearest the spectators. "We have."

"How do you find the accused at the bar, guilty, or not guilty?"

"Guilty as charged," he declared in a firm, clear voice. Legere's face was a frozen mask. The faces of the jurors betrayed only relief that it was over. Members of the Glendenning family, sitting barely six feet away from Legere, said nothing.

"Members of the jury. Harken to your verdict as reported by your foreman and as the court records it," Martin called out, reciting the formal language of the court. "The accused, Allan Legere, has been found guilty of second-degree murder. Members of the jury, by the verdict as announced by your foreman, do you find the accused guilty? So say you one, so say you all? Are you content?" The jurors nodded their agreement.

David Hughes asked that each juror be polled individually for his or her verdict. Martin began reciting the names of the eleven men and one woman. Each juror stood up and, speaking so everyone could hear, said "guilty."

Wally Jimmo's name was the last one called. The eighty-seventh person interviewed for the jury and the final juror to be selected, the Chatham high school teacher's voice nearly failed him as he rose to speak. "Guilty," he managed to squeak.

Godin asked the convicted killer if he had anything to say before he was sentenced.

"Well, just one thing, your honour. I still maintain that Mason Johnston misinterpreted me. That's about all I can say. I don't know how much evidence – I don't know how much it weighed upon me, but I know he misinterpreted me."

Godin then sentenced Allan Joseph Legere to life in prison with no chance of parole for at least eighteen years.

Outside, about 125 people stood waiting for Legere to come out of the building. He appeared at noon, under heavy guard.

"Allan, Allan. Do you have anything to say?" a TV reporter called out.

"Well, I told you about Mason Johnston, didn't I?" he replied, his voice level.

"How do you feel?"

"Well, I wasn't there, was I," was his only reply.

"Will you appeal?"

"Yes."

About a dozen school-age children, mostly young girls, stood near the sheriff's car and shouted at Legere.

"Allan, Allan," they called out between giggles.

Legere ignored them as he climbed into the car. Then suddenly he turned and through the window stared at them before turning again and looking straight ahead. The car pulled away slowly, heading for Moncton.

About an hour and a half later, as he was being taken out of the sheriff's car in Moncton, Legere made a desperate bid for freedom. Using a plastic fork that he had fashioned into a key, he managed to unlock his shackles, and made a run for it. An off-duty Moncton police officer moonlighting with the sheriff's department tackled him to the ground. As required, the officer reported the incident to the sheriff's department, but no one passed the information on to local police or prison officials. It would later prove a mistake. A fatal mistake.

The next week, Todd Matchett and Scott Curtis were each sentenced to life with no chance of parole for sixteen years. At the sentencing, Matchett managed to slip a note to a reporter. Neatly printed in pencil, but full of misspellings, it said: "I Todd Matchett, was involved in an arm robbery at the home of Mr. and Mrss'es Glendennings. But I'm truly telling the truth when I say that I wasn't planing on beating or hurting anyone of the Glendening's ... It just so happened that I was accompanyed with a (nut), better known as a (sicko) ... Well as you can see Allan Legere really did a good job on putting everything on use me and Scott that is and taking everything off himself."

Legere filed an appeal less than two weeks after his conviction. Since David Hughes didn't want to handle the appeal, he arranged for Fredericton lawyer Tom Evans to take over.

In May, Evans took the highly unusual step of writing letters to the jurors. He wanted permission to interview them and submitted a list of questions about what they knew prior to the trial: did they know Legere and reputation, did they know the Glendennings? In less than a page, the lawyer used *Marimichi* for Miramichi, *Glenndenning* for Glendenning, and *tiral* for trial.

Evans failed to follow through with the interviews and began missing legal deadlines. Legere angrily fired him on December 22 and Evans sent a letter to Hughes three weeks later, in effect, handing the case back to him. (Evans later quit the law society after being convicted and jailed for sexual misconduct with a minor.)

Hughes quickly filed an appeal saying Judge Godin should have disallowed Johnston's testimony and the hair samples, and should not have mentioned section 213(d) of the criminal code. The court heard the appeal on April 14.

The year-long delay proved lucky for Legere. In December,
the Supreme Court of Canada struck down section 213(d) of
the criminal code. The court said a Québec man, Yvan Vaillancourt, deserved a new trial because he had asked his
accomplice in a pool hall robbery to remove the bullets
from his gun before they went inside. Vaillancourt had been
convicted of murder under 213(d) because the gun went off
in a scuffle, killing someone. The Supreme Court said a person should only be convicted of murder if he or she
*intended* to kill someone, or was so reckless that they
clearly didn't care what happened to the victim. Simply
taking part in a robbery wasn't enough.

The decision rocked the legal community. Two days
after its release, the director of public prosecutions for New
Brunswick, Robert Murray, issued a memo warning prosecutors to stop using *any* part of 213. Legal analysts predicted the end of the section. Sections 213(a-c) topped a
federal justice department list of sections which might be
ruled unconstitutional next.

Preparing for the Legere appeal, Crown prosecutor Fred
Ferguson and co-counsel Bill Corby were forced to admit
that using 213(d) had perhaps been a mistake. They would
have to try to defend the conviction on other grounds. In
fact, their argument was straightforward: the Glendenning
attack had been so brutal and so reckless that those responsible *had* to know death was likely. Moreover, evidence
pointing to Legere as the third man was so overwhelming
that a jury would have convicted Legere with or without
213(d).

In August 1988, Legere's appeal was duly rejected by all
three appeal court judges. They agreed with Godin's decisions on Johnston's testimony and the hair. They accepted
the assertion that Legere was the mastermind behind the
attack and was as guilty of murder as Curtis and Matchett,
even if he perhaps had not actually hit anyone. The court
said Legere directed, instructed and "generally supervised"
the teenagers.

The court's legal argument about the use of 213(d), however, stunned the lawyers. The judges ignored warnings about the section's future and said Legere would have been convicted under 213(a) and (c)!

Hughes promptly asked the Supreme Court if it would hear an appeal. The court only accepts cases it thinks involve laws needing clarification.

While Hughes was preparing for that hearing, Allan Legere was busy too. In a three-page hand-written letter, he urged the jurors to come forward and admit they had been prejudiced against him. Underlining the words for emphasis, he said, "I simply ask each of you, to kindly fill in the answers to the 4 questions on the form enclosed. There is no need to inverview you as you only need be fair & honest, – Period!" The letters were handed over to the RCMP by the attorney general's office because they were considered "veiled intimidation."

On February 20, 1989 the Supreme Court listened to Hughes' arguments about why it should hear the case. An answer was expected later in the year. Hughes was confident that Legere would eventually get a new trial because "there was no evidence that Allan had struck any blows to either Mr. or Mrs. Glendenning." He would then ask to have the trial moved out of the Miramichi. The lawyer remained convinced that it had always been impossible for Legere to get a fair trial in Newcastle. "Feelings were running too high and the jury panel had to be prejudiced against my client. If a new trial had been granted, the most that Allan could have been convicted of would have been manslaughter. His sentence would not have been more than ten years, and he would pretty well have been eligible for parole at this point."

# FIVE

# Plotting Escape

By early May 1989, Allan Legere's patience with the appeal process was running out. He sat fuming in his cell at the Atlantic Institution, a maximum security prison in Renous, about twenty miles south of Newcastle in New Brunswick.

Waiting for the Supreme Court to announce its decision was unnerving Legere. Ever the paranoid, he suspected the court was being controlled by New Brunswick's justice department and the "rich people" of the Miramichi, who, he felt, had always used their influence against him. Well, he would wait no longer.

At this time, Legere was in the segregation wing of Renous because prison officials thought he might be killed if allowed to mingle with other inmates. He knew he had little chance of escaping from the prison itself. He needed to convince prison authorities to let him out on a medical pass where, hopefully, he would have only a couple of guards to worry about.

His plan had been laid with consummate patience. After poking sharp objects in his ear to infect it, he demanded medical attention, pestering the prison's doctor for a referral to a specialist in Moncton. Escorted there on October 27, 1988 he furtively examined the layout of the doctor's office and surrounding area, and found it perfect. A bathroom directly behind the nurse's desk meant he could slip out of his handcuffs in private, then burst out and grab the nurse as a hostage. Once outside, he could disappear before the guards could run him down. Moreover, the office was in a part of the city he knew well.

Legere visited the specialist again on November 24, but made no attempt to escape. Perhaps the impending winter stopped him. Perhaps it was the upcoming Supreme Court hearing. Maybe his guards were not the kind to believe his mix of light-hearted banter and polite manners. A nurse in the doctor's office remembered a guard refusing to shut the door while Legere used the bathroom, thereby making any attempt to slip out of his handcuffs impossible.

However, by spring, ten weeks after the Supreme Court hearing, Allan Legere was ready to go. He had been due to visit the ear doctor on May 15, but the appointment was moved to May 3 because it had been scheduled on an "as-soon-as-possible" basis. The change meant meeting the specialist at the Dr. Georges L. Dumont Hospital instead of his office. No one told the hospital the patient was an inmate serving life for murder and his name was misspelled in the appointment book as *Allaine Legere*.

The movements of inmates on medical leaves are monitored by a computer system based in Ottawa. The prison files a report with the computer each day, the computer then notifies police in the area concerned. In 1989, the system was handling 4,000 to 5,000 reports a day. It took more than a day to warn about an impending visit, so word of trips made on short notice weren't passed on because the inmate would be back before the police knew he was coming. To compensate, the system's organizers asked for at least 72 hours notice before moving anyone. In an emergency, the prison was supposed to call the police force on its own to explain what was happening. Officials at the Atlantic Institution, however, didn't know about the rule.

This lapse was indicative of the prison's troubled history. Opened in early 1987, the prison quickly ran into problems, even though it housed less than half of the two hundred and forty inmates for which it was designed. Angry workers criticized the way it was run. Experienced guards coming from other prisons said they had never seen an institution run so poorly. They talked about prisoners intimidating new guards. The manufacture and consumption of illegal alcohol – called brew – was out of control. There were fears the inmates might riot. Workers blamed the warden, saying he was inexperienced and unable to command respect.

Tensions boiled over in July 1987 when a female guard was attacked. More than one hundred workers met and called for an independent investigation into the way the prison was run. The warden suggested one of the protest leaders was trying to get even because he'd been disciplined a few days earlier. A few months later, both the warden and union president were transferred.

The problems continued. In April 1989, three inmates armed with homemade knives attacked a black man in the industrial shop area. There were large seizures of brew and brew-making equipment. There were rumours of a sitdown protest by inmates. Prison officials suspected a power struggle among the inmates was fueling the problems. An inspection team visiting the prison in early May called it "dirty" and scolded the warden for the way it was being run.

Legere's escape plan was designed to exploit the problems inside the prison. He had become a virtual recluse after arriving in Renous, papering over his windows to block out the light and letting his hair and beard grow long and matted. Now, with spring on its way, he seemed to return to normal and began to use his remarkable charm on prison officials. Unlike other inmates, he went out of his way to be cooperative and polite, disarming even local people who knew his reputation for violence. Guards, case

workers, unit managers – they all found Legere easy to talk
to, not one to make trouble, a welcome break from the ten-
sion-charged atmosphere in the rest of the prison.

Correctional Services Canada had a computerized program it used to ensure workers knew when they were dealing with a dangerous prisoner. There was nothing in it to
indicate that Allan Joseph Legere was a threat.

At about seven o'clock on the morning of May 3, 1989
guard Bob Hazlett walked along the cement corridors of the
Atlantic Institution to the shift supervisor's office.
Assigned to outside escort duty for the day, he was briefed
on the trip he was scheduled to make that morning.

He was handed a standard prisoner's card, which provided little information – a photocopy of a photograph of
the prisoner, his name and number – *Allan Legere, FPS
112120A*. There was no mention of any risk of violence or
escape, nothing about his behaviour inside the prison, not
even a physical description mentioning his weight or the
colour of his hair and eyes.

Hazlett and his supervisor talked for about ten minutes
about what to expect. Hazlett had once escorted Legere to
hospital in Chatham and well remembered the police who
accompanied them as a special precaution. Moreover, the
Escorted Temporary Permit Form 23321 filled out for this
trip included a special note in the *extra conditions* section
on the bottom of the page. "Escorting officer must maintain visual surveillance of inmate at all times," it said in
capital letters.

The briefing over, Hazlett walked to the central control
area to pick up handcuffs and a body belt. The belt wraps
around the prisoner's waist and is used to lock his hands
close to his body. Hazlett spent a few minutes checking the
equipment to ensure it worked. He signed it out at 7:19 and
left to join guard Robert Winters, the junior officer assigned
to the escort job, in the keeper's office. Both men worked
on Unit 3 where Legere was housed and they knew his

reputation for getting along well with the staff. Legere, who had seen the prison nurse at 7:03, had just finished his breakfast and was waiting in his cell.

After waiting for a few minutes in the office, Hazlett and Winters arrived at Legere's cell door at 7:40, only to have him say he was using the bathroom and needed a few more minutes. The guards walked down the hall and sat for about ten minutes in the common room until Legere pressed his call button to tell them he was ready. Legere stuck his hands through the slot in his door used to slide in his food and the guards clamped a pair of handcuffs on him, then took him out of the cell.

"My watch," Legere declared, "I need my watch."

"We're wearing watches," one of the officers replied, "we can tell you the time if you need to know it."

Legere insisted. He had to have his watch so he would know the time when they arrived in Moncton. Unwilling to drag the conversation out any further, they told him to go find it, and hurry up, they were falling behind schedule. It took a couple of minutes for Legere to find the watch, which he dug from behind his television set. Satisfied, he handed it to Hazlett, who put it on his wrist.

When the three men arrived at the security area near the entrance to the prison, Legere announced he had to go back to his cell. He was wearing slippers and had to change into his running shoes. He also wanted to bring along a crossword puzzle. The guards agreed to both requests.

After passing through three electronically controlled security areas, Legere and his two guards arrived at the admissions and departure area at 8:10. Waiting for them there was the driver of the van, Douglas Sweezey, a term employee hired in 1987. Sweezey searched the van. Regulations said the search was supposed to be done by the officer in charge and his subordinate, but Sweezey usually ended up doing it instead. Legere was taken to a cell and ordered to strip, so he could be searched. The officer assigned to the departure area came in during the search.

"Do you want to see my prick too?" Legere demanded. The officer quickly left the room.

Hazlett and Winters began to check Legere from head to toe, peering into his nose, ears and mouth, under his arms, between his toes and fingers. They picked through his hair. Finally, they demanded his spread his legs and Winters checked his rectum. Neither officer used the electronic hand scanner, which was available, to check Legere. Guards inside the prison mistakenly thought such equipment, similar to the portable units used to check passengers at airports, could not be used as part of a strip search. Had they used it, they would have discovered a collapsed television antenna which Legere had shoved up his rectum just minutes earlier.

Hazlett went through Legere's belongings – a newspaper, ball point pen and two Old Port cigars in individual plastic wrappers. Even though Legere didn't smoke, nothing about the items struck Hazlett as odd. Other prison workers, however, knew Legere didn't smoke. In fact, records kept at the prison canteen showed during the entire time he had been there, Legere had bought envelopes, stamps, chips, Pepsi and a jar of peanut butter – but never cigarettes. Such information was not a standard part of the file given to guards escorting a prisoner, however, nor did the prison keep a list of prisoners considered potential escape risks.

Less than ten minutes after it began, the search ended. Legere was allowed to dress before Hazlett fastened leg irons to his ankles and locked his hands into the body belt and attached handcuffs. Legere's parka was thrown over his shoulders and buttoned at the top and bottom. The parka's arms covered the cuffs on his wrists and body belt.

As Legere left the departure area he turned to the officer in charge there and said he wanted to store some of his things. The officer explained the proper procedure to him; Legere said he'd do it when he returned. It was 8:20 a.m.

Legere walked over to the van, jumped into the second

bench seat on the passenger's side, and settled in for the ninety minute drive to Moncton. The guards were not armed, a precaution taken in case a prisoner manages to get free and tries to grab the weapon. The officers did carry, however, cannisters containing eighty grams of Mace, a type of tear gas which could be sprayed in an inmate's face.

Legere talked briefly about his appeal, then fell silent, ignoring the officers and his crossword puzzle. The guards would later testify they watched him for all but about five minutes of the trip.

Inside the Atlantic Institution, an officer was supposed to telephone Moncton City Police to let them know Legere was on his way, but he was too busy to do so. There were problems with the electronic security system guarding the outside of the prison – it kept going off without reason. Tied up trying to figure out what was going on, he asked another officer to make the call for him. It wasn't done.

Arriving in Moncton, the prison van crossed over a small humpback bridge and drove past the turn-off normally used when taking Legere to the doctor's office. For the first time during the trip, Legere became angry. He demanded to know what was going on. They had missed their turn. He calmed down when told they had to go the Dr. Georges L. Dumont Hospital instead.

The van arrived at the hospital at 10:31. Legere insisted someone help him get out. Sweezey did so. He noticed Legere kept his arms oddly stiff against his sides as he climbed down. No one noticed that one of Legere's cigars now lay on the floor in the back of the van. It had been broken in half.

Hazlett and Winters escorted Legere into the hospital's reception area while Sweezey radioed back to the prison to announce they'd arrived. Inside, the officers, who had never been in the hospital before, took a service number and sat down at a cubicle to fill out the required paperwork.

When Legere announced he had to go to the bathroom, Winters volunteered to take the prisoner while Hazlett finished filling out the forms. When the admissions clerk pointed to the emergency area on the left, however, Legere balked, saying there were too many people there and he would be embarrassed. The clerk suggested Winters take Legere to the washroom behind the nearby canteen. Misunderstanding the instructions, Winters spotted a pair of washrooms through a nearby archway and led Legere across the hall into an adjoining wing of the hospital to a washroom used mainly by staff. Unlike the suggested washrooms, which featured stalls opening into an area containing sinks, this one opened directly into the hallway.

Legere stood in the hallway as Winters opened the door and inspected the windowless room before letting his prisoner go inside alone and close the door. Winters leaned against the wall next to the washroom. A minute or so later Legere opened the door slightly and, apparently leaning forward as if he was still sitting on the toilet seat, asked Winters if he could find some toilet paper.

"I'll get it for you," volunteered a woman walking past the door. She headed into the adjacent women's washroom to look for it.

At this point, Legere exploded out of the mens' washroom, bolted past Winters, and careered off a table in the corridor before cutting to his left and out the exit. "Don't come after me," he screamed at Winters as he shot past him. Behind him in the sink were the unlocked leg irons and handcuffs – still attached to the body belt which, mysteriously, remained locked.

Momentarily stunned by Legere's escape, Winters recovered quickly and charged after him. Outside, Legere shot past Sweezey, who was still in the van, and started clambering up a grass embankment. Sweezey leaped after him, closing to within just a few feet when Legere wheeled and slashed at him with the TV antenna, which Sweezey mistook for a sharpened screwdriver.

"Stop following me," Legere screamed. The confrontation gave Winters enough time to catch up, but as he lifted his Mace cannister Legere ducked and turned. The three-gram burst of tear gas harmlessly hit the back of Legere's parka as he started running again. Sweezey sprinted back to the van to call in the escape while Winters went after Legere, who was now heading toward the hospital parking lot.

Inside the hospital, Hazlett had finished the paperwork and said he was going to the washroom which the admitting staff had directed Winters and Legere to use. He was still standing there minutes later when the admissions clerk saw Legere run past, chased by Winters. The clerk rushed down the hall looking for Hazlett.

"Votre prisonnier s'est echappé!" she yelled when she found him. Your prisoner has escaped! She then turned and ran back down the hall, leading the guard to the exit.

Hazlett met Sweezey running the other way, back toward the prison van. "Bob," Sweezey shouted, "I'm going to phone the institution, okay?"

"Yes," Hazlett yelled back as he sprinted after Winters. Ahead, Legere had outdistanced Winters and disappeared around a corner.

At that moment, Peggy Olive was sitting in her car waiting to pay her parking lot ticket. An attractive woman with dark, curly hair reaching to her shoulders, she was well-known in the Moncton area for her horsemanship. An animal lover who worked for the SPCA, she had an empty cat's cage in the seat next to her.

A man suddenly rushed up to her car, glanced underneath its body, shouted there was something underneath it, then pulled the driver's door open. It was Allan Legere.

"He told me to move over. I just did not move," Olive said. "He had what looked like a screwdriver in his hand. He pushed me and half sat on me."

Ramming the car into gear, Legere burst through the barrier and veered right, speeding away from the hospital area. "He told me he was doing eighteen years for murder. He had nothing to lose." He was going to drop her off, he said, and he demanded that she contact a CBC reporter he knew to say he hadn't killed anyone.

"He was very aggressive. He wanted to a be a good guy. He kept changing from the good guy to the bad guy." The empty cat cage separating Olive and Legere bothered him. He kept trying to throw it in the back seat, so she moved it. "There we were, me, him and the cat cage."

Back in the parking lot, Hazlett and Winters were desperately searching for Legere but he was gone. All that remained was his parka, which the two men found lying on the ground. The parking lot attendant told them what had happened. It was 10:40 a.m.

Minutes after kidnapping her, Legere dropped off Olive. She ran into a nearby store and called police. Legere, in the meantime, left her car in the parking lot of a private radio station in the city's upper middle class West End, an area he knew well. He grabbed Olive's blue ultrasuede coat and took it with him.

City police were dumbfounded and angry. Allan Legere, a convicted killer, was on the loose in one of New Brunswick's largest communities. Roadblocks were set up. Patrols began. Traffic backed up for blocks.

News of Legere's escape travelled quickly. In Newcastle, the husband of one of the *Miramichi Leader*'s reporters picked up the news on a scanner and called the paper where they played the scanner's reports over a loudspeaker. People stood motionless, unbelieving.

In Saint John, ninety miles southwest of Moncton, RCMP officer Kevin Mole heard a news report about the escape. He jumped in his car and raced to the scene, hoping he might be able to help.

Moncton's West End is part residential, part industrial. There are houses, then an industrial park surrounded by woods, and beyond that, at the extreme western edge, a rail yard. An estimated 2,000 rail cars were passing through there daily in 1989. Police concentrated their search in that area, knowing Legere had consistently eluded them and their dogs there during a series of 1982 burglaries.

One night shortly after Legere's escape, they came close. A police dog was on Legere's trail, chasing him through the woods; a police helicopter flew overhead, searchlight glaring down. Then fog rolled in, a light rain fell, and the dog lost the scent.

Each time there was a sighting or possible sighting, each time food was stolen, dozens of policemen were there with a dog and a helicopter. But Allan Legere seemed to be gone.

On May 7, Max Ramsay was shoeing his horses in a barn at the Truro Raceway in Nova Scotia, about a two-hour drive south of Moncton when an attacker jumped the 62-year-old man from behind. Ramsay was kicked, beaten and tied up. He told police his attacker matched Legere's description, but they were doubtful.

Sixteen hours later, someone walking along the banks of the Miramichi river near the Morrissy bridge in Newcastle found Ramsay's wallet floating in the water. Searchers later dragged Ramsay's 1986 Chrysler New Yorker out of the river. It was empty.

# SIX

# Back Home

THE first reported sighting of someone prowling around the Miramichi who matched Allan Legere's description occurred on Wednesday night, May 10, 1989.

Mary Susan Gregan of Chatham had been playing bridge at a neighbour's house and arrived home just after midnight. She removed her jewelry – a twenty-four inch gold chain with a gold pendant on it and a diamond cluster ring with thirty-one stones in it – and put them in her jewelry box on a bureau next to her open bedroom window.

"It was quite warm that night and I didn't have the screens on yet, so the window was wide open. There was just a little micro-blind covering the window."

Gregan watched the Stanley Cup hockey semi-finals from Western Canada until about two in the morning, then returned to her darkened bedroom. She was walking towards the open window when she saw a head pop up, then back down outside.

"I saw the head come up and the dark, wiry hair. The size, the hair, I thought it was Allan Legere." They had been neighbours in a trailer park on the outskirts of Chatham earlier and Legere had been a customer at the bank where she worked. Certain he hadn't spotted her, Gregan dropped to the floor and crawled out of the bedroom down the hall. "I was going to call the police from the hall, but I thought he might hear me there, so I went downstairs to my husband's desk." She gave the operator her address in case something happened and asked the operator to call the police. Gregan then crawled back upstairs and sat outside her sons' rooms until the police arrived. The man was gone. Four days later, while preparing for church, Gregan reached for her pendant and ring. They were gone.

On May 16, Joe Ivory of Chatham noticed someone in a field near his home, but when he went to investigate, the person ran away. Six days later, Cathy Mercure was enjoying a sunny spring afternoon knitting when she looked up and spotted a man hiding in a ditch near her home. He had dark, wavy hair and was wearing a brown winter jacket and white, highcut running shoes.

"There's Allan Legere," she screamed. He darted across the road and out of sight. Mercure called police. She recognized him because he was acquainted with her husband Norman and had visited their home on occasion.

A few days later, Michael Sproull of the Kelly Road area reported seeing someone in the woods behind his house. It was in the same area where the Glendenning's safe had been found in 1986 and where police suspected Legere had hidden some of the money.

There was another episode on May 27. Someone broke into the garage beside Joe Ivory's home and stole a duffle bag, a piece of pie and about $100 worth of frozen meat. The incident happened just around the corner from Annie Flam's corner store.

PART TWO

# SEVEN

# The First Attack

ANNIE Flam opened her store in Chatham in 1939. The small store in a corner of the two-storey century-old house on Water Street was the heart of the neighbourhood – and Annie was the reason.

The tiny 75-year-old woman opened her shop at eight in the morning and closed at eleven at night. The only times she wasn't behind the counter was when she was hanging out clothes or taking care of her sick mother upstairs. When her mother died, Annie continued to keep the room spotless, like a shrine. On Wednesday afternoons long ago she had golfed with her friends, but now many of them were dead. Annie talked occasionally of retiring, but so far she hadn't been able to bring herself to do it.

The Flams moved to the Miramichi from Montreal in the 1920s and found themselves at home in what was then the largest Jewish community in New Brunswick. They even had their own synagogue. Over time, however, the families drifted away. By the 1960s, they couldn't even get the required ten men, or *minyan*, required for evening prayer. They'd bring in a few gentiles off the street, put skullcaps on them and say: "Pray with us, and we'll have a poker game after." By 1989, there were fewer than a dozen Jews left in Chatham.

Annie continued to observe all the Jewish holy days and

kept a kosher house. Her sister-in-law, Nina, was a great cook and helped prepare the special food. Because Nina was a Christian, her marriage to Annie's brother, Bernie, initially upset the Jewish community. The anger soon dissipated, however, and Nina and Bernie Flam went on to have four girls and adopt another. A big man, Bernie owned a furniture store next to the grocery store. The couple would fill in for Annie, especially on golf Wednesdays.

A hairdresser until she met Bernie, Nina then quit work, but still cut hair for friends. Said a friend, "For forty years I did her sewing and she did my hair." Eventually, Bernie attached his house to Annie's store, and added a connecting door between them.

Bernie was elected mayor of Chatham, the first Jewish mayor of any municipality in the province. He died in office in 1973. His photograph hung in a hallway of the Flam home. Nina and her daughers always touched it before leaving the house and said, "Bye, Daddy."

Annie mothered the neighbourhood children. Mike Bowes, a former mayor himself and now a lawyer, remembers being grilled by her. "She always wanted to know what you were doing. It was like an inquisition, but a kind one."

A long-time customer said, "You went there for an ice cream, and got a half-hour of wisdom." Another said, "You were expected to pay her a call if you hadn't seen her for awhile. I remember one time I came home from somewhere and didn't stop in right away. A day or two later my sister said, 'Annie's been asking for you, you should drop by.' I forgot. The next night my sister came in from Annie's. 'For Jesus' sake, will you go over and visit Annie's,' she said. I dropped in a bit later, bought a quart of milk and talked for an hour."

Proud, tough, and kind, this Jewish woman had a tea for one of the neighbourhood Christian girls on her first communion. "She was the most strong-willed woman on the Miramichi," said cousin Sam Rubenstein. One of the most respected, said a former police chief.

There had been just one incident in the store. In the 1970s, two young toughs had robbed her store, shoving her against the freezer so hard she hit her head. After that, she kept a hatchet for protection and put a pair of scissors under her pillow. Still, the Flams continued to keep money in the house, in drawers mostly. "Quite a sum," police would later say.

On the evening of May 28, a Sunday, Nina and Annie Flam sat in the corner store on Water Street and talked.

"Normally, I would [stay] while she closed the store, but this night I didn't," 63-year-old Nina recalled. Instead, at about 10:30 she headed upstairs to her bed.

The home was old, but well-kept, filled with polished furniture and knick-knacks. The layout was confusing for someone who hadn't been there before, as might be expected when two houses are joined. Nina's bedroom, overlooking the front street, was at the top of a flight of stairs. Annie's bedroom also overlooked the front street, but was on the opposite end of the two-home complex, directly over the store, which faced the sidewalk.

As Nina headed upstairs, Wendy Jenkins walked into the store to buy a bottle of pop just before Annie closed. She knew the Flams well. She lived nearby and dropped in two or three times a day. Annie by this time was hard of hearing. One day Wendy dropped in while Annie was watching the TV, which was blaring. Jenkins had to shout to get Annie's attention. "I could have gone right through to her apartment," Wendy said, "and she wouldn't have heard."

Allan Legere was still on the loose, but the Flams didn't seem worried, even though there had been a curious incident a couple of weeks before. Nina had found the back door on her side of the house unlocked. That was odd, she'd kept it locked day and night for more than thirty years.

This night, Nina was upstairs on the telephone talking one of her daughters, Natalie, on the phone. Afterwards she read for a little, then dozed off with the lights on.

A few doors away, Kaye Legresley-Johnson was working at the Pizza Delight restaurant. Around 11:15 she spotted a man wearing blue jeans and white running shoes walking briskly through the alley, but thought nothing more of it.

Rita McKendrick was going to bed at around 12:30. She looked out her window facing the back of the Flam home one street down the hill. A man was standing in the shadows, peering intently up at a window of a nearby building. A light was on in the window.

"He was medium size," McKendrick said. "I don't know about his height. His clothes were tight on his body and I think he had a short jacket on. I must have watched for maybe two minutes. And I went to tell my husband, but he was watching TV. I came back and watched another two minutes before the man walked away to the left and towards the Flam's place."

Nina Flam awoke with a start. There was a man standing in the doorway of her bedroom, and he was wearing a mask with part of the face cut out of it.

The moment Flam's eyes opened, the masked man rushed over, clamped a hand over her mouth and jammed a knife up against her throat. "Don't make a noise and I won't hurt you," he warned. She did as she was told. He shoved a pillow over her face to block her view, grabbed panty hose from a drawer, and tied her to the bed.

"My name is Gerald and I need $3,000. My girlfriend's pregnant and she needs an abortion." He said he lived nearby. "I've been away for awhile."

"Where does Annie keep the money?" he demanded. "She must have money."

Nina tried to tell him, but he couldn't seem to understand what she was talking about. Several times, he rushed out of the room, only to return. "Each time when I couldn't tell him where it was, he would either slap me, or punch me." Twice he throttled her with his bare hands.

"You rich people think you have everything your own way," he snarled.

"What have you done with Annie," Nina begged.

"Annie's all right," came the reply. He began to tear through her jewelry, things which belonged to her or her late husband. "Junk," he shouted. He grew angrier. The voice sounded familiar to Nina. He spoke like a Miramichier and seemed to know who she was, although he kept mispronouncing her name, calling her *Neen-a* rather than *Nine-a*. He also kept calling her "Mrs. Bernie," a reference to her late husband.

He talked about her daughter, Nancy, asking if she still went out with John Smith. He said something about Nancy being 23, which was wrong, she was 30 and no longer dated Smith.

He demanded to know more about what he thought was a safe in the store downstairs. It was, in fact, a lottery machine. He threatened to rape her if she didn't tell him where the money was.

"I couldn't tell him and he did rape me. And when I didn't do what he wanted, he'd hit me. Then he went away, and he came back, and did it again."

He performed oral sex on her, asking her as he did if her husband had ever done that to her. He was amazed when she said she hadn't made love since her husband died. He tried to force her to perform oral sex on him, inserting his penis in her mouth. He had light brown pubic hair. When she refused to do what he asked, he beat her harder than before.

He kept explaining himself, saying he "had to get hard" and "you know what it's like when you've been away for awhile."

"You like to torture people," she sobbed.

"Yes."

"You're killing me," she cried out.

"You're killing me," he mocked in return.

There was a chain around his waist and a small, metal

box on its right side. A ten-inch piece of the chain dangled at his side.

"I felt the chain, but I don't know whether he put the chain in me," Nina said.

Finally, he said he was going to burn down the house. "I'll make it look like an accident and that you died in the fire. The bad guy will be blamed for this," he predicted.

Nina couldn't see what he was doing because her head was still under the pillow. Using a match or lighter, he proceeded to set fire to the clothes in her closet and to the mattress on which she was lying. Nina didn't know it, but he had set a smouldering fire in Annie's room nearly an hour earlier. In all, there were four or five fires burning throughout the Flam property.

Then, inexplicably, he cut Nina loose and pulled her clothing back down over her body. "He tucked me into bed like a little child and told me I was going to die." He only left the room once he seemed certain the fires were catching.

Bruised and terrified, Nina Flam thought she was dead. It took her a few moments to realize she wasn't. She struggled to her feet and staggered to the door, only to discover the man was waiting in the hallway. "He shoved me back in and I fell on the flames. I know I screamed." Somehow, she got back on her feet and fought her way once more through the smoke and growing flames, lurching to the door. This time, the man was gone. She staggered into a small bedroom on her right. "I knew I couldn't stay there." The house was burning down. She had to get out. She forced herself to keep moving, back into the hallway and down the stairs.

Outside, Howie Preston of Newcastle was driving home from work. It was 3:50 a.m. As he passed the Flam store, he saw smoke pouring out of the eaves. He stopped and pounded on the front door, but it was locked. Officers Dan Pugh and William Dickson were passing by in a police car. They notified the fire department, then ran up to the house.

Pugh broke down the back door. The house was dark and full of smoke. He tried a light switch. It worked. In front of him on the floor was Nina Flam, partially clothed and barely conscious.

"Where's Annie?" he asked.

No reply.

"Where's Annie?"

Nina gestured weakly with her right hand. Upstairs, Pugh thought, she must be upstairs. He looked up. Too dangerous. The smoke was thick and growing thicker.

He picked up Nina and carried her through the downstairs to the front door. He unlocked it and took her outside. She's obviously incoherent, in shock, Dickson decided as soon as he saw her. She seemed a bit frightened of him.

"Give me your coat," Nina said. "Give me your coat." Dickson took off his jacket and gave it to her, then led her to the police car and called for an ambulance.

Firefighter Tony Lloyd ran up to the house. Wearing a fireproof suit and breathing gear, he climbed the stairs to find Annie Flam. It was impossible. The heat and smoke were too intense now. He had to turn back.

Outside, ambulance driver Fred Pitre helped Nina. He gave her oxygen and applied first aid to her burns before getting her in the ambulance and rushing her to the hospital about a mile away. Dickson called ahead and told the doctor to have a rape kit ready.

When the ambulance arrived at Hôtel Dieu Hospital, nurse Marjo Palmer tried to keep Nina Flam talking. She'd been raped, Nina said. No, the rapist hadn't worn gloves. No, she couldn't say how big he was, but he sounded older, 40 or so.

"I was afraid she might not make it," Palmer said. Nina vomited twice while being examined for evidence of the rape. Three swabs were taken from her.

Doctor Gerard Losier noted her injuries: second and third degree burns around the face, mouth, torso, back and legs. Her pelvis was also badly bruised. Her groin was also bruised and burned. Third degree burns covered forty per cent of her body.

Back at the house on Water Street, firefighters had managed to save part of the the building, but not Annie Flam. Inside, partially buried under smoldering rubble, they found her body. Her jaw had been broken. Hours later, police searched for signs of how the man had broken into the house. It was a mystery. The doors were still locked. No windows were smashed in. The damage was greatest at the front of the building, where Annie had sat each day minding her small store.

The police investigation included questioning about sixty potential suspects. And as Nina began her slow, painful recovery, RCMP officer Kevin Mole played recordings of four voices for her. One of the voices belonged to Allan Legere and had been recorded during a Court of Queen's Bench hearing. Nina Flam said she remembered Legere – he had dropped by the store often, standing around, talking to Annie – but she didn't think Legere's voice was the one she'd heard. In fact, the voice of a neighbour sounded more like her attacker's. Even though she hadn't seen Legere in years, she felt the man who'd attacked her was too small to be Legere. And her attacker had light-coloured pubic hair. Or at least that's what she believed. The hair on Legere's head was dark.

Flam's inability to recognize Legere's voice didn't deter Mole. "I was aware from speaking with Legere before that his voice, the intonation of his voice, changes depending on the mood he's in," Mole said later. "He'll often change his demeanour when you're speaking to him. He'll go from being very vocal, to being very reserved and quiet. The voice comparison that I gave Mrs. Flam to listen to was a very controlled Allan Legere testifying on his behalf."

More important, thought Mole, was the way the man behaved while in the house, the way he seem to flip from one emotion to another. This was a Legere trademark. As for the pubic hair, well, Mole suspected Nina Flam had simply made a mistake. "If Allan Legere didn't do this," Mole thought to himself, "I'll jump off the Chatham bridge."

Annie Flam's funeral was held in Saint John. The rabbi led the mourners in praying the Kaddish, the Jewish prayer of life and death. *Yisgadal v'yiskadash shmai raba.* Magnified and sanctified be His great name.

Later that summer, Nina's daughters came and took away whatever was salvageable. A crane showed up after they departed and flattened what was left of the building. The rubbish was carted off. An empty lot was all that remained.

Allan Legere's name was on everyone's lips following the Annie Flam murder, yet few thought he was responsible. True, the similarities to the Glendenning murder were obvious – the robbery of a store, an attack on elderly people, the use of extreme violence. But Legere had blamed the brutality in the Glendenning attack on Scott Curtis and Todd Matchett and many people believed him. He was considered a break-and-enter specialist, a professional criminal, to be sure, but not a wanton killer. Besides, why risk an attack in the middle of Chatham – a one-minute drive from the police station – with the police after you? And leave behind so much money? It didn't make sense.

It all made perfect sense to Kevin Mole, however. He remained convinced that Legere was their man. *Everything* pointed to him. The attacker knew the community. He was excited and in a hurry during the attack. As in the Glendenning attack three years before, he was preoccupied with finding a safe. During the rape of Nina Flam, the attacker had talked about being *away* for a long time. Legere had, after all, just escaped from prison. And Legere had been spotted in the area just days earlier. Finally, there was the attacker's use of fire. In 1986, Legere, Matchett and Curtis had quarreled over the idea of burning down the Glendenning house. Mary Glendenning said one of the men wanted a fire to destroy the evidence, but the other two had refused to allow it. Left to his own devices in the Flam house, however, the attacker set a series of fires. The killer, Mole reasoned, *had* to be Legere. But how to prove it?

The Flam investigation changed hands at the request of the provincial government, with the RCMP taking over from the Chatham town police. Information to the public about the investigation began to dry up, in part because Staff Sergeant Ben St. Onge, the completely bald and barrel-chested head of the Newcastle detachment, disliked reporters. The feeling, not surprisingly, was mutual. Still, St. Onge did break the silence long enough to tell one radio reporter that Allan Legere did not match the description of the killer provided by Nina Flam.

Sergeant Ernie Munden was named the official spokesman of the Flam investigation. A twenty-two year veteran, Munden would eventually become the most familiar RCMP face on the Miramichi. His greying moustache and almost white hair made him look older than he was, and he seemed uncomfortable with his new job. But at least he was approachable, and that seemed like a good beginning. Munden, for his part, said Legere hadn't been and couldn't be ruled out as a suspect. He had spoken to St. Onge and the evidence didn't show one way or the other that Legere was involved.

On May 29, the Supreme Court of Canada announced that Allan Legere had until the beginning of October to give himself up. If he did not surrender, or had not been captured by then, he would lose forever his chance for an appeal. Lawyers familiar with the court couldn't remember such a deadline ever being set before. It prompted speculation that Legere had an excellent chance of convincing the court to hear his appeal.

Meanwhile, people were still coming to terms with the Flam murder when an incident in Chatham set off another round of jitters. At 11:30 on the evening of June 1, Joe Ivory and his wife were pulling into the driveway of their home after a day at the cottage when they spotted a man trying to break into their garage. The man was wearing a light grey jacket, tight jeans and white sneakers and carried a knapsack. Caught in the glare from the headlights, he bolted through a gate. Shaken by the murder a few days earlier, and furious that his property was again being violated, Ivory hit the gas and roared off after the prowler.

With his wife still in the car, Ivory sped through the neighbourhood, tearing past neighbours' homes, knocking over a lawn chair and crushing a ladder as he tried to run down the man. Ivory was forced to give up when the man dashed up a driveway and vanished. Ivory rammed a fence in one final attempt to hit the man.

The next morning, Chatham contractor Lloyd Hannah arrived at a downtown home to do some landscaping work. He spotted a pair of smoke-gray men's glasses in a hole next to a pile of deck lumber. The glasses were close to the spot where Joe Ivory last saw the prowler the night before.

On June 3, Kevin Mole took the glasses to a Moncton optometrist to compare them to Legere's prescription. According to the acting police chief in Chatham, Jack Bell, "These glasses were checked by an optometrist and are the same type, style and prescription as worn by Allan Legere at the time of his escape from custody in Moncton."

Crown prosecutor Fred Ferguson, considered a potential target by police officers who knew of Legere's hatred for him, broke the news to his wife. She began to cry. Allan Legere, it seemed, was indeed back, it wasn't just a rumour anymore.

At a press conference a few days after the Ivory sighting, Munden warned people that trying to catch an escaped killer like Allan Legere isn't like what they see on television. "It's very, very difficult to go ahead and locate somebody, a resident of the area who has in-depth knowledge of crimes, having committed crimes, who is very aware of the police situation."

"This is his home," he said of Legere. "He's quite

comfortable in these surroundings. There could even be people helping him."

The killing of Annie Flam and reports of more than fifty sightings of Allan Legere or someone people thought was Legere set off a spree of security system purchases. Elderly people who could afford it had metal bars installed on basement windows. Hardware stores reported a jump in the sales of dead bolts and door chains. To make matters worse, two other convicts were on the loose as well. Brothers David and John Tanasichuk had been serving time for break-and-enters. One was in the Westmorland minimum security institution at Dorchester, New Brunswick, the other at a correctional facility in Parrsboro, Nova Scotia. On May 22, David had escaped. John followed soon after. The Tanasichuks knew the Flams, and police considered David, along with Legere, a suspect in the murder of Annie Flam.

Ferguson called the Tanasichuks "disorganized criminals." They were so inept one of the brothers accidentally shot his partner while using a motorcycle to escape after a robbery. The RCMP found the Tanasichuk brothers an hour's drive south of Newcastle in the Harcourt area. They'd been hiding at a hunting camp. After questioning them, police quickly eliminated David as a murder suspect and the two were later charged with being unlawfully at large.

From time to time that summer intensive police manhunts for Legere took place. Helicopter, dogs and search teams were used, but nothing turned up. Police pressured Legere's friends, but if they knew anything, they weren't saying. Suspects were asked for and supplied hair samples and, in some cases, recordings of their voices. Crime Stoppers offered a $2,000 reward for information leading to Legere's arrest. Nothing, however, seemed to work.

A manhunt in mid-June involved police with dogs and a helicopter combing woods around the industrial park in Chatham, apparently acting on a tip. Again, nothing turned up. The next week there were reported sightings of Legere in both Fredericton, more than 100 miles to the south, and, amazingly, the Caledon East area northwest of Toronto. Newcastle RCMP said they believed Legere was still in the Miramichi, but they had no proof. By late July, they thought he might be gone. Many Miramichi residents agreed. After all, hadn't he apparently been spotted shortly after his escape in the area where the Glendenning's safe had been found in 1986? Everyone knew there was supposedly thousands of dollars still missing from that robbery. Perhaps, people surmised, he had returned to dig up his hidden money, then taken off. Hopefully, for good.

What people did not know was that intense work was going on behind the scenes by RCMP officers to try to prove Allan Legere had killed Annie Flam. In June, after reading about a relatively new laboratory technique called DNA fingerprinting, Kevin Mole had tried to find out if it might help police connect Legere to the murder. What Mole needed was a sample of Legere's blood or hair. Worried about using the hair sample taken in 1986 because of a New Brunswick Court of Appeal decision, which had called the seizure of the hair illegal, Mole hoped there was an alternative. Calling the RCMP crime laboratory in Sackville, he was told the knife used to stab Legere in Dorchester Penitentiary in 1986 might have enough blood on it to be used in such a test.

Mole gave serologist Sandy Lumgair the knife and a semen swab taken from Nina Flam. He asked her if they were suitable for DNA analysis. They weren't. For one thing, there just wasn't enough blood on the knife.

With Legere still at large and the Flam investigation at a dead end, the RCMP officer felt he was out of alternatives. A request for permission to use the controversial hair samples taken from Legere in 1986 was refused. The appeal court had spelled it out: the seizure of the hair had been illegal. Yes, it had been allowed as evidence in the Glendenning case because the police hadn't realized their mistake

and were acting honourably. If they tried using that hair
again, however, three years after it was taken, they could
expect no sympathy from a judge. By July 6, the question
appeared academic anyway. The RCMP Central Forensic
Laboratory in Ottawa said it could not do DNA analysis
using hair because it didn't have the necessary equipment –
and would not for some time.

One alternative remained – a method of analyzing secre-
tions like semen and saliva to determine a person's blood
type. Mole was told this test could determine whether or
not the blood from a suspect belonged to the same group as
that of the attacker. The test wasn't as exact as DNA fingerprinting, but it was something.

The investigators thought it over, then rejected the idea.
They had little physical evidence, just three swabs of material, and they didn't want to sacrifice any of it to a test that
wouldn't point a firm, convincing finger at a suspect. The
officers felt they had to pin their hopes on DNA fingerprinting, even though their understanding of the process at this
time was sketchy. Mole, for instance, thought the DNA
tests would provide a complete physical description of the
attacker, right down to the colour of his hair. Meanwhile,
the officers explored the possibilities of having the work
done by the FBI in the United States or Scotland Yard in
England.

While they waited, Mole and Corporal Gaetan Germain
drove to the Atlantic Institution in Renous on July 25 to
meet with Peter Roberts, the institutional preventative
security officer. They wanted to search Legere's cell. They
hoped something there might help them in their hunt.
They spotted a piece of paper with the name of a doctor and
the date March 28, 1989 on it. The note mentioned a wart
and said it was now available for analysis. The next day,
Mole talked to William Scarrow at the Moncton Hospital
and was told the regional pathology lab for Northumberland County had the wart in storage. Search warrant in
hand, jubilant RCMP officers picked it up July 28. The cele-

bration was short-lived. On August 2, the RCMP lab in Ottawa said the wart wouldn't work. They needed hair. Worse, the officers discovered there were just three independent DNA labs recommended or accepted by the courts – two were in the United States, the other in Ontario. Each was too busy to do the work until 1990.

The officers reconsidered the semen-blood type test. It could do one of three things: eliminate Legere as a suspect, include him in the group who might be a suspect, or tell them nothing. They gave the lab the half of a swab which had already been examined by the lab in Sackville. The other two swabs would be kept for DNA testing, should it become available.

The results came back quickly and devastated the police. The test couldn't tell them anything because "substances" released by Nina Flam's body contaminated the test, making it impossible to pinpoint the blood type of her attacker.

For most Miramichiers, the summer and early fall passed peacefully, uneventfully. Then, less than two hours before the Supreme Court's October 1 deadline for Legere's appeal, violence struck the region again.

At 10:30 on Saturday night, September 30, Morrissy Doran of Newcastle struggled to his phone to call the police. The 70-year-old man had been shot in the back with a shotgun. He described his attacker as an unshaved man about five feet, 11 inches tall with a medium to heavy build wearing what might have been a black leather jacket, dark clothing and a ski mask. The attacker crawled into the house through a basement window, and came upstairs into the house. He demanded money, but Doran fought back and was shot before his attacker fled.

The next night, 76-year-old Edwin (Sonny) Russell and his 63-year-old wife Evangeline were attacked in their home, just a five minute walk from the Doran residence. Just after nine o'clock, they had heard someone struggling to get in through a basement window. The man managed to force it open, but then suddenly turned and ran to the back door leading into the kitchen and burst inside, a shotgun in his hand. He lashed out with the weapon, knocking both Russell and his wife unconscious, then started to roam around the house.

Evangeline regain consciousness first and ran outside, her attacker pursuing her out into the street. The Russell home was barely a minute away from the Newcastle police station. Sonny, in the meantime, regained consciousness and went after his assailant. The two men fought briefly in the street, then the attacker broke off and ran, heading south, leaving behind his gun.

Police had barely arrived at the Russell home when a second call came in. Someone had tried to break into the home of Todd Matchett's father, Billy, about two miles away on the south end.

Police cars roared off, arriving minutes later at Matchett's where a man matching the description of the attacker in the Doran and Russell incidents was spotted running away.

A door-to-door search turned up nothing and the investigation quickly stalled. Still, police said they had a good composite sketch of the attacker. The incidents rekindled the fear of the previous spring, but for most there were too many differences between the Flam murder and the assaults. These attacks seemed amateurish compared to the Flam murder.

A week later, newpapers noted the Supreme Court of Canada was set to officially drop Allan Legere's appeal case the next day, Thursday, October 12. The next day, RCMP officials in Fredericton received good news from their Ottawa laboratory. It could do a DNA analysis in the Flam case this fall. The letter announcing this arrived too late for word to reach those officers working on the case before the weekend, but it looked like a link between the killing and Legere might soon be established. It was Friday, October 13.

# EIGHT

# The Second Attack

THAT Friday dawned sunny and mild – a perfect day, thought 56-year-old Bernard Geikie of Newcastle, to take a drive to his camp upriver. Coming out of his house, Geikie glanced over and saw Donna Daughney in her backyard hanging out the wash. He waved. She waved back.

They had been neighbours for 33 years, ever since Bernard and Mary married. That's the way it is on Mitchell Street. Tucked in behind a saw mill and a set of railway tracks leading to the Newcastle wharf, it's working class and proud of it. People know their neighbours, their children. They look out for each other.

"I can remember when they were both born," said Geikie of Donna and her younger sister Linda. "They were paving the street for the first time. I saw them grow up. When Donna graduated, she got dressed here to go to her prom." He could remember her getting her first new dress when she was 12.

"We considered them our daughters. You couldn't have girls come into your house every day and have the relationship they had with my children and grandchildren and not think that way. Donna would light up your room when she walked in. If it was a dull day, she'd light it up."

That evening, Margaret Murray stepped out of her home beside the Daughneys' to remove a wash from her clothesline. The sun was setting and the night felt like it was going to be cold. As she reeled in the wash, Murray glanced across the driveway to her neighbours'.

The Daughneys were having their house renovated. Workers were putting on robin-egg blue exterior siding. They were more than half done by quitting time; the siding reached above the windows and doors of the first floor. Three long cardboard boxes of siding sat a few feet from the back door. Nearby, old windows and plastic were stacked against a white shed. A fence enclosed the yard. The few trees had lost most of their leaves in the past couple of weeks.

Murray could see Donna standing inside her home painting the frame of a window. "Donna was a perfectionist. They just had new windows installed and she was standing in one window painting it."

Murray knew the sisters well. Life hadn't been easy for them – or their older sister Frances. Their father, Charlie, was an alcoholic. He didn't beat the girls when they were growing up, but he often yelled at them and sometimes locked them out of the house if they hadn't come home when he demanded. Saturday mornings, their mother, Willa, would cross the railway tracks to the saw mill, her children holding her hands. She stood in line with the men, waiting for Charlie's cheque. If she didn't get it before he did, he'd drink it away. The sisters rarely talked about those early years, but when they did, it was with bitterness.

Frances Daughney moved away, eventually settling in Alaska. Donna moved to Ontario to work, but returned after her mother died to take care of her father and Linda. When Charles Daughney died, the sisters stayed on in Newcastle.

The two women were quite different. Donna, 45, was more outgoing than Linda, who was four years younger, wore glasses and suffered from the skin condition eczema. Linda loved earrings, sometimes wearing as many as three in each pierced ear.

"Donna was very protective of Linda," said a girlfriend who remembered going to the local Legion with them. "Linda wasn't slow or retarded, as some people said, just extremely timid, to the point of being frightened if someone asked her to dance. If Donna thought someone was bothering her younger sister, she could be fiercely protective, to the point of telling men to get lost."

Donna Daughney worked hard at staying in shape, walking miles each day and lifting weights at a downtown gym when she wasn't working part-time for the local welfare department. Rings were a passion and she wore several at one time. A large red one, in particular, rarely left her finger. Neither woman had a boyfriend. Donna had gone out with someone for a while, but it hadn't worked out. She never wanted to marry, she told friends, because she was afraid her husband would treat her the way her father had treated them.

Like everyone on the Miramichi, the sisters had heard about Allan Legere still being in the area, but didn't take any special precautions, even after the Doran and Russell attacks just two weeks earlier. The sisters had a routine that rarely varied. Supper was at 4:30, and at 5:10 Linda would walk to the Geikies' for tea.

Friday the 13th was just like any other day. That evening, Linda shared a small drink with Donna, then got ready to visit a friend, Faye Hachey, who lived a short walk away. The two women had known each other for about five years and were close friends. Linda pulled a jean jacket over her knitted sweater and glanced in a mirror to check her earrings before leaving. She didn't take along a purse as she walked out the rear door. The door on the side of the house couldn't be used because the steps had been removed so the new siding could be installed. Daughney and Hachey went to a nearby Tim Horton's franchise for a coffee and talked to some friends they met there. It was about 10:00 p.m.

On Mitchell Street, William White was just going to bed when he looked out his front door. He'd glanced out periodically during the evening to see if Donna Daughney was still painting the window frames next door. She was. White waved, then turned and went to bed. It was 10:15 p.m.

At Tim Horton's, Linda and Faye were ready to head home. It was about 11:00 p.m. "We went down the King George Highway," Hachey said. "I left her where I live. She was going home, across Pleasant Street to Pond Street."

Walking the final few steps down the slight hill on Davidson Lane, Linda Daughney could see her house on the corner. There was no street light at the intersection, as there is now, so it was dark. The light at the back door of her home was out. Usually, Donna left it on for her. It must have blown, Linda thought. She'd have a difficult time unlocking the door in the dark. Perhaps she'd just knock on the door and Donna could open it.

Margaret Murray was watching TV next door to the Daughney home. "I went to the kitchen to make a lunch for my husband. I heard a noise, like wind blowing. I knew the wind was blowing, but this noise was worse. I turned off the kitchen light and went to the door." She peered into the night. "I was looking straight across at the Daughneys' house, but everything was pitch black. I didn't see a thing, so I thought it must have been the wind blowing."

Odd, she thought as she reached for the light switch, the sisters always left the outside light on until the last one was home. Margaret flipped on her kitchen light, finished making the lunch for her husband and took it to him.

Meanwhile, a few feet away, Linda Daughney had walked into a killer's hands.

He may have been peeking in the windows, staring at Donna as she painted the inside frames of the windows. Intent on what he was doing, Linda may have surprised him. Or maybe he had been waiting for her to come home. Perhaps the urge was welling up inside of him and her arrival was the trigger.

A few feet from the back door he leaped at Linda, driving a fist into her face. She stumbled backwards in the darkness, probably unconscious before she hit the ground. The blow broke her upper and lower jaws, ripping lose a pair of her earrings. Blood spewed from her shattered nose and mouth, soaking into the ground. A gold earring with a white stone landed on the gravel driveway. A heart-shaped earring sailed onto the grass beside a box of siding in the backyard. Her shattered glasses landed amid tufts of pink fibreglass insulation on the driveway.

Inside, Donna Daughney leaped to the kitchen window and strained to see what was going on. She ran to the back door to turn on the light, wondered why it was off in the first place. Later, it was found to have been partially unscrewed.

The killer charged the few feet to the back door, stumbling briefly over a ladder left there by the men working on the house. Catching his balance, he yanked open the screen door, tearing apart the plastic lock, then crashed into the inside door, splitting it and shattering the casing. Splinters of wood flew across the kitchen.

A stunned Donna Daughney tried to scream. She fought back, but her powerfully built attacker overwhelmed her easily. Downstairs, furniture was scattered about as she struggled. Bits of flesh were torn off her legs and the trunk of her body as she fought to stay alive. Trying to run upstairs, she was grabbed by the hair and her head rammed against the wall, leaving a blood stain the size of pumpkin. With her blood covering the bannister, she ran towards her small bedroom to the left at the top of the stairs, vainly trying to keep her attacker from coming after her.

Her fingers made patterns in the blood that splattered on the inside of her door as she tried to claw her way past her attacker. Her fingernails dug into his flesh, tearing at it. He grabbed her by the neck, leaving deep bruises on the right side as he squeezed.

By this point, Donna Daughney's face was shattered and covered in blood. Like her sister, her upper and lower jaws had been broken, her nose smashed almost flat against her face, her eyes blackened, and swollen. A hail of punches and kicks had broken five ribs. One blow to the head was so severe it had ruptured a blood vessel in the brain.

Still, Donna Daughney's nightmare wasn't over. The attacker hauled the now-unconscious sister onto the bed. He pulled out a knife and poked her in the throat, but not so deep as to kill her. It opened a wound about an inch deep and an inch wide, puncturing her voice box, forcing Donna to gasp for air.

He then slashed at her chest and face, making shallow, S-shaped cuts in her body. Her blood soaked the mattress, leaving a large stain in the middle. The pillowcase was red with blood. More blood splattered on the wall behind her head.

The attacker proceeded to pull down his pants. The excitement of the attack made it easy to get an erection. His semen stained her lower abdomen and genital area. Her body, unable to cope with the attack, went into shock and Donna Daughney vomited. The contents of her stomach flooded her lungs, and she began to drown her in her own vomit.

At this point, the killer remembered Linda Daughney, still lying unconscious outside on the lawn, hidden by the darkness. He pulled on his pants, grabbed a piece of blue cord and ran outside. He bundled up the younger sister and dragged her into the house, her blood dripping on to the back steps as she was yanked inside.

Going up the staircase, he pulled off her jean jacket, throwing it behind him to the bottom of the stairs. He tore at her pants and pantyhose, turning them inside out as he yanked them off, leaving them behind on the stairs. He dropped Linda on the floor of Donna's room.

With both sisters unconscious, there was no longer any reason to hurry. He calmly picked his way through Donna Daughney's clothing and poked in dresser draws. Finding her underclothes, he procceded to toss panties around the room.

It was quiet. The killer looked out the window on to Mitchell Street. The neighbours were all in bed, their lights off. He left the bedroom to wander around the house. The upstairs was set up rather like a donut with the stairs forming the hole in the middle. Just outside Donna's door stood a walnut-coloured bureau. He spied a jewelry box and purse. He dug through both, taking whatever seemed valuable, dumping the rest on to a white rug at his feet.

He looked across the hall into Linda's room. Next to it was the bathroom. Inside, several toothbrushes sat in a holder on the counter. On a shelf next to the sink were brown, red and blue towels – neatly folded and put away. He disturbed nothing. Walking clockwise around the donut, he noted the large number of potted plants in the window overlooking the back yard.

Completing the circle in front of Donna's room, he headed down the unusually steep staircase, steep because of the small size of the house. Looking to his right, his eyes swept across the living room, taking in the yellow-orange floral print on the couch by the window overlooking Mitchell Street. He saw the coffee table in front of the couch where a few books and box of Kleenex sat on top. The linoleum squeaked under his feet as he ran a hand along the panelboard on the wall.

He turned left into the kitchen, enjoying the silence, the soft light from distant street lights filtering through the windows. He noted the brown, patterned wallpaper, the plants hanging from rope baskets, the plastic bag full of cloth sitting on the counter. A kettle, toaster, wooden butcher's block and knife stand stood undisturbed, all the knives still in their places.

A pile of eighteen rolls of quarters, wrapped in brown paper, formed a flattened pyramid on the counter. A bluish green vase held flowers. He leaned over the sink to look past the curtains and out the window. As the thirteenth became the fourteenth, he felt matters were sufficiently in hand that he could turn on the lights.

Around 3:30 a.m., a teenager, Terri Mazerolle of nearby
Pond Street, drove past the Daughney residence on her way
home from a date. "That's strange," she thought, "the
lights are on in the house." The Daughneys weren't the
kind of people to be up at such an hour. They usually went
to bed early. Still, it didn't seem something to worry about,
so Mazerolle continued on home to get some sleep.

Inside the Daughney home, the killer headed back
upstairs to Donna Daughney's room. He looked down at
Linda Daughney, sprawled on the floor in front of the bedroom closet. Glancing up, he saw a pair of eyeglasses on the
nearby dresser. A large pile of clothes cluttered the floor.
Tangled in the clothing were a set of false teeth, a bra, a
facecloth, and a short length of blue rope. Donna's body was
already growing cold. But Linda, although unconscious,
was still alive. Once again the killer pulled down his pants.
Later semen was found in Linda's pubic area and there was a
bite mark on her breast.

Dawn was little more than an hour away. The killer prepared to leave. In Linda's room he pulled open the door to
the closet and, using a lighter, set the clothing on fire, then
shut the door. He stopped in the doorway to Donna's room
for a final look. He went inside and pulled the covers over
her body and tucked her into the bed. Then he left the
house.

Joseph Wayne Williams and his son, Joseph Roderick Williams, were busy that morning driving trucks for the Gold
Line transport company. They were hauling material from
the Repap pulp mill in Nelson-Miramichi across the river
to the Newcastle mill.

At 5:10 Wayne noticed a man standing at the railway
tracks near the intersection of Mitchell and Jane streets, a
few feet from the fire station and about three hundred yards
from the Daughney house.

"He had long, dark hair and a beard," Wayne remembered. "The left side of his head looked wet, dirty or matted.

I was going to tell the police about it if I ran into any of them on the street, but I didn't see any police cars that night."

Roderick passed by twenty minutes later and saw the man in the same place. He had a narrow face and looked like he weighed about 200 pounds.

At 5:45 a.m., Mark Manderson of Bushville was driving to his job at the Miramichi Pulp and Paper mill on the south end of Newcastle. "I crossed over the Morrissy Bridge, turned left onto Mitchell Street and Davidson Lane. At the corner of Davidson, there was an individual on my right side. It was very dark and I could only see in the headlights of the car. I travelled the route for a year and I never saw anyone on the road at that hour before. The headlights lit the individual's back."

As Manderson drove by, the man turned to his right, raising his shoulders at the same time. "This severely limited my view of his face. He acted suspicious." Manderson decided to stop and look in his rearview mirror. "I saw a figure standing there fifty to a hundred feet away. I noticed the individual was wearing a hat or liner from a helmet. His clothing was baggy and didn't fit very well and it seemed his clothing was layered. They were poor quality clothes."

Manderson couldn't tell the colour of the man's clothing or much about his appearance. He did notice, however, that the man *wasn't* wearing glasses and *didn't* have a beard. It was still too dark to see more. It was a cold morning and the man seemed to be bobbing up and down to keep warm.

"It was quite a spectacle to see. His upper body was literally bouncing and weaving side to side, but his feet were stationary. His head was canted toward the ground and his arms were out. I was convinced it was a male and judging from his agility, he was not an old man. He was bouncing his upper body. He was about five feet 11 inches, slight build. It appeared to me the head was a bit bunchy on the side, that his hair wasn't cut very tight on his head."

Inside the Daughney house, the fire was smoldering, there

were no flames, nothing that was visible from outside. Returning to check his "handiwork," the killer was upset to see that the home was not a conflagration. He went inside. Donna was still on the bed, Linda on the floor. Linda was still breathing.

He stepped over Linda and started a second fire, this one in Donna's closet. Then he crossed the hall to check on the first blaze, opening doors, doing what he could to speed it along. Now the fire took off. Flames exploded across Linda's empty bedroom, scorching everything. The door caught fire. Her headboard and window frame were charred and paint peeled from the walls, turning them greyish black. Flames chewed at the floor, eating their way towards the kitchen below. The house smoke detector began to bleat.

The killer ran from the house, shut the door behind him, and disappeared. Upstairs, the fire continued its voracious search for wood, oxygen, flesh. Linda's unconscious body fought for air as well, struggling to survive the smoke that was billowing through the house. But it was no use: with her airways blackened and the house burning around her, she stopped breathing.

At 7:35 a.m., Danny Sullivan and his girlfriend were on their way to the swimming pool at the CFB Chatham base for a scuba diving lesson. Driving through Newcastle, Sullivan looped down Davidson Lane and on to Mitchell Street. Workers, he noticed, had put up some siding on the old two-storey house at the corner. A renovator himself, he checked their work as he pulled up at the stop sign, then swung left past the home.

"I was looking at the lines of their siding to see if it matched up at the corner," he said. There's nothing worse than siding that's crooked, he thought to himself as he measured the work with his eyes. Then something caught his attention. Smoke. It appeared to be pouring out of the eaves. Could be the fireplace acting up, Sullivan thought.

A volunteer firefighter with the Newcastle department for six years, Sullivan hit the gas and raced around the corner to the fire station. He pulled on his gear, leaped into a pumper truck and roared back to the house, radioing for help as he did. At the house, he jumped out and started setting the engine up to pump water.

Newcastle police officer Charlie Barter was just two blocks away when the call came in. He arrived at the house just as Sullivan was dragging a hose off the fire truck. "We met at the rear of the house," Sullivan said. "I went to the rear door and Constable Barter was on the landing. The screen door was open and the other door was shut.

"Should I go in? Should I kick the door in?" Barter asked.

"No," said Sullivan, "stay out of there. We don't know what we're up against."

The fireman touched the door gingerly with his fingertips, checking to see if it was hot. Nothing. He tried it with his palm. Still okay, but the door looked pretty solid and was probably locked. He crouched down, preparing to break it open, staying low to try to avoid a possible explosion of flames when the outside air hit the fire. He told Barter to do the same. The moment Sullivan's shoulder hit the door, it popped open.

"I fell through the door and I landed on the kitchen floor on my hands and knees. I ducked first. I thought there might be a chance of an explosion. The kitchen was full of smoke and the smoke detector was bellowing. I wasn't prepared to go any further and I closed the door."

He had to get an air pack. Passing the door, he noticed what looked like a split in it near the lock. The crack ran from the top to bottom.

"What do we do now?" yelled Barter over the noise of the smoke detector and sirens of approaching fire trucks and police cars.

"Hell, I don't know," yelled Sullivan. "We can't go in there."

"There should be a couple of girls in there," shouted a

neighbour. A growing crowd watching the firemen. Another fireman ran into the house, checked the downstairs as best he could, then ran out again. The upstairs was full of smoke.

Next door, the shouting woke up the Murrays. Margaret smelled smoke. She turned to tell her husband, who jumped up to see what was going on.

Another fireman, Reg Falconer, raced up to the back door wearing a Scot air pack, hip waders, hard hat and face shield. He was determined to make it upstairs. Fighting his way through the smoke and heat, he struggled to the second floor, feeling his way with his hands, using a flashlight to try to cut through the blackness. The only sounds were that of the fire. No one was crying for help. Turning right at the top of the stairs, he began a frantic search for the two women who were said to live there. It was hot, but the bull-necked fireman had been in worse. Still, the smoke was so thick in the hallway that his flashlight was practically useless. Reaching out with his left hand, he groped for the wall. He found Linda's empty room first. It was badly burned, there were melted shoes and smoking bits of clothing on the floor.

Circling clockwise, he passed the bathroom, a window, and a spare bedroom. There was one room remaining. Straining to see as he entered the room, he saw the shape of a fireman on a ladder at the window straight ahead. To the right, the white of a fluffy quilt on the bed in the corner caught his eye. The room was a haze of smokey shadows.

Then, through a break in the smoke, he saw at his feet what he feared most – a woman lying face down on the floor. She was wearing a T-shirt – no, two T-shirts – and pair of socks. Her head seemed to be resting against a dresser. She wasn't moving. He dropped down, turned her over and grabbed her in the classic, fireman's rescue position. Her head rested against his chest as he hugged her unmoving form and started backing out of the room.

Outside the window, fireman James Matheson was

smashing the the glass so he could get his water hose inside.

"I've got a body!" screamed Falconer. "I've got a body!"

Matheson dropped the hose and leaped through the glass. He grabbed the woman's heels and helped lift her out into the hall. Then he turned and ran back inside, frantically looking for the second woman.

In the hall, Falconer was in trouble. He was forced to drag the dead weight of the woman backwards down the steep stairs. No longer able to use his flashlight, he could only twist his head around and try to squint through the visor of his breathing gear.

It proved an impossible task. Partway down the stairs he lost control, lurched and fell backwards, still grasping the woman in his arms. She crashed down on top of him, and they landed in a pile at the bottom. Firemen rushed up, lifted her off him and headed outside with her. Among them was fireman Roy Geikie. "I was looking to see who it was because I knew Linda and Donna very well." But what he saw left him confused. "I couldn't tell who it was. I noticed that she wasn't wearing any clothing, just a blue top. The colour of skin was darker beneath it. The face was bruised and swollen. Both eyes were quite puffy. Blood covered the eyes."

Gently, the firemen put the woman on the ground nearby. "She was covered in soot or debris," Barter noted. "In my mind I thought it was an accidental fire. [But] I noticed the eyes were swollen. She had blackened eyes and there were people gathering to see." The constable grabbed a piece of pink insulation from the back yard and used it to cover the body.

Upstairs, fireman Glen Tozer had climbed through the window into the room. He and Matheson knew there was probably a second woman in the house. But where?

"I think there's something on the bed," yelled Tozer through his breathing equipment. Smoke filled the room.

"Are you sure?" shouted Matheson. "You sure it's not part of the hose you're tripping on?"

"I know there's somebody there!"

Desperately, Matheson reached out through the smoke, his hands running over the blankets on the bed. A hand hit something. A foot!

Air from outside was finally driving some of the black smoke out of the room and Matheson was able to see it was a woman lying face down on the bed, covered by blankets. Only her head was showing, her face turned to one side.

"I yelled and screamed and shook the body, but there was no response," Matheson said. "I crawled on the bed and knelt. It was almost like she was tucked into the bed under a sheet and a comforter." He tugged at the woman, jerking her free. All she had on was a T-shirt.

"I put her in a clinch. I noticed she was naked from the waist down," Matheson said. "I wasn't sure until then whether it was male or female. She was lily white. I tried to comfort her. I held her head off the floor. I just assume everybody's alive. I was thinking we had a limp, heavy form who'd just been rescued from a flash fire in the ceiling. I cradled her head in my left hand." He looked at his hands. "I noticed the back of the head was very matted and wet. There was blood on my glove." He and Tozer lifted her up and carried her out.

At about eight o'clock at his home, funeral director Brandt Adams received a phone call. There was a fire at the Daughney home on nearby Mitchell Street. Perhaps he'd like to check it out. Adams dressed quickly and dashed out to see if he could help. He'd known the Daughney sisters for fourteen years and considered them quiet, personable people who kept to themselves. As he arrived, he saw a body being brought out of the burning house, but, like Roy Geikie, he couldn't tell if it was Linda or Donna.

Meanwhile, St. John Ambulance attendant Ernie MacLean of Chatham Head was struck by what he saw when he looked at the women. "I noticed the faces. Both eyes were black and swollen." Odd, he thought. He asked Const. Barter to come with him to the Miramichi Hospital in Newcastle. A closer look at the bodies told the officer that this had been no accident. The blackened eyes, the puffy lips, the broken noses, the disfigured jaws. Obviously these women had been beaten. He, MacLean and a nurse stayed with the women until RCMP arrived later in the day.

At 8:10 a.m. the bodies of Linda and Donna Daughney were wheeled into the morgue at the Miramichi Hospital. Dr. Basil Blanchard pronounced both women dead. He noted the badly bruised faces and broken noses. At 9:30, Brandt Adams arrived at the hospital to look at the bodies. Unable to identify them by looking at what was left of their faces, he had to rely on what he knew about the sizes of the two women. "Donna was heavier than Linda," he said. "Donna's face was fuller and she was taller than her sister."

Plastic bags were placed over their hands to preserve any possible evidence and the bodies put in cold storage. Later that day, a hearse, escorted by an RCMP car, headed for Halifax. There they planned to shine a special laser on the outside of the bodies, hoping it might spot evidence invisible otherwise. After that, the bodies would be taken to Saint John for an autopsy.

Back at the house, firefighters had managed to save the house, although the fire had burned a hole in the floor separating the kitchen and Linda's room.

Whereas October 13 had been sunny and mild, the fourteenth was cloudy, gray and gloomy. Margaret Murray watched as police combed the Daughney sisters' yard. They found a pool of blood on the lawn. A metal detector uncovered a piece of metal, a long-lost quarter. Two cigarette butts turned up, one under the fence behind the shed, one on the back steps.

"There was a Mountie and a dog going around the house," Murray said. "There was a step ladder and he moved it and it clicked. It was the same noise I heard the night before."

# NINE

# Keeping Secrets

Among the RCMP officers called to Newcastle to help investigate the double murder was Kevin Mole. A quick look inside the house, as well as photographs of the victims, convinced him the killer had to be Allan Legere. The similarity to the earlier attacks was, he felt, striking: the battered faces, the torture involving a knife, the sexual assault, the tying-up of the victims, the setting of fires to try to destroy the evidence, even the timing of the attacks. Nina Flam had estimated her attacker had broken into their home around 11:30 at night – about the same time Linda Daughney had walked into her killer's grasp and the front door of the Glendenning home had been broken down.

After months of pushing, the announcement that the Ottawa laboratory was ready to do the DNA analysis, provided "unencumbered" samples of Legere's hair could be found, was welcome news. Mole was certain it would prove him right. It set off, however, a renewed debate about using the Legere hair sample taken in 1986. Lacking an alternative, this time the RCMP decided to risk it. In the meantime, Mole hoped there might be sufficient physical evidence in the Daughney home to link Legere with the sisters' deaths.

If police were getting anywhere with the rest of their investigation, however, they weren't telling anyone. The first statement issued after the murders of the Daughney sisters simply said the women had been beaten and that police were trying to find out if the killings were related to any other cases.

Three days after the murders, Sgt. Ernie Munden met with reporters in the small coffee room of the Newcastle detachment. He told reporters a composite sketch of a suspect would not be released because it might give the attacker a chance to change his appearance. He confirmed the women had been brutally beaten and sexually assaulted, but said nothing else would be released to ensure the investigation and family would be protected. He acknowledged there were similarities between the Flam and Daughney murders, but it wasn't conclusive proof. Yes, it might be a serial killer, but that had to be determined. Yes, Legere was a suspect, but he wasn't the only one.

"If Legere is responsible," Munden added, "he must be apprehended. If he is not, it is important not to mislead people into thinking he is the prime suspect." He pleaded for the public's help, even help from local criminals. "The criminal community have their own code of ethics and would not and should not tolerate this and previous crimes." He urged people not to buy or use guns for protection.

Although not involved in the day-to-day investigation, he had seen what the killer had done and it unnerved him. As the news conference ended he picked up photographs of the Daughney sisters. The tightly controlled voice broke. "I've only seen these people in the hospital, in the morgue. It is very difficult to see the loss of human life, especially when it comes to women, even more so, children. The person or persons who took their lives has to be brought to justice very, very quickly. It is a terrible crime."

There were tears in his eyes.

Shortly after the double murder, the telephone rang in the home of Crown prosecutor Fred Ferguson. His wife picked

it up. A man asked to speak to Fred. When told the prosecutor was out, the man asked if he was speaking to Mrs. Fred
Ferguson.

"Yes."

"Well, you're next," the caller snarled.

The RCMP's attempt to impose a news blackout only served
to magnify the significance of the little information that
was available.

Word spread of two attempted thefts committed the
night of the murders. A Chatham businessman living in
Newcastle heard a noise and suddenly his cable TV picture
went fuzzy. He flipped on the back light just in time to see
someone running away. The cable wire had been cut, possibly after being mistaken for a telephone line. Around midnight, at a home just minutes from the Daughney house, a
man surprised a thief upstairs in his home. The thief
jumped out a window taking some money and jewelry with
him.

Desperate to protect themselves, terrified residents set
off another mini-boom in security equipment sales. The
provincial utilities company, N.B. Power, was forced to add
extra crews to try to keep up with the demand for
dusk-to-dawn lights. Staff ordered an additional two hundred lights and crews installed as many as fifteen a day.
They might have done more, but they could work only during daylight hours because people refused to answer their
doors after dark.

Residents selling dogs were flooded with calls and set up
waiting lists for puppies not yet born. Town officials scrambled to assure organizers of a meeting of a thousand teachers planned for Newcastle that it was still safe to visit the
area. Scanners capable of picking up police broadcasts
disappeared from stores as fast as they arrived. One man
bought a $200 unit in Yarmouth, Nova Scotia – hundreds of
miles away – and had it delivered by visiting relatives.
Communities cancelled Halloween – fearing the killer

might use the chance to strike again – and organized parties for children in local halls instead. Police warned potential trick or treaters that anyone found walking the streets wearing a mask would be hauled in for questioning.

Creative Security Systems of Moncton expanded into the Miramichi area three weeks earlier than planned. The home safety business increased even in Moncton as people clambered for a panic-button system capable of setting off an alarm at the police station.

In Newcastle, people living around the Daughney home set up their own security system. "Every door and window is secure," said Edith Russell, an elderly, white-haired neighbour of the Daughney sisters who worked as a cross-walk guard at a nearby school. "And I've told my neighbours what to do if they need my help. All they have to do is bang on the wall and I will be able to hear them. My neighbours across the street have my telephone number. Also, if they come outside and yell, I will be able to hear them."

Still, the precautions seemed to offer little comfort. "They don't want money, it seems, they just want to beat and kill," Russell said. "It's just terrible. Everyone is so scared and nervous. They're all old people on this street. The Daughneys were the youngest ones living here. You have to think of everything. Nina Flam's brother lives on this street, right across from where the girls were murdered. Maybe whoever did this to them mistook the house for his."

Edith Russell's willingness to talk to reporters at a time when few were willing to take the risk of having the killer or killers seeing or hearing them turned her into a media star and helped make the Daughney murders a national news story. She appeared on CBC Radio's national program *As It Happens* and CBC-TV's *The Journal*. (Her family opposed the interviews, however, and a few weeks later, when *The Journal* tried to get her back on the show, her family forbade it.)

On October 17, Liberal MP George Rideout of Moncton

stood up in the House of Commons to call for more help for
the police working on the Miramichi murders. "These
crimes are most violent and heinous," he said. "On the
basis of information that I have been given, the RCMP is
short-staffed in New Brunswick due in part to the new
peacekeeping role." (Five RCMP officers from the province
were in helping police an election in Namibia. None were
from Newcastle.) I am further advised that some members
of the force who have an intimate knowledge of Newcastle
have not been utilized," Rideout said. "Would the minister
commit the additional staff necessary so a full, complete
and expeditious investigation can be carried out immediately?"

The next day, just over one hundred people braved the
cold and wind to attend the funeral of Linda and Donna
Daughney. Although the sisters were Anglicans, the service was held at in the larger St. James and St. John United
Church nearby. The service was brief. The choir sang "The
Lord is My Shepherd" and "How Firm a Foundation." The
Anglican pastor, Father Barry Thorley, urged the congrega-
tion not to lose hope. "It is not our town, nor the community around this town, that is wicked and evil. Rather it is a
presence within the town, and consequently amongst us,
which is based on evilness and wickedness."

As the pallbearers led the caskets out of the church,
Frances Daughney, now the only living sister, stood up and
tried to touch the coffins, but her husband and Bernard
Geikie gently restrained her.

That evening, about three hundred people jammed into
the main auditorium of the Newcastle town hall for a
forum organized by CBC Radio. Organizers wanted to talk
about ways people could cope with the violence. The
crowd, however, wanted the police to tell them what was
going on.

Former local hockey star Gordie Graham of Newcastle
stood up and vowed that if the killer tried to break into his

home and threatened his wife and infant son, the police would carry that man out feet first. The crowded roared its approval.

"There's not jury in the world that's going to convict you for shooting scum like that," shouted another man to more cheers.

Sgt. Ernie Munden pleaded with people not to take the law into their own hands, saying a homeowner must be able to defend his or her actions in a court of law. Shoot someone, he warned, and you could face criminal charges.

His caution was ignored. People cheered when a man stood up, said his home is his castle and he would do what he had to do to protect it.

"What's a person supposed to do," another yelled, "wait for an attacker to come in and shoot him?"

A senior citizen, Don Whalen, warned about the effect the news blackout was having on the elderly. "There's no information, none whatsoever to satisfy and cool the feelings down so that at least we know that someone is out there working for their interests."

Although a CBC event, few people walked up to the microphones in the audience. "More of us wanted to get up and say something, but we were too scared with the TV cameras there," one woman explained afterwards.

The next day, Newcastle town council voted to give $10,000 to a Crime Stoppers' fund aimed at ending the crime wave. Within a day, public donations pushed the total to nearly $30,000.

Also, Newcastle police released a sketch of a heavy-set man with a stubble of beard and dark, curly hair thought responsible for the Doran and Russell attacks. Calls flooded in as people mistakenly thought the sketch was of the man who killed Annie Flam and the Daughney sisters.

A manager of a donut shop became the centre of speculation. He was new to the area and looked vaguely like the person in the sketch. Rumours spread quickly: he beat his wife; abused his children; was involved with drugs; police had marched into his shop and dragged him away in chains. Finally, the man had to go to the local paper to refute the gossip.

Stories in the national media began to appear; some portraying the Miramichi as a violent place inhabited by hicks infuriated residents. One article, which called the Miramichi a "little Detroit," prompted Newcastle councillor Rick Matthews to spring to his town's defence. "We have a bad situation and everyone is fearful, but Newcastle certainly can't be compared to a small Detroit. People still walk our streets in Newcastle, but with great concern."

Criticism of the police appeared in the letters to the editor section of the *Miramichi Leader*. Said one writer: "I am afraid our local police, often called Canada's finest, are doing a terrible job. Annie Flam is dead and buried, yet little has been done. I am afraid this last double murder will go the same route. I am sick of hearing how good the RCMP are. Let's have a demonstration to prove it so my family and I can relax in our home."

At an October 27 news conference, Sgt. Ernie Munden announced police had no evidence linking Legere to the Daughney killings. He answered a variety of questions: calling in a psychic would be a last resort; there was no evidence the double murder was a cult killing; there was no description as yet of the attacker in the Flam case.

Hours after the meeting, RCMP headquarters in Fredericton issued a terse media release saying there would be no further news conferences. If any more information became available, it would be released in a written statement. This was to ensure consistency in the information provided to the public, the RCMP explained.

The timing of the information crackdown could hardly have been worse. Late on October 28, a man broke into a truck parked next to the Morada Motel, located on a hill above the police station in Chatham. He stole two guns and fled on foot. Constable Robert Bruce heard a shot. Town police and the RCMP quickly sealed off the area, but the man was gone.

Just after midnight on the other side of Chatham, John MacLean of Tweedie Street was watching the World Series on television. He started into the kitchen for a drink of water when he saw a figure pass by the window. He thought it was just a child taking a shortcut, but went outside to investigate anyway. A man was standing at his front door. He was just under six feet tall, dark and slim with pronounced jowls. He was wearing a burgundy sweater and had a black knapsack slung on his back.

"I saw him and he saw me. We sort of surprised each other. I went to say something, but he turned around and pointed a gun at me, so I threw my hands in the air."

"Go back in the house and go back to sleep," the man snarled. MacLean quickly did as he was told. He backed into the house, hands still in the air, shut off the lights and hit the floor. He crawled to the phone, pulled it down on the floor, then, using a lighter to see, called the police.

Outside, the man with the gun coolly smashed the windows of MacLean's car and truck and rummaged through the glove compartments. Nothing was taken. (The next day, police discovered the home once belonged to Wally Jimmo, a member of the 1987 jury in the Glendenning case. Jimmo had moved, but was still living on the Miramichi.)

Police rushed to the MacLean home. RCMP dogmaster Corporal Gaetan Tomassin's dog Sam caught the man's scent and took off, straining against his leash. Two officers followed as they raced west, heading out of town, down a hidden trail through dense woods and holes in barbed wire fences.

"I was running flat out with the dog pulling me along," said Tomassin. He knew they were close because several times the dog's ears perked up and its tail stood on end each time it caught a trace of the man.

Dog and master ran about a mile through the misty, moonless night until the woods opened up at a set of enormous Texaco fuel storage tanks overlooking the Miramichi River. Tomassin realized he had lost the two men following him, and he didn't know where he was. He hesitated a moment, then continued running, across an open field and through a large patch of tall weeds, downhill towards the river. Crossing Upper Water Street near the vacant lot that was once Annie Flam's store, the trail led him between two houses to a fence. The dog strained at its leash, eager to leap the fence.

Tomassin jumped over the fence and fell thirty feet down an embankment to the shore. He jumped up and looked around. He thought he saw a shape ducking behind something not more than two hundred yards away. He ran to the spot. He reeled in the dog and drew his gun. Barely twenty feet ahead was a man with a rifle in his left hand. Tomassin dove for cover.

There was an orange flash and the explosion of a shotgun going off. "Give yourself up," the officer shouted.

"Don't come near me or I'll fucking kill you," the man snarled back. Tomassin was astonished at the man's remarkable calm. He didn't even sound out of breath. There was a second explosion.

"As I heard a second shot, he was going up the ridge," Tomassin said. "It was too late to release the dog. I could hear vegetation crushing under the suspect's feet as he ran away."

Tomassin jumped up and started to run again, prepared to shoot back, but determined to hold fire unless he could see his target. The man ran into a driveway and darted between two houses. Tomassin rushed after him, stopping at a trailer just long enough to call for backup.

Two officers joined Tomassin and his dog and once again they started running. The dog caught the man's scent along a set of railway tracks that circled behind the 18-hole

Miramichi Golf and Country Club outside Chatham. Suddenly, the dog's tail rose up.

"Heads up," Tomassin hissed. Another explosion of orange light flash through the night, this one less than a hundred feet away. The officers heard bits of lead tear past as they dove for cover in a ditch. The dog's leash slipped from Tomassin's hand and Sam charged the fugitive.

"Sam," Tomassin yelled, "get back here."

Conditioned to obey, the dog turned just feet from the man and returned to its master's side. The officers crouched in the ditch for about thirty minutes, straining to hear the man. It's just a matter of time before someone gets ambushed, Tomassin realized.

The game of cat-and-mouse was over, however. The fleeing man slipped into the night, leaving behind on the railway tracks a knapsack containing eighteen bottles of beer stolen from the van of a Theatre New Brunswick worker.

By 2:00 a.m. more RCMP were being brought in and roads leading out of the area were sealed off. Some homes were evacuated, other people were told to stay inside with their doors locked.

A few hours later, near the area where the chased ended, William Skidd hung up his phone after talking to a friend about the incident. As he headed to the bathroom, he glanced out the window. A man was standing on his lawn and he was carrying two rifles. Skidd assumed it was a police officer and rapped on the window to get his attention so he could ask him what was happening. Instead, the man calmly turned and walked back into the woods.

Only then did Skidd realize the man didn't look at all like a policeman. He was about six feet tall, with brownish hair and a thin, unshaved face. There seemed to be freckles, or perhaps they were pine needles, on his cheeks. He was sloppily dressed in a pair of brown pants and work boots. There was something strange on his head, not a hat exactly, it looked more like a knapsack.

Police combed the area until just before noon, then returned later and tried again. On Monday morning, a woman living in the area looked out her window and saw two police officers wearing fatigues roar by in a Jeep. Their faces blackened, they carried special glasses to enhance night vision.

Meanwhile, people with camps in woods a few miles to the south of Chatham called to report earlier break-ins and people helping themselves to food.

By Monday, telephone lines were jamming as reporters and a public frantic for more information tried to figure out what the RCMP were doing. The police, however, weren't just refusing to answer questions; they wouldn't come to the phone. An RCMP handout said only that there had been a complaint about a shot being fired and that a man with a gun was spotted near the golf course.

This infuriated *Miramichi Leader* editor Rick MacLean, who criticized the RCMP in a television interview and the lead editorial in the paper on Wednesday. "The force has asked for help for the public in solving the recent series of crimes in the area," he wrote. "But they seem to think they will get the help they need without providing anything meaningful in the way of information to the public ... We're *eager* to help. *Desperate* to help. We're frightened and we want this to end. Yet the RCMP feels it should treat us like children who deserve only to be seen, but not heard. Such treatment is outrageous ... this province should rethink the idea of setting up its own force – one that is more sensitive to the concerns of the people it is paid to serve and protect."

RCMP Superintendent Al Rivard of Moncton visited MacLean's office the next day and said the news blackout was a misunderstanding. He'd meant for Sgt. Munden to respond to calls, but not to appear on camera unless there was something new to report. He was concerned about talk that the police forces might not be cooperating with each other.

Rivard confirmed that the RCMP were about to set up a special unit in the area. He also said there were about eighty police officers in the area ready to help if needed. That included the various local police forces and twenty-six members of the RCMP detachment in Newcastle.

*Miramichi Leader* publisher David Cadogan criticized the RCMP in his column on Friday. "The RCMP are nationally renowned for their arrogant and ignorant treatment of the public with regard to information about their activities ... On the one hand, the police work hand in hand with Crime Stoppers, an organization that writes and films re-enactments of crimes in sometimes sickening detail to jog the memories of the public. On the other hand, the RCMP plays 'I've got a secret' with the most horrible series of crimes we can remember."

At a news conference that day, the police forces banded together in a display of solidarity as police chiefs Jack Bell of Chatham and Dan Newton of Newcastle joined Rivard and Munden to field questions.

Complaints about a lack of information, Munden charged, weren't coming from the public. "I think criticism is being directed through the media. Whether it is a co-ordinated response, or by some member of the media, I don't know."

A great deal of work has been done, the RCMP told reporters. More than fifty suspects have been interviewed and their alibis checked. Annual leaves for officers have been cancelled.

(The police work failed to learn, however, about a curious series of thefts at the Governor's Mansion, a bed-and-breakfast, about one mile southwest of Chatham Head. A number of people staying at the sprawling home of a former lieutenant-governor lost personal belongings that fall: clothing and boots, identification papers belonging to a Fernand Savoie of Bouctouche, a radio, and, oddly, Volume 13 from a set of the Encyclopedia Britannica.)

The mounting pressure to do something had created a

debate within the RCMP about what to do next. There were two choices: throw as many men and squad cars onto the streets as possible to try to ease public fears, or set up two-man teams to stake out wooded areas believed to be used by the killer and wait for him to surface. Hoping to quiet the public outcry, the RCMP decided to throw more officers onto the streets.

It would prove a fatal mistake. Had they chosen to concentrate on searching the wooded areas, they would have discovered a series of improvised camps strung out south-east of Chatham. Virtually invisible from the air or at a distance on the ground, the camps – one made using trees shaped in the form of a teepee, and another built using scraps of plastic and a stolen tarp – contained makeshift stoves and cooking utensils. The campsites, it would later be discovered, belonged to Allan Joseph Legere. From one night to the next he would shift from camp to camp, avoiding detection.

Now a rumour began to circulate that the Daughney sisters had been killed by a cult whose members tore out the sisters' eyes, broke their legs and slashed their faces. On November 9, Munden felt sufficiently perturbed to officially debunk the stories: "Donna and Linda Daughney sustained severe injuries in the facial area and elsewhere, the result of a severe beating. They were sexually assaulted. The bodies were not mutilated. There is no evidence of a Satanic cult." With that the RCMP said there would be nothing else released until the next Wednesday, November 15.

Those plans changed after they received a call from the crime lab in Ottawa. The RCMP quickly announced what everyone had suspected all along: it appeared the Flam and Daughney murders were the work of the same person. Something had turned up in lab tests, but police wouldn't say what.

A prepared statement hinted at a link between Legere and the killings. "Allan Legère continues to be a suspect in this murder investigation and a warrant continues to be held by the Moncton police department for his escape from lawful custody." Legere was not called the prime suspect, but his name was the only one mentioned.

Reporters strained to confirm the link. On Monday, November 13, CBC-TV's André Veniot reported that lab tests had found something identifying a "prime suspect." Hair, semen or both had been tested using the new technique of DNA fingerprinting and a match of the genetic makeup of material found at the crime scenes had been made with samples previously taken.

On November 15, Newcastle police announced they had arrested a man in connection with the attacks two months earlier at the homes of Morrissey Doran and Sonny Russell. Allard Joseph Vienneau, 30, of the Newcastle area was charged and ordered to undergo a thirty-day psychiatric examination.

In the meantime, the RCMP felt Allan Legere's recapture was just a matter of time. They narrowed the search to the Chatham Head area, certain Legere was cornered there.

At noon on November 15, two Roman Catholic priests dropped into the Renous Recreation Center for lunch with a church group. The clergy were Father Leo Sullivan of St. Patrick's Church in Nelson-Miramichi, and Father James Smith of the Church of the Blessed Virgin Mary in Chatham Head, about two miles to the north.

At 2:30 Father Smith left. He had a busy afternoon ahead of him, including a trip to the Miramichi Hospital in Newcastle to visit the sick, something he did at least once a week. Among those he visited was Joe Pineau of Newcastle, a parishioner he had known for more than a decade.

"Father Smith visited me about quarter to five and stayed till about 5:30," Pineau remembered. "He came to see me and he was talking to the fella in the next bed. I think he mentioned something about having to go to a meeting."

After completing high school classes for the day, Peter McCafferty was asked by his grandmother to take an envelope over to Father Smith. In it was money to pay for a mass. McCafferty agreed to do the chore. He ate supper, then around 5:30 walked the short distance to Father Smith's rectory in Chatham Head.

"When I got to the rectory, the sun was going down," he recalled. "I entered the walkway, using the concrete steps going up the back porch. The porch was lighted." The priest answered the door bell, nodded his head when told what the money was for and placed the envelope on the kitchen table. "He seemed perfectly normal. It was my first time in the rectory, so I took a real good look around before I left."

Inside the rectory, Father Smith was sitting down to a meal of corn, onions, mushrooms, carrots and apple slices.

Just before nine o'clock, neighbour Anna May Chevarie looked out a window and noticed the priest standing on the patio above the garage attached to the right side of the rectory, the side farthest away from the church. There was a light on in the yard.

Chevarie had known Father Smith for nineteen years and had seen him out on the patio many times before, his hands clasped behind his back, often gazing up at the stars. This time, though, was different. "He was staring towards the light in the backyard. He was looking down around and toward the garage door. He stood up then with his hands behind his back. Once he stood under the light I got kind of nervous. He gave me the impression that he heard something."

Father Smith went back inside. The parish had installed an alarm system after a series of break-ins. Twice thieves had entered the house by climbing onto the garage roof and forcing open the sliding doors on the patio. There was a walk-in safe in the house, but Father Smith rarely kept much money in it. Former altar boy Vince Pineau, who lived across the street and still did odd jobs around the house, remembered putting away $50 and $100 bills after collection on Saturdays and Sundays, but that money was usually taken to the bank the next day.

The security system included outdoor lights controlled by a timer that turned them on each afternoon at four and shut them off at eleven. There was also a burglar alarm activated by distruptions to beams of invisible light. One beam was aimed across the lawn near the garage wall. Another beam scanned the inside of the garage. The system was very sensitive. Frequently, blowing leaves or drifting snow triggered it, so Father Smith usually switched it off during the day, but turned it on again before going to bed.

Before leaving the patio, Father Smith glanced at the windows of the house. He was planning a trip to the Holy Land and was winterizing the rectory before he left. Workers were replacing most of the storm windows.

While the priest was on his patio looking around, all eyes were shifting to the Chatham Head area as it became obvious that police were concentrating their search there. Two dogmasters were called to the Dickson Road after a suspicious man was spotted. The trail, estimated to be about an hour or two old, petered out near Father Smith's church.

On November 16, the RCMP announced that a news conference would be held the next day, Friday. Speculation was rife that the police would confirm that DNA testing had linked Allan Legere to the killings. At 6:00 p.m. Thursday night, Rick MacLean and André Veniot broke the story in advance of the media conference. The news was the talk of the province – until 7:05.

# TEN

# The Third Attack

JAMES V. Smith grew up tall and skinny in Lower Newcastle in the Dirty Thirties. Everyone had a nickname back then and it seemed natural that his was "Slim Jim."

Third-born in a family of nine boys and girls, he was considered a bright student. "He'd read something once and remember it," recalled older brother Leonard. The closest to Jim in age, he watched his brother skip Grade 7 and end up in his class, much to his childhood embarrassment.

The top prizewinner when he graduated from high school, Jim had kept his desire to become a priest private until then. "There was a big storm the summer before college," Leonard remembered. "The streets of Newcastle were covered with pulpwood, pine trees were broken. We were walking along and it was then he told me he was going to become a priest." He was ordained on May 6, 1945. (Another brother, Percy, would also rise to prominence as a local lawyer and MP for the area.)

A lover of photography and travelling, Father Smith took pains to combine these passions, taking along his camera when he visited the Holy Land (four times), and Rome (six times), among other locales. On his last trip to the Middle East, he had gone as a tour guide to save money.

He was known to be a careful man with a dollar and

earned a reputation as a good parish administrator. He managed to turn around the finances of Chatham Head after he was appointed its priest in the 1960s. Before his arrival, the parish seemed to lack the ability to pay the interest on the church mortgage. With Father Smith in charge, however, the mortgage got paid off, the oil furnace replaced with electric heat, and siding put on both the church and rectory.

If he could cut a deal to save parish money, he would. He once asked the clerk at a Zeller's store for a church discount for a popcorn popper. When asked if he could provide the store with a letter for their records to explain the lower price, the priest smiled his dry smile, pointed to his clerical collar, and said, "Isn't this good enough?"

Father Smith loved to use his camera to record events in the community – events at school, graduations, skating parties. He was strict, however, when it came to the shennigans of the young people involved.

"I remember him going to take our picture when we were in Grade 11," recalled a former student. "We were acting the gawk [fooling around].

"'Okay', he said, 'if you don't want your picture taken, then ...'

"'No, no, father,' we said. 'We'll behave.'

"In those days, you were brought up to stand and listen everytime a priest or nun walked into a room."

The priest also doubled as an unofficial archivist, saving and cataloguing the photographs he took. Once, when asked by students who were planning a high school reunion for a photo to put on a wall, Father Smith invited them over. When they arrived, he had the boxes waiting, the years neatly labelled on them. A student recalled the visit: "We were looking through and I remember saying, 'Look at that, that was in Grade 7.' 'No,' he corrected me. 'That was in Grade 6.' And it was."

Just before a planned cruise with Leonard in the early 1980s, Father Smith had a heart attack. He recovered and

continued his busy life. By 1989 he was 69, but refused to
consider retirement because he preferred to stay in the parish.

He kept the family home in Lower Newcastle and went
there when he could, enjoying walks along the sandy beach
by the Miramichi. A friend once asked him if the priest-
hood was a lonely life. Sometimes, Father Smith replied,
but sometimes he enjoyed that loneliness.

As he had every year, Father Smith organized a cook-out
for the choir during the summer of 1989, even though it had
been a difficult time. His sister Alice, a nun, had died in July
of cancer.

The hunt for Allan Legere didn't seem to affect the
priest. He encouraged his parishioners to stay calm and
embrace their faith. The fear would pass, he predicted. "He
never appeared frightened or worried by it or think he was
in danger," Leonard said. In fact, the brothers were making
plans to visit Hawaii, even though Father Jim had just
returned from a visit to Korea.

Jane (not her real name) bumped into Father Smith in
early November 1989. "We talked about the escape of Allan
Legere and all the killings that had gone on. He wasn't
afraid. I said to him, 'Father, why don't you move out of that
rectory until this is over? You could move into the rectory
here in Chatham.'"

"He had this funny way of holding his hands behind his
back. Then he'd start rocking on his heels and lick his lips,
as if pausing to think. 'Oh no,' he said. 'How would it look
to my parishioners. Me leaving and them having to stay in
their homes.'"

She suggested he stay at the church during the day and
sleep in the Chatham rectory, five miles away. He
dismissed the suggestion. After all, although he lived alone,
his rectory was only a hundred yards from the main road at
the back of the large church parking lot and was surrounded
by houses – except for a patch of trees and some high grass
on one side.

"'I don't think he's looking for God," Father Smith replied calmly. "He'll not come where God is."

A few days later, Father Smith noticed two RCMP officers outside his home. Police and dogs used to hunt Legere were now concentrating their efforts in the area. Knowing Legere had grown up in the Chatham Head area, police suspected he might try to hide there, perhaps even in a church basement. Smith nodded to the officers on his way by, but didn't stop to talk.

The killer knew where he was going. It was November 15 and he was trapped in Chatham Head and running out of time. Police were tightening their net, concentrating the search, using dogs, helicopters, infrared scopes. It was getting to be too much. He needed to hide for a little while to let the searchers pass by and what better place than a church?

A ladder banged against the corner of the one-storey garage attached to the first floor of the rectory on the side opposite the Nativity of the Blessed Virgin Mary Church. Before he could clamber up to the patio and break in through the sliding doors, however, he heard the doors open. Caught off-guard, he wheeled and ran behind the house just as Father James Smith walked out to investigate.

At the back of the house, the killer had run up a set of stairs onto the porch and was trying to pull open the back door. Finding the screen door locked, he tore it open, sending the plastic striker plate normally attached to the doorframe flying into the back yard. Thankfully, the inside door wasn't locked.

Father Smith heard the noise from the patio and went back inside to check. By looking diagonally across the house, the intruder could see into the living room through the dining room entranceway. He rushed at the elderly priest, giving him no time to react and dragged him to the kitchen, away from the front of the house where a passerby might see or hear something.

He demanded money from the safe he said he knew was built into the corner of the study next to the front door. Perhaps Father Smith tried to tell him there was no money there. Perhaps the priest refused to open the safe. Maybe he tried to fight back. If he did, it was an uneven battle. The killer pulled out a knife. As Father Smith tried to fend off the slashing attack, the blade sliced into the ball of his right hand and cut through his left index finger.

The intruder began to pummel the priest with his gloved fists. Father Smith's glasses flew across the room as he was knocked down and tried to crawl away from the blows. He was kicked repeatedly. Experts say it usually takes about six strong blows at any one point to draw blood. Twice, as he lay on the floor, kicks sent the priest's blood splattering against the kitchen baseboard. Other blows sent blood flying against the walls. There were smears of blood on the linoleum floor as Father Smith rolled across the floor. In the hallway, kicks drove blood through the air and on to the walls.

Smith was dragged from the floor onto a folding chair facing the back door in the kitchen and tied with a blue towel and blue plaid shirt. Then, his attacker began to systematically torture him.

One knife cut zig-zagged from the middle of his face to the back of his neck. Another cut began on his forehead and extended on to a cheek. There was a small cut on the left side of his head. He was nicked below his left ear.

Eager to keep the priest alive so he could get the information he needed, intent on prolonging his victim's agony, the intruder poked Father Smith in the throat, leaving only a superficial cut in the centre of his neck. He did, however, puncture his left cheek. A triangular pattern was hacked on the priest's face, as if trying to peel away the skin on an orange.

Seeming to tire of the knife, the intruder began to kick his prisoner again, smashing ribs with every blow. Sensing he needed more leverage, the man reached up to grab the frame of the back door and used it to drive his feet forward, into the priest's body. Father Smith was now barely able to breathe because of the broken ribs. His brain was bleeding internally and swelling from the punches and kicks that snapped his head from side to side.

The man hauled the priest from his chair and carried him into the study. The locked safe stood in the corner. Unwilling, perhaps unable, to tell his attacker what he wanted to know, Father Smith was beaten again. The attacker slammed him against a wall in frustration, leaving a bloody smear behind. He then threw the priest into the sharp corner of the desk, tearing open a bloody wound on Father Smith's right shoulder before he hit the floor.

The man bent down beside the priest and wrapped his powerful fingers around his neck, determined to squeeze out what life might be left. The pressure shattered a small bone used to anchor the muscles of the neck. Shock and the beating forced Father Smith to vomit. Food and blood flooded his lungs, choking him – just as had happened a month earlier to Donna Daughney.

Once again, the attacker resorted to using his feet. Leaping into the air. Crashing down on the priest's ribs. Crushing them. Caving in his chest. The results were devastating: seven shattered ribs on the right side and another six on the left. Father James Smith was dead.

The frenzy eased as the attacker realized he'd killed the only person who might have helped him open the safe. He turned to it and tried to decipher the combination, but failed. Seething, he turned back to the priest, lashing out at the body, kicking and punching it as if that might somehow force the secret of the safe from the dead priest's lips. He pounded Father Smith's face with his boots, seemingly determined to obliterate the man's features. The priest's nose shattered. One kick sent a crack snaking up through his upper jaw all the way to a spot behind his left eye, which was promptly filled with blood. The priest's face broke free from the front of his skull and slid slightly to one side, like a mask that had come loose.

The killer's head began to clear. The beating stopped. He turned to the safe once more. He searched the house for tools to use to break open the lock. He ran down the stairs to check the storage room, saw only a photocopier and shelves of cardboard boxes, books and church documents lining the walls. He missed the door to the garage tucked into a far corner of the house. He ran back upstairs, a trail of blood on the walls and beige carpet tracing his route.

He dashed through the house and out the kitchen door, leaving a partial bootprint on the grass as he circled the house to the garage. Although it was a double garage, it had only one door. He managed to pry it partly open, just enough to enable him to roll underneath. Inside, he grabbed an axe, electric drill, crowbar, chisel and a set of screwdrivers. Seeing the door to the basement, he grabbed the handle. It was locked, the deadbolt still in place.

He twisted the metal handle, nearly bending it in half as he tried to force the door open. When that failed, he kicked it, leaving blood stains on the wood. He then hacked at the door with the axe, finally splitting it in two.

He dragged the tools to the main floor and tried opening the safe. When that failed, he hacked at the wall around it, seeking a way inside. Bits of plaster fell on the priest's body. He tried breaking into it from the back, through the other side of the wall. He ripped away a V-shaped section of plaster from the wall in the hallway next to the front door, but discovered red brick underneath.

Defeated, he looked around the rectory. There was a large puddle of blood on the kitchen floor underneath the chair used earlier to hold the priest. The kitchen table teetered on its side, two of its legs having buckled. Blood was dripping from the walls of the kitchen and study.

Outside the sun was coming up. The killer knew he couldn't run away now. He would have to wait for nightfall when he could use the priest's car in the garage. In the meantime, he could check the house for any evidence that might link him to the attack.

He walked over to the sink and washed himself as best as he could. He wasn't worried about fingerprints, he knew his gloves would protect him from that eventuality. His boots, however, were covered in blood, so he removed them and washed them inside and out. He dug two bread bags out of a drawer to use as liners to keep his feet dry when he put the wet boots back on. He changed his clothes, jamming his bloody clothing into a bag he had brought with him. For all his precautions, though, he didn't notice a copy of *Candle* magazine, a church bulletin, lying on the floor. On it was the distinct herring-bone shape of his boot print.

Hungry, he ate some food he found in the refrigerator and washed it down with a mix of Bacardi coolers and Pepsi, throwing the empty pop bottle into the puddle of blood on the floor.

A ringing phone shattered the morning stillness. Calmly, the killer picked up the receiver. The caller, not recognizing the voice, asked for Father Smith. "Wrong number," the killer said and hung up. Neighbours noticed a man walk across the kitchen and pick up the phone, but thought it was the priest. A second call late in the day went unanswered because the killer was busy hotwiring Father Smith's car.

Morning turned into afternoon and soon dusk settled over the Miramichi. No one had come to the rectory. The killer's luck had held. Nonetheless, he knew there was a mass planned at the Blessed Virgin Mary Church for seven o'clock. He had to get going. Earlier the killer had searched the priest's body, tearing out the back pockets of his pants to find car keys, but he had found nothing. Kicking open a window of the locked car, he proceeded to tear apart the steering column to get at the ignition system. He ripped out two pieces of blue plastic, one of them containing the word *horn*, and threw them onto the concrete floor. He yanked out the ignition system, pulled off what he didn't need, then connected the two wires he thought would start the car. Instead, the horn started to honk.

He grabbed at the wires again, pulling them apart once more. He tried another combination. This time the car started. He lifted the garage door, jumped in the 1984 Oldsmobile Delta 88 and, driving through the parking lot, turned right and headed north, towards Bathurst. It would be close, but if all went well, he could just make the train to Montreal.

At 6:35 that evening, Clara Ramsay left her house in Chatham Head to go to mass at the Nativity of the Blessed Virgin Mary Church. Passing the rectory, she stopped when she noticed a ladder leaning up against the front of the garage. Peculiar, she thought. Nevertheless, she decided to continue into the church. There were no lights on when she went inside, so she sat in the darkness until someone turned them on a few minutes later.

Marvin Muzzeroll didn't realize half of his extension ladder was missing. The resident of Brown Road, located roughly two hundred yards east of the rectory, had a male guard dog, but it was 12-years-old, and going deaf and blind. It was tied to a twenty-foot length of chain in front of the garage, so it couldn't chase anyone.

A few minutes after Clara Ramsay had entered the church, Judith Ann Murdock and her daughter left their house in Chatham Head to buy groceries. As they walked to the car, they heard a noise across the street. It seemed to be coming from the garage of the rectory.

"My daughter asked me, 'Why is Father Smith honking his horn?'" Murdock recalled. "We got in the car and started to pull out when we glanced over and saw what seemed like the brake lights of a car in the garage."

The honking of the horn continued and it was difficult to tell if the driver was entering or leaving the garage. Murdock started her car and drove away.

Cabbie Robert Blair Hancock was driving past Father Smith's around 6:45 when he noticed a light blue car speeding out of the church parking lot towards Chatham. He caught a glimpse of the driver. The man looked to be of medium build, with dark hair that was rather long in the back.

At 7:00, Katharine Johnston looked out a window of her home. The elderly woman noticed something odd across the street: the rectory was dark. "Father Smith must be away," she thought. "Or maybe he didn't make it back in time for mass." That was unusual. The priest was well-known for his punctuality. One evening he visited a Chatham Head woman who was dying. It was about 6:30 and he had a mass at seven. Smith stayed until 6:55, then raced across the field to the church in time to conduct the service.

By now a small crowd of about thirty parishioners was waiting inside the church. They, too, were thinking it odd that Father Jim had yet to appear. Someone checked behind the chancel to see if Father Smith was there, but he wasn't. By 7:10 it was obvious he was not coming. Parishioner Nick Verriker decided to go next door to check the rectory. The father of full-grown triplet girls sometimes did odd repair jobs for Father Smith and the priest had given Verriker a key to the rectory so he could check it when he was away.

Arriving at the back door of the rectory, Verriker noticed the light on the porch and another one lighting up the back yard weren't on, as was Father Smith's custom. The door was locked, so he unlocked it. He tried the light switch, but it didn't work. There was enough light, however, to make out shadows, enough to tell Verriker that something was terribly wrong. The kitchen was a mess. There was blood on the walls and floor. Verriker backed out, slammed the door and started screaming. "Call the police! Call the police!"

Inside the church, stunned parishioners clutched their rosaries and began saying Hail Marys. "All of us were praying Father Smith would be all right," recalled Irene Roach, former president of the Catholic Women's League and a woman who knew the priest well. "But we knew in our hearts he wouldn't be. Everyone was crying, even the men."

The first police car roared up to the house bare minutes after the call came in. RCMP Const. Joseph Yvon LaFontaine was the first to arrive. One look at Nick Verriker told him there was trouble; the man was panic-stricken.

"It's torn apart!" Verriker cried out. "The house is torn apart!"

It was dark by then, so LaFontaine pulled out a flashlight and headed to the back of the house. It was dark on the porch, which ran for more than half the length of the house, but he managed to unlock the door using the key given to him by Verriker.

When he stepped inside the kitchen he saw puddles of blood on the floor, a chair facing the back door and an over-turned table. LaFontaine closed the door and called for backup. Then he began stringing yellow police tape around the house.

RCMP Sgt. Jacques Ouellette was on patrol when the dispatcher called. Ouellette hit the gas. There was already a crowd gathering at the rectory when he arrived. LaFontaine's police car was parked in the yard. Ouellette was briefed quickly by LaFontaine before he entered the house through the back door. He was taking no chances.

"I drew my revolver. I held my flashlight in the other hand. I entered very carefully and stayed close to the right hand side of the walls," Ouellette recalled. He needed to know who was inside, but he didn't want to destroy any evidence. "The wind was blowing and I could hear all these things going on. I really had sort of an eerie feeling. I had a feeling something was wrong. The blinds in the house were drawn. I looked on the floor of the kitchen for evidence. It was messy with paper and books."

Working his way along the right side of the kitchen, he came to the entrance to the dining room. Seeing the flickering glow from the television in the livingroom, he worked his way there. The sound on the TV had been turned down and the digital clock on the VCR was flashing 12:00. The room was empty.

Heading back into the hallway, Ouellete continued his counter clockwise search of the house, finally working his way to the rectory office. The room was a shambles. Father Smith was lying face down on the floor. Blood had pooled next to his face. His left hand was turned palm up. A shoe was missing. Ouellette rushed over, bent down and put his hand to Smith's neck, searching for a pulse. There was none.

Local doctor Basil Blanchard of Newcastle was called in to check the body. He had viewed the bodies of the Daughney sisters barely a month earlier. Wearing gloves, he knelt down to check for breathing. He and Ouellette lifted the priest by his belt so the doctor could use his stethoscope to check for a heart beat. There was none. Blanchard noticed the overstuffed filing cabinets and the papers scattered on the floor. "This man gets a lot of mail and reads a lot," he thought.

Father Leo Sullivan was called at about 7:30. "The Father has been murdered," said the voice on the other end of the line. Could he come and administer the last rites? Sullivan rushed to the house, only to be told he couldn't go inside. He was allowed into the church where he spent the next few hours with parishioners. Finally, police escorted him next door. "I recited the prayers at the entrance of the office. It was Father Smith."

For once, police didn't hold back much relevant information. That night, they released a two-page report of what they knew.

Telephones started ringing throughout the Miramichi as the news spread, jamming circuits. The RCMP went on radio and television, appealing to people to stop using the phones because police couldn't make or take calls.

Everyone seemed to be thinking the same thing: he has killed a priest, no one is safe.

# ELEVEN

# Where Is He?

Wʜɪʟᴇ Miramichi residents struggled to cope with the third attack in six months, police tried to figure out if the killer was still in the area. Compelling evidence suggested he was gone, perhaps slipping away just minutes ahead of police road blocks.

Thursday evening, Malcolm Wilkinson, a Saint John petroleum inspector, was driving to Bathurst for a service call. At 7:15, about ten miles north of Chatham, he caught up to a blue car trying to pass a tractor-trailer on a bumpy stretch of isolated highway. Time and again over the next six miles the car swerved out to try to pass, only to be forced back by oncoming traffic. In a hurry himself because he was scheduled to inspect a truck at eight that evening, and not wishing to stay behind an apparently drunk driver, Wilkinson eventually passed the car, glancing over as he roared past. "I noticed two people," he recalled, "a middle-aged male and an elderly looking female, haggard looking." The middle-aged man driving was heavy-set and clean-shaven. The woman had large, pointy features.

About a half-hour later, ᴠɪᴀ Rail ticket agent Michael Murty and a second worker were selling tickets and taking care of baggage at the counter of the Bathurst train station. A man entered and walked up to the wicket next to

Murty's, but the agent was busy counting receipts, so he turned to Murty.

"He didn't stand directly in front of me," Murty recalled. "Usually, people stand right in front of the counter, but he stood to one side. I kind of suspected he was hiding something. He asked for a day-nighter seat to Montreal on the 8:28 p.m. train." His cash register recorded the time as 7:47.

Up to then, the man had carefully kept his head turned sideways permitting Murty to see only his profile. He turned towards Murty when he paid for his ticket, however, giving the ticket agent a good look at him under the bright, flourescent lights.

"He looked familiar. He was roughly five foot eight or five foot ten, one hundred and seventy pounds, probably somewhere in his forties and spoke English. I believe he was wearing some kind of coat. I noticed his hands were awfully dirty and he seemed to have black and grey hair. He seemed to be in kind of a hurry. He went outside the station when he could have sat and waited for the train."

Malcolm Wilkinson was also in Bathurst. He had arrived on time for his appointment to check a truck, only to discover the inspection had been postponed. At 9:30 he drove through the cold and rainy night to Keddy's Motel, about fifty-five miles from the home of Father Smith and a half-mile from the Bathurst train station.

As Wilkinson walked through the motel parking lot he noticed the front window on the driver's side of a blue car was open, so he went over to close it. When he leaned over, he spotted the steering column. It had been ripped apart. Thinking someone had tried to break into the car, Wilkinson ran into the motel to tell the staff. Cook Hel Gauthier had just finished his shift and was eating a late supper. He jumped up and ran outside with Wilkinson to check the car.

Wilkinson pulled open the driver's door to look for identification. When he lowered the visor, a business-size

envelope fell out. Gauthier picked it up. The address on it
was *J. Smith, Chatham Head, N.B.* He put it back. The two
men spent several minutes checking the inside of the car
before Bathurst city police officer Walter Lavigne pulled up
at 9:52.

A quick look convinced him the car had been stolen.
The side vent window on the right rear door was broken.
The steering wheel was damaged, the ignition plug
removed and the centre torn out. There were four small
pieces of brown plastic on the driver's seat. A hat of a kind
often worn by older men was sitting on the passenger's seat.
Under the seat was a blue vinyl tote bag with a screwdriver
sticking out of it. Inside were a pair of pruning shears. An
old kitchen knife and a pair of religious books – *Pastoral
Care of the Sick* and *Rites of Anointing* – were lying on the
floor. Jammed under the front seat was a hunting knife in a
sheath. A GM car key was hidden under a floormat, a
Miramichi telephone directory was on the back seat.

Lavigne radioed in details on the car – a 1984 blue
Oldsmobile Delta 88 with a landau-style vinyl roof and
licence plate number AKW 470. Within ten minutes, RCMP
arrived to take over.

The RCMP also checked the VIA train schedule and
noted a train had left Bathurst for the twelve-hour trip to
Montreal less than two hours earlier.

At 2:25 a.m. on November 17 at Riviere-du-Loup in
Québec, RCMP officers Regis Coté, Richard Poule and
François Dollard boarded the nine-car train from Bathurst.
They were looking for a white male in his forties, weighing
about two hundred pounds with dark hair and perhaps a
beard or moustache. Coté and Dollard were in plainclothes.
Their job was to spot any suspects, then wait for police
from Lévis and the Sûreté du Québec to come on board to
help them. No one got off at Lévis, and despite walking the
entire length of the train, the RCMP officers failed to find
anyone matching the description they'd been given.

Allan Legere circa the mid-1980s
(*Times-Transcript/Moncton*)

The general store and home of John and Mary Glendenning, Black River Bridge, N.B.

A door at the Glendenning residence, shattered during the brutal attack of June 21, 1986.

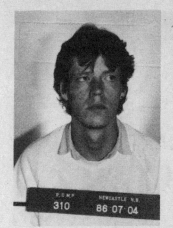

Scott Curtis, 20, (left) and Todd Matchett, 18, were two of three men charged with the murder of John Glendenning. They entered guilty pleas in 1987 and are currently in jail.

Allan Legere was also charged with the murder. A jury found him guilty in January 1987 and he was sentenced to life imprisonment.

Annie Flam (*Guy Aube*)

Annie Flam's store in Chatham, N.B., May 29, 1989 – the day after she was murdered and her shop torched.

Donna Daughney (left) and her sister, Linda: murdered October 1989. (*Guy Aube*)

The gruesome death of Chatham Head priest Father James Smith in November 1989 sent New Brunswick into paroxysms of fear. No one, it seemed, was safe from "the Madman of the Miramichi." (*The Miramichi Leader*)

Relations between the media and the police were often strained during the intense manhunt. Attending a press conference (left to right): Chatham Deputy Chief John Foran, RCMP Supt. Al Rivard, RCMP Sgt. Ernie Munden, Chatham Police Chief Jack Bell, Newcastle Police Chief Dan Newton.

The police sketch of a man investigators believed was an accomplice of Allan Legere. (*The Miramichi Leader/Willie Wark*)

One of the camps south-east of Chatham believed to have been used by Allan Legere during his six-month jail break.

Clerk Joy Levesque was working at the Irving gas bar and convenience store near Sussex, N.B. the night of Legere's capture. (*Kings County Record*)

Trucker Brian Golding had his rig hijacked by a gun-toting Allan Legere that same night. (*Willie Wark*)

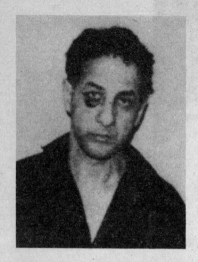

A bruised, hungry and tired Allan Legere at the time of his capture. (*Canapress*)

Hoping to catch a glimpse of the recaptured Allan Legere, a crowd gathers outside the RCMP station in Newcastle, N.B. November 24, 1989.

At 4:45 a.m. the train pulled into Lévis, located on the rocky cliffs opposite Québec City, and about eighteen police officers jumped on board to help in the search. Heavily armed, they began sweeping through the train's interior, which was in semi-darkness because only the overhead reading lights had been turned on.

They checked each male passenger, shining flashlights into their faces as they rummaged through suitcases in overhead racks and peered into sleeping berths. They were looking for someone with a tattoo of an eagle head and star on his right forearm and an eagle on the right bicep. That someone was Allan Legere.

One of two passengers sitting in a pair of seats in the middle of the second car prompted special attention. Passenger number 30 matched the general description of Legere, although he wasn't anywhere near two hundred pounds in weight. Sgt. Denis Lemelin of the Lévis police force asked him in French to identify himself. The man seemed to be groggy, as if the demand had awakened him. Replying in English, the passenger told Lemelin he was Fernand Savoie of Bouctouche.

Lemelin asked RCMP officer Regis Coté to speak to the man in English. Coté was familiar with the Bouctouche area of New Brunswick because he was originally from the province and when he vacationed there he often went to Moncton, about a half-hour drive southeast of the village. It struck him as odd that someone from a largely francophone area was unable to speak French. Both Coté and Lemelin looked at Savoie's identification papers, straining to see them in the dim light. Satisfied, they handed them to a couple of the other officers, who also checked them.

By this time the rest of the train had been checked and a crowd of officers was gathering around Savoie, who was told to remove his coat and roll up the right sleeve of his long-sleeved shirt. Lemelin edged closer, determined to be as close to the man as possible in case he tried to pull out a gun. Savoie stood and turned sideways, pulling up his shirt-sleeve to his elbow as he did so. When told to roll up it right to the shoulder, he complied. There was no tattoo. At least that is what police would later claim. Savoie was told he could sit down and continue his trip.

What the officers didn't know was that the description on the wanted notice they had been sent was accurate but for one crucial detail – the tell-tale tattoo of the eagle head and star would be found on Allan Legere's *left* arm, not the right.

Later that morning, around the time the Bathurst train was arriving in Montreal, contractor Leonard Doucet arrived at Keddy's to work on a swimming pool being built near the parking lot. He and his crew were just getting started when a worker spotted pair of boots and a winter parka with red trim hidden behind a pile of plywood. They were soaking wet. Doucet called the police.

When city police officer Steve O'Neil picked up the clothing, he couldn't help but notice the overpowering smell of wood smoke on the coat. He failed to notice a tiny, rusted nail protruding ever so slightly into the heel of the left foot.


Angry Miramichi residents now focused their anger on the police and their inability to catch a killer who, it seemed, slipped past them at will, tortured and murdered people in their very midst, then escaped undetected.

The morning after Father Smith's body was found, people driving to work and children on school buses peered out their windows at the yellow police ribbon and sawhorses blocking the parking lot of the church in Chatham Head. Neighbours looked out windows, trying to find out what was going on, then called friends.

RCMP officers and their white and blue cruisers were everywhere. An RCMP dogmaster with a German shepherd combed the grounds of the rectory searching for clues. The curious stood on the steps of a senior citizens' home across the street. Father Smith had been on the board of directors and visited it often. (The home would later be named Father Smith Manor in his honour.)

Cars pulled over just to look, others drove by slowly. "I almost had two accidents so far today from staring at the other drivers," one woman told a reporter. "Everybody looks like Allan Legere today." Asked if he knew when police first arrived at the rectory, one man said yes, "Too fucking late, that's when."

Later in the day, reporters from across the country jammed into an anteroom off the auditorium at the Newcastle town hall to hear what police had to say. The series of murders had electrified not just New Brunswick, but the rest of Canada as well.

Supt. Rivard and Sgt. Munden told reporters they now believed that Allan Legere had an accomplice – a tall, thin man. They handed out copies of a composite sketch of the suspect. The face looked mousy and pock-marked, with long, narrow features. The man was shown wearing what looked to be the liner of a snowmobile hat on his head.

Yes, they said, Allan Legere was indeed the prime suspect in the murders of the three women and a suspect in Father Smith's death. Munden refused to comment when asked whether or not a weapon was used, but he did respond when asked if Legere had ever threatened anyone. "A lot of people have received threats from Allan Legere. He said he would come back to the community and the community would pay. He has voiced that he would go ahead and seek retribution upon the community."

If it was Legere, why was he still hanging around? "This individual, he loves the chase. He thrives on the attention. He loves the chase. This may be the reason for him still being in the area," Munden said.

The discovery of Smith's car in Bathurst, however, presented police with a problem. They could no longer be confident that the killer was still hiding nearby. "Up until last night, I believed he was in the area. Today, I'm not certain," Munden said.

They warned any friends of Legere who might know his whereabouts to surrender the information. "A word of caution to friends and associates of Legere. Allan Legere is considered one of the most dangerous and wanted criminals in Canada," Munden said.

Both Rivard and Munden bristled when asked if it might not be a good idea to bring in armed forces personnel to help with the search. "I don't need more people," Rivard shot back, "I need more information." Already, more than one hundred policemen were looking for Legere, the problem was someone had to know something, but that someone was refusing to tell police.

Indeed, no one was telling them about an elderly man in the Chatham Head area who suddenly that fall had taken to keeping piles of newspapers in his shack, even though he couldn't read. No one was telling them about the time a friend had dropped by the elderly man's place and casually asked why he had such a large pot of stew boiling on the stove, far more than he could eat. In fact, police would only hear these stories years later.

In the meantime, the provincial government was telling the RCMP to get whatever they needed to catch Legere. Rivard could have as many officers as he needed, as much funding as he needed. "Money is no problem. This is more important than money," said Solicitor General Conrad Landry.

Premier Frank McKenna, MLA for the riding which included Chatham and Chatham Head, announced he was returning to the area from Fredericton so he could be with the people of his riding. He would stay with friends and run the government from Chatham, he said, while his family remained in Fredericton. McKenna announced that more RCMP officers were coming to join the investigation, prompting questions about why the officers were needed now when police had said just days before that they had plenty of men. An emergency 911 number was planned for the Miramichi, McKenna promised, as was money to set up Neighbourhood Watch programs.

Some accused the premier of grandstanding, but the daily newspaper the Moncton *Times-Transcript* praised the premier for his actions, saying it was the right thing to do at the right time.

Meanwhile, the price on Legere's head was climbing. Munden announced the Crime Stoppers' reward was now $50,000 for any information leading to the arrest of Legere and another $50,000 for information helping end the crime wave on the Miramichi.

A sketch of a man believed to be helping Legere was released by the RCMP and drew considerable attention. It was the first bit of "real" evidence people saw which suggested police might have a solid lead in the case.

The drawing was of a thin man, possibly 20- to 25-years old, with a long face and nose. His cheeks were pitted with what appeared to be acne scars or moles. His hair was described as being reddish brown and straight. His eyes were distinctively light, perhaps blue or green. He was tall, about six feet, with narrow shoulders. Still, he was described as having a big bone structure. He had a patchy beard and moustache.

Police had always suspected Legere was being helped by someone, but had offered no evidence to back up their claim, other than to say there had to be an accomplice for him to avoid recapture for so long. The suggestion infuriated people who felt the community was being unfairly blamed for harbouring a convicted killer. The sketch of the accomplice was so precise in its details, however, that it suggested someone must have had a good look at the man, perhaps even known him.

Former Chatham police chief Dan Allen thought the person in the sketch looked *very* familiar. He started to turn the sketch around in his mind's eye until he could picture the face in profile, then he added weight to that profile.

The drawing, he concluded, could only be one man – Allan Legere. True, he was thirty or forty pounds lighter, but living in the woods and stealing food as best he could would explain that.

Allen passed his conclusion onto the RCMP. Added to the intense pressure the police faced to catch the killer, it made the decision to keep the focus on Legere easier. The search for an accomplice – if there even was one – would have to wait.

More than one thousand people jammed into St. Mary's Roman Catholic Church in Newcastle the night after Father Smith was found for a prayer service. Bishop Edward Troy of Saint John said Father Smith's fellow priests remembered his gentleness, kindness and asked people not to give into the anger and frustration they felt, but to turn it into prayer.

The hunt intensified with startling speed. Police refused to acknowledge that officers were camping in woods, hiding in sleeping bags, waiting. They refused to confirm if a special search team had been flown in from British Columbia to join the search. They refused to say if tired dogs had hampered a search in the Chatham Head area a day or so before Father Smith was killed.

But such stonewalling was pointless. People could see the sudden increase in manpower for themselves. There were police officers and police cars seemingly everywhere. Outside Chatham, the building housing the Major Crime Unit was surrounded by cars and four-wheel-drive vehicles every hour of the day. At night, they would disappear, apparently dispatched to patrol various key areas of the region.

Most obvious was the RCMP's Emergency Response Team, the ERT squad. A specialized unit of ten men, they spent all of October and November searching for the killer, sometimes for twenty-four hours at a stretch. Easily visible in their dark, almost black uniforms during the day, they became close to invisible at night. They often slept in the woods, enduring freezing temperatures, unable to set fires for warmth, hoping for that one chance. They were armed with heavy-calibre weapons, knives and special glasses that let them see at night.

Still, demands for military help persisted. Surround the area, use as many men as you need, comb it inch by inch. Get him. Whatever it takes. Get him.

The RCMP's response was always the same. Manpower isn't the problem, information is. What do you surround and search, when you don't know where to look?

The lack of success frustrated RCMP officers flown in from across the country, away from their families for weeks at a stretch. One eight-year-old boy sent his father a note saying in French, "I love you, even if you're never home."

Searches were ordered at the slightest provocation. Each time, RCMP would dispatch dozens of officers and a chopper equipped with a heat-seeking device capable of spotting a man in any weather.

One Saturday afternoon, police swooped down on an area west of Chatham, combing woods there. Reporters scrambled to find out what was going on. When it turned out to be a reporter from a daily paper and a friend out for a walk, angry police later suggested privately that the "walk" was actually an attempt to test the response time of the police.

Monday, November 20, brought cold weather and the first snowstorm of the winter. With it came hope. No longer could a woodsman's tricks work against men and dogs. A dog's nose might be fooled by doubling back, but no man could walk on snow without leaving footprints. Plus, it was cold. Few could hide for long in a tent or lean-to in the bitterly foul weather. It was a ray of hope, the first in weeks, and people held on to it desperately.

A worker in a half-ton truck spotted a bearded man matching the photos of Legere sneaking around a cross-country ski club clubhouse a couple of miles north of New-castle. The man wore a checkered shirt, carried a gun and had a large knife strapped to a leg. The worker headed down the hill hoping to get a better look and nearly ran down the man when he bolted in front of the truck. "He looked right at me when he ran past," the eyewitness reported. "He had this look on his face, he looked terrified." The man leaped over a bank of snow and disappeared into the woods. Confusion about where the sighting happened delayed a search by about two hours, but police, dogs and a chopper soon blanketed the area.

People hugged their scanners, praying this would be it, keenly aware that it was early afternoon and the light would fade in a couple of hours. Some people in subdivisions a mile north of the sighting fled their homes as the chopper headed their way.

At nightfall the word shot from house to house, phone to phone. It was all over! They had him! He was in a cop car behind a mall! "He," however, turned out to be a hunter chasing rabbits.

Rumours continued to feed rumours. *Miramichi Leader* editor Rick MacLean was moving that week. His house had sold earlier, with the deal set to close that Friday, November 24. A Chatham resident called on Tuesday, before all of the furniture was to be moved. "Was it true?" MacLean was asked.

"Was what true?"

"That you're moving out, that the police said you'd better leave because you've been saying all those things about Legere on the television."

Crown prosecutor Fred Ferguson, who had to this point refused the demands of friends to seek protection, or perhaps even to leave the area for a while, discovered the matter was no no longer in his hands. One night, after his children had gone to sleep, he opened the door to find his friend, RCMP Sgt. Vince Poissonnier, carrying a .38 calibre service revolver, a .12 gauge pump action shotgun and an ammunition belt with spare shotgun shells. A police radio dangled from one hip, a mobile telephone from the other. Poissonnier had called earlier and insisted he be allowed to spend the night. Ferguson had relented, but on one condition. "I don't want the children to see you in the morning so please slip out before they wake up."

Convinced Ferguson would be Allan Legere's next target, RCMP officers pressed both him and their superiors for permission to provide ongoing protection. Eventually, after senior officers had been convinced that a successful attack would leave them unable to explain why they hadn't taken such an obvious step, the RCMP stationed a van and armed officers on Ferguson's waterfront property. Even with this, Ferguson took his own precautions. When he heard a noise one night, he searched the house in his underwear, a rifle in hand, fearful that Legere had somehow slipped past the guards. A few days later, he was moved to a local motel while his family left the area to visit relatives.

The hunt took its toll on the RCMP officers too. Dogmaster Gaetan Tomassin had been staying at the the Journey's End motel in Newcastle since May. His dog, Sam, stayed with him. There are seventy rooms in the motel. By the end of November, about ninety per cent were occupied by the RCMP. The clerk working the night shift quit because she was too frightened. The RCMP asked that the motel entrance be locked, but were told it was against the rules. Eventually, the door was locked. "It's not for your safety any more, it's for ours," the RCMP explained. Off duty officers sat in the lobby overnight to watch the front desk. The manager remembers one officer coming up to her after Father Smith's body was found and saying, "We're here to protect you and we couldn't stop a priest from being killed." Then he broke down and cried.

Supt. Giuliano Zaccardelli, the head of criminal operations for the RCMP in New Brunswick, did what he could to try to boost the morale of his officers. Soft-spoken and well-liked, he visited Newcastle to talk to the investigators, praising their work, assuring them that the killer would make a mistake and when he did, they would catch him.

As public pressure mounted, the *Toronto Sun* ran a story about police in-fighting hampering the investigation. "Police feud in N.B. killer hunt," blared the front page headline of November 20. "Police in-fighting is the reason a fugitive killer hasn't been caught, municipal sources here say," wrote reporter Tom Godfrey. Unidentified officers described a deep rifts between them and the RCMP. They blamed the RCMP for refusing to share information.

It was potent criticism. People on the Miramichi were already questioning the effectiveness of bringing in outside RCMP officers who didn't know the Miramichi. Munden, however, denied any problems. In fact, the relationship between the departments was good, he said.

Police continued to say they suspected someone of hiding Legere. Why, the public asked, when it made no sense? It was too dangerous. "He seems to possess the ability to motivate people to do things for him," Munden reasoned. "There are people out there who don't believe he's guilty of anything." The more dangerous it is, the more he likes it, Munden suggested. "This is a game of 'I can scare you, I can do what I want and you can't catch me. I will outfox you.'"

It all seemed so futile, so frustrating. How could a man be out in that weather, his footprints clearly visible in the snow, and avoid capture? Police worried the killer was waiting for some sort of sign or omen before striking again, something like the full moon on December 12.

A police officer wearing combat fatigues and carrying an assault rifle with the word *Snake* on the stock compared it to a lottery. "It's like playing 649. One of these day, we're going to hit the jackpot."

As police officers fought the cold and snow of another Miramichi winter in their hunt for Legere, a man calling himself Fernand Savoie and carrying his ID was staying in one of the most expensive hotels in downtown Montreal.

Hours after arriving in Montreal on Friday, November 17, Savoie had walked into the Queen Elizabeth Hotel just above the train station. Carrying only a couple of plastic bags as baggage, and sporting a bruise on one cheek, he produced two pieces of identification, checked into a non-smoking room for the night, and paid for it with $130 in cash.

It was the beginning of a bizarre few days for chambermaid Roslyn Antoine, the Trinidad native who had worked at the hotel for nineteen years. Savoie rarely left room 1036, preferring to lie on the king-size bed watching television for hours on end, a *Do not disturb* sign hanging on his door. He checked out each day, then checked back in a few hours later – each time paying cash for the room. He never seemed to sleep under the covers, preferring to lie on top of the bed.

On November 20, Antoine entered the room to make up the room and discovered the bathroom was flooded, the toilet blocked and the bed soaked with water. Apparently, Savoie had attempted to wash some clothes in his room instead of going to a laundromat or asking the hotel to do it for him. He had spread the clothing on the bed in an attempt to dry it. The bedspread and mattress, in fact, were so wet they had to be replaced. Antoine stripped the bed, then left for lunch at 2:30 p.m. When she returned, she was so nervous she brought along her supervisor, Adelaide Escalerira.

"I told the supervisor there was something strange about the guest, something funny about him," the chambermaid said. "I was uncomfortable going into the room by myself."

They discovered the man in the hallway, pulling towels off a cart and using them to try to mop up the mess. When Antoine said she would call a plumber to have the problem in the bathroom fixed, he talked her out of it, saying he was a plumber and could do it himself if he had a plunger. Antoine began mopping up the water.

Throughout the entire half-hour it took to clean up, the man watched nervously and kept up a non-stop barrage of chatter. In a quiet voice, he enthusiastically praised the large bed in the room. He asked Antoine what country she was from, adding that one of his best friends was a black man who once helped him when he was attacked from behind. At one point, he said he was in town from Ottawa on business with two other men. That comment stuck Escalerira as odd since he was sporting a two-day growth of beard, wore a grey sweat shirt with orange lettering and construction boots. "The way he was dressed was like a lumberjack," she recalled.

Once Antoine had completed her work, he wasted no time talking further with the two women. "He hustled us out of the room very quickly," she remembered. "I asked him if he wanted the room vacuumed and he said that he wasn't fussy."

While in Montreal, Savoie visited optometrist Dr. Raouf Greich. He said he needed a new pair of glasses because he had lost his. He said his birthday was January 12, 1948 and described himself as a self-employed artist who needed the glasses right away so he could "see far."

Back at the hotel, he made a series of phone calls to area pawn shops. He finally settled on one of the classier ones, called Mercury National, a five-minute walk from the hotel. Jewelry buyer Morley Thompson and partner William Hextall had been in the business for twelve years, reselling jewelry or removing the precious stones and melting down the gold. At around noon on November 20, a man identifying himself Fernand Savoie of Bouctouche rang the doorbell and said he had several pieces of jewelry he wanted to sell. Thompson checked out the man in the television monitor, then let him in.

The man pulled out some jewelry and spread it on the counter. He wanted $500 for it. Thompson gave him $450 and wrote down a description of the items. There were two seven-point diamonds, a box-link chain, a pendant, and a number of rings including two wedding rings, a ladies' moonstone ring, two with purple and green stones respectively, and one with a distinctive square red stone set at an angle.

Father Smith's funeral was held on November 21, during the first snowstorm of the winter. St. Mary's Roman Catholic Church in Newcastle was packed with about two thousand people as more than fifty priests helped celebrate the mass. Bishop Edward Troy pleaded for calm: "We are shocked and filled with revulsion, but we must not be afraid, we must not give in."

Monsignor George Martin, a friend of Father Smith's for forty years, delivered the homily: "We have lost a friend, a good pastor and a gentle man. The person or persons who have done this thing have violated their own humanity, their own dignity, the very humanity and very dignity that Father Smith affirmed all his life, by the proclamation of the gospel of Jesus Christ."

Vince Pineau, the neighbour and former altar boy who did odd jobs for Father Smith, pressed his face hard against the staff of the cross he carried as he led the funeral procession outside. He was crying. That same day – at his own insistence and with the permission of the police – Pineau cleaned the rectory. It took eight hours.

Father Smith's casket was taken to the cemetery where his father, mother and a sister were buried, next to the church where he had been baptized sixty-nine years earlier. Leonard Smith pulled out a vial of red earth from Cardigan, Prince Edward Island – his brother's first parish, the place he returned to every summer – and sprinkled it on the grave.

## TWELVE

# Profile of a Serial Killer

WHILE the people of the Miramichi struggled to come to terms with the grim reality of a serial killer in their midst, police faced the daunting task of trying to track down the man they suspected was responsible – Allan Legere.

Serial killers are notoriously difficult to capture. Many serial killers attack strangers, making such usually reliable police techniques as checking on friends and relatives useless. Some attack people they know will not be missed, like teenagers who have run away from home, making the chances of being noticed unlikely. Others move from place to place, never staying in one place long enough to risk detection. If Legere was indeed the Miramichi killer, then he was attacking people he had met, then using his knowledge of the area to avoid being found. That ability to avoid detection left him free to pick the time and place of each attack, a common trait of the serial killer.

Jack the Ripper is probably the most famous of all serial murderers, and he was never caught. In 1888, he killed five women in London's East End, always following the same pattern. He would pick up a prostitute, slit her throat, then mutilate the body with a knife. Each mutilation was more violent than the one before. In the final attack, where the killer, for the first time, used the victim's room he tore off her nose and breasts, slashed open her body and practically emptied it of its internal organs, which were then strewn around the room. His need to kill, then mutilate the women was clearly overpowering. Once, when interrupted after killing a victim, but before he could mutilate the body, the Ripper struck again within the hour, despite a police search going on nearby. The repetitive nature of the attacks – always committed in the same part of the city – the careful planning that allowed him to strike and escape, the urgent need not only to kill, but to mutilate, and the escalating violence of the attacks all marked the Ripper as a classic example of a serial killer.

Serial killers, then and now, are usually white males in their mid-twenties to mid-thirties. They usually start killing when they're around 27, says Robert Ressler, a former FBI criminologist who has interviewed dozens of them. The late start is unusual for killers: an FBI study found that whereas forty-five per cent of murderers are under age 25, eighty-five per cent of serial killers are *over* 25. Experts suspect the reason is that the factors influencing the development of a serial killer's personality require decades to culminate in murder.

Abuse as a child seems to play a key role in creating a serial killer. An FBI study done in the early 1980s looked at thirty-six murderers, twenty-five of them serial killers. Nearly half had been sexually abused.

Researchers have found that, as children, serial killers tended to wet their beds, deliberately set fires in occupied buildings to try to hurt people, and tortured animals. The first victim of "Co-ed Killer" Edmund Kemper of California was the family cat, which he buried alive, then later dug up and decapitated so he could jam the head on a stick in his room. In 1963, at age 14, he murdered his grandparents. He was released from a mental hospital at 21, and two years later began an eleven-month rampage, killing eight women.

In some cases, the killer 'graduates' from less serious crimes to murder. Canadian serial killer Clifford Olson of British Columbia was one of those. "As a child, Olson was a bully and a con artist. His teachers remember him as a promising young boxer who liked being the centre of attention. He grew up to be a part-time carpenter, and was convicted of ninety-four offenses ranging from fraud to armed robbery," say Jack Levin and James Alan Fox in *Mass Murder: America's Growing Menace* (Plenum Publishing, 1985). Married, with an infant son, Olson is known to have killed eleven boys and girls between November 1980 and August 1981. The number, in fact, may be much higher.

A 1989 study of forty-one serial rapists found three-quarters had been sexually abused. Since some serial rapists, like "Boston Strangler" Albert DeSalvo, eventually move from rape to serial murder, the link is a compelling one. Canadian social scientist Elliott Leyton looked at the family lives of twenty-four killers in his 1986 book *Hunting Humans: The Rise of the Modern Multiple Murderer* (McClelland and Stewart). All but five were either adopted, illegitimate, their mothers had been married at least three times, or had been institutionalized in a juvenile home, mental hospital, or orphanage. Clearly early abuse helps serial killers develop the brutality needed to commit their horrific crimes.

The fact that few of these men begin killing until they're at least in their late twenties suggests it takes considerable time for their development as serial killers to be complete. That development includes a rich fantasy life, which they use to rehearse their first killing over and over. For years, they dream about murder, slowly embellishing the fantasy, making it more real. Finally, the day comes when the need is so overwhelming that he feels ready to attempt his first attack.

Ted Bundy was 25 when, while making love to a casual acquaintance, he found himself nearly strangling her just before achieving orgasm. Soon after, he risked following a woman after she left a bar, but his attempt to ambush her failed when she turned into her home just before the place where he was waiting with a two-by-four. A second attempt came closer to succeeding when he actually hit a woman with a club. When she screamed, however, he fled. It was another two years before he was ready to try again. In January 1974, he slipped into a basement apartment and crushed the skull of a woman he'd never met. He later admitted to killing more than twenty women in a spree that lasted for years before he was caught and executed.

Such attacks follow a pattern. There is building up of the need to kill someone, followed by the hunt for a victim, then the killing, which is often part of an elaborate ritual involving torture, rape, murder and mutilation. The murder satisfies the killer's need and he enters a "cooling-off" period. It never lasts. Slowly, the cycle begins again. Often, the cycle grows shorter and shorter, driving the killer to take ever greater risks. Bundy, for example, preferred attractive women in their twenties, but in the final days just before his capture he was so desperate he killed a 12-year-old girl because he couldn't find a more "typical" victim in time.

Victims are usually chosen at random, although the killers have a specific *kind* of person in mind. Jack the Ripper attacked prostitutes. Bundy preferred white, upper middle-class women.

Most prefer to stay in one area. The usual victims in that area are people who cannot defend themselves – women, children and the elderly. Few serial killers use guns, perferring the physical contact required by a knife or club. David Berkowitz, the "Son of Sam" killer who shot New Yorkers with a .44 in the 1970s, is an exception.

It's not unusual for serial killers to continue denying their actions, even after they've been caught and convicted. Used to years of fooling people into believing they were normal, they remain utterly confident of their ability to convince others that they are right. Some make up wild

stories to explain away damning evidence. John Wayne
Gacy of Chicago, the famous killer of young male prostitutes and men who worked for his construction company,
claimed the twenty-seven bodies buried in the crawl space
under his house in Illinois must have been put their by
someone else. Bundy didn't admit he was guilty until
shortly before his execution; up to that point he simply
refused to accept that the evidence presented against him
proved his guilt.

It's unclear how big the serial killer phenomenon is, but
the FBI estimates there are anywhere from thirty-five to
one hundred serial killers in the United States at any one
time. The number seemed to surge in the past twenty years,
but that may in part be the result of better detection and
reporting. The United States, especially California, seems
to be the centre of serial killing, but there have been cases
reported around the world.

Part of the problem for experts estimating the number of
killers is deciding exactly what a serial killer is. Killers like
Jack the Ripper, Olson and Bundy are just one small group
of a larger class of serial murderers that includes people
who kill elderly patients in hospitals; mass killers who grab
a gun and kill as many people as possible before being killed
themselves; and professional thugs who kill for a living.
Lust killers like Bundy, however, receive the most public
attention, because of the fear their random attacks cause.

Lust killers tend to fall into two groups, and police can
usually tell which kind they are dealing with by looking at
the crime scene. Killers who are good at convincing people
that they are normal tend to be methodical murderers who
hunt for their victims far from home to decrease the
chances of getting caught. They bring a weapon with them
and are more likely to torture and mutilate their victims
before carefully hiding the body.

The second group are loners who graduate from being
Peeping Toms and thieves of women's clothing to killing.
Less organized, they often use whatever weapon they find

at the scene in their more frenzied attacks. They leave the body behind to be discovered because they love the publicity and fear the murders cause.

It's not unheard of, however, for a killer to show tendencies from both groups. Jack the Ripper, for one, was well organized, yet left his victim's bodies where they would be found. The Ripper's case also appears to be an exception because he apparently stopped killing in November 1888, while most serial killers keep going until caught.

Theories as to what causes someone to become a serial killer abound: abuse as a child, a brain injury, some sort of genetic problem, insanity. Psychiatrist Donald Lunde believes some are driven by paranoid schizophrenia: they hear voices that tell them to kill. Others, he says, are sadists who torture and kill to arouse themselves sexually.

University of British Columbia psychologist Robert Hare has studied psychopaths, people defined by psychiatrists as feeling no empathy or pangs of conscience, for nearly thirty years. He sees a link between the way they use language and the organization of their brains. Psychopaths use language oddly, contradicting themselves from one moment to the next, yet dominating a conversation because of their charisma. Tested to see how they react to the emotional impact of words like *love* and *death*, they respond the way "normal" people would to neutral words like *tree* or *car*. Hare has found the brains of many psychopaths are set up in an unusual way. In normal right-handed people, language is controlled by the left side of the brain. In psychopaths, both sides of the brain are involved and the left does less than normal. This unusual use of language makes it difficult to interview a serial killer about why he kills.

Most refuse to accept any responsibility for what they've done. Some blame drugs and alcohol, saying they caused the attacks. Some claim they have multiple personalities. Research has not found a case of a person with a multiple personality being a serial killer, however, although "Hillside Strangler" Kenneth Bianchi tried to fake the disorder once captured. Some, like Bundy, blame pornography. FBI experts agree serial killers are drawn to sexually sadistic pornography more than other people, but such an appetite, they say, simply *fuels* their violent fantasies, it doesn't create them. Control, experts say, is the killer's goal, control over the life and death of each victim.

The need for control, and the desire to blame others for their actions are common traits among psychopaths. They demand control of everything around them and can become violent if challenged. Devoid of feelings themselves, they are master manipulators who can fake emotions at will to get what they want.

"He lacks a conscience, feels no remorse, and cares exclusively for his own pleasures in life," say Levin and Fox in *Mass Murder: America's Growing Menace.* "Other people are seen merely as tools to fulfill his needs and desires, no matter how perverse."

Not all sociopaths become killers. Many retain enough control over their desires to avoid committing murder. Some become very successful, in part because their lack of concern for the feelings of others makes everyone easy prey for their business ventures.

Elliott Leyton believes the real motivation for serial killers is their belief that society has somehow conspired to prevent them from achieving the proper station in life. "These killers are not alien creatures with deranged minds, but alienated men with a disinterest in continuing dull lives in which they feel entrapped," he writes in *Hunting Humans.* "Reared in a civilization which legitimizes violence as a response to frustration, provided by the mass media and violent pornography with both the advertising proclaiming the 'joy' of sadism and the instruction manual outlining correct procedures, they grasp the 'manly' identity of pirate and avenger. If they no longer wish to live, they will stage a mass killing whose climax is their execution; but should they wish to live, and to achieve notoriety

– even celebrity – they will prepare their careers in serial murder. In doing so, they settle old scores in a manner which often yields a double dividend of sexual pleasure and defiance of the authorities." Many – like Bundy, Gacy and Olson – seem to revel in the attention showered on them after they are captured, all the while demonstrating a remarkable ability to ignore the horror of their actions.

Eric Hickey, a member of the criminology department at California State University, Fresno, interviewed a serial killer in 1990 for his book *Serial Murderers and Their Victims* (Brooks/Cole Publishing). The killer calmly described in chilling detail what he felt during each attack: "Sex was sort of a vehicle. When that was done, climax was reached. You've already terrorized this person. You've already hurt them, beat them, whatever. But there would be a feeling of letdown. You're excited, and then all of a sudden you come down. Kind of like a ball game. All this had been acted out for years and, in particular, it always involved stripping the victim, forcing them to strip themselves, cutting them, making them believe that they were going to be set free if they cooperated, tying them down and then the real viciousness started. The victim's terror and the fact I could cause it to rise at will ... their pain was proof to me that I'm in control, I am playing the star role here, this person is nothing but a prop. I'm growing and they're becoming smaller. Once both the violence and the sexual aspect were completed, then that was it. That was the end of the episode."

## THIRTEEN

# Hostages to Fear

THE murder of Father Smith attack ended all pretence of a normal life for people on the Miramichi.

None felt the fear more than the members of the jury from the 1987 Glendenning murder trial. The very moment parishioners were discovering the body of Father Smith in his rectory, those jurors were meeting with RCMP in Newcastle. They didn't know precisely why they had been summoned, but Ron and his wife, Lois (not their real names), arrived full of concerns. Since Legere's escape, Ron had heard the rumours that he had sworn to return and seek revenge on those who helped put him away for life.

"At first, I wasn't too concerned because I figured they'd catch him before too long," Ron said. "Then it was one week and two weeks." He had followed the news of the hunt for Allan Legere closely, but it was only after the Daughney murders that he began to worry. Even though it took RCMP another two weeks after the Daughney deaths to name Legere as their "prime suspect," Ron had reached that conclusion the moment he heard of the sisters' killings. He remembered the photographs from the Glendenning trial, including those of John's battered body. He remembered Allan Legere staring at the jury with his piercing pale blue eyes.

He put two loaded guns underneath his bed. One was a shotgun with a slug in it and the other was a high-powered .22. Despite the precautions, even slight changes in routine provoked panic. "One night I was snoring in the den and Mark could hear me. I stopped snoring, and when I did, Lois started coughing. That scared him so bad that he come out of bed and tiptoed down with the gun and peeked in to see if we were all right." When their son took the dog out at night, he would carry a long knife in his sleeve.

Just before the meeting with the RCMP started, Ron talked to a fellow juror, Wally Jimmo, for a few minutes. Jimmo confessed he was terrified. "He didn't sleep at all at night. He sat up with a loaded gun and let his wife sleep." He had good reason to be afraid. On October 28, a man carrying a gun had appeared at his former home and smashed the windows of the new owners car and truck, apparently searched for identification papers.

The news the RCMP had for the jurors wasn't encouraging. "The officer more or less told us that night that if Allan Legere wanted to break into your house, there was nothing you could do to stop him. His words were, 'He's an expert escape artist.' He said he would probably sit on a hill somewhere and study someone's house for a month. He would sit across the street and watch your house for a month. He would know that house inside out without ever being inside of it."

The RCMP dodged questions about whether or not the jurors might be targets for Legere, yet clearly that was why they had been called to the meeting. The officers would only say they were talking to many groups about their safety. The police told them to make their homes safer, lock their basement windows and install deadbolts on doors. Pamphlets on home security were distributed.

When Ron and his wife arrived home after the meeting, they heard Father Smith had been murdered. Ron was downcast. He wondered if they would ever catch Legere.

"You run it through your mind, what you'd do if something happened. You lay at night and think about it. I keep thinking about the way they broke into John Glendenning's house. They just smashed the door and in they come. So you start figuring out how you're going to work it if they come in. It mightn't be like that, but that's the way I had it planned if they come in.

"I was right over me gun and I was just going to flop down behind the bed and I was just going to lay it down on the bed. I was going to take Lois with me. I didn't tell her that. I was just going to grab here and haul her down behind the bed. I was going to use the bed as a shield.

"I'm not a gun man. I shot one deer in me life, that was back when I was 18 or 20, and I knew that wasn't for me and I never hunted after, maybe shot the odd partridge. But after this started happening, I often thought what would I say if somebody asked me could I shoot a man.

"Up until this here episode, I know I would have said no way could I shoot a man, there'd just be no way. But you know, during the last few weeks of that, I think I could have shot him, if he'd come through the door. If he come through the door and I knew it was him."

Bishop Troy's plea for calm was ignored. People were panicking now. An elderly woman had been killed. Then two sisters. And now a priest. Anyone, it seemed, could be next. Anyone.

Tom and Betty (not their real names) made immediate changes in their lives. A mill worker who usually travelled often, Tom told his wife he was staying home. They nailed shut a basement window under the sundeck and jammed sliding windows with pieces of wood. "We blocked off our sliding door with chairs," Betty said. "We thought if they did get in, at least we'd hear the racket. We put kitchen chairs right up against the doors."

They refused to buy a gun, but Betty kept a hammer next to her side of the bed and Tom had an eleven-pound pipe wrench on his side. They changed their daily routine. A teacher, Betty came home from school a few minutes later so Tom would get there first and search the house.

"When we went out at night, we'd leave all the lights on and leave the radio on," Tom said. "I remember us noticing that the town looked so strange because there was nobody walking around hardly. One Friday evening, we went downtown about ten and we saw one person."

It was the same everywhere. A young music teacher at Betty's school so terrified she wouldn't stay alone. "Her parents wanted her to resign, they were so worried about her. She lived in an apartment by herself. One of the other teachers had to go and stay with her."

Even Legere's mother seemed to be frightened, heading to Ottawa to stay with a daughter. Ironically, her son-in-law was a civilian employee with the RCMP.

Susan (not her real name) knew both Allan Legere and Father James Smith.

"I grew up with Father Smith. My mother has picture of him in a photo album. He was at a card party twenty-five years ago. He was the most gentle man. When we were children, he'd play with us in the snow, teach us how to make snowmen. He was so down to earth. My brother was killed when he was 21. Every year on November 16, the anniversary of his death, Father Smith would visit with Mom. He saw Mom at hospital on November 15 and told her, 'We'll have our visit today, in case I can't get over tomorrow.' Mom still can't talk about it."

Susan remembered being frightened of Legere when they were both adolescents. "We would swim at the wharf in Newcastle when we were 12 and 13. If Allan was in the water, we weren't. He'd haul your leg and pull you down. He held that fear over everybody. When we were teens we weren't allowed to go to a dance in Chatham Head because Allan Legere was from there. He was always intimidating. He made you fear him. And we never walked across the

Morrissy Bridge (connecting Chatham Head to Newcastle) at night because of that fear. After he came back from Ontario, you'd go to the Hi-Tide (a club in Newcastle). He'd walk in and you'd leave. He could empty a club just by walking in. If he asked you to dance, you didn't say no. I danced with him twice. It was stressful for me. I kept praying for the dance to be over. I've never seen Allan mad or raise his voice. It was part of his intimidation."

Even though she was now living in Moncton, Susan slept with a loaded gun next to her bed.

Todd Matchett's father, Billy, just *knew* Allan Legere was after him.

Divorced, in his mid-fifties, under five foot six and overweight, Billy usually spent his days at a local tavern. He combed his gray hair forward, covering his forehead, making him seem even shorter. His moustache was the same colour as his hair.

On October 1, there had been a fire at his McArthur Street bungalow in the south end of Newcastle. Certain the fire, a Legere trademark, had been set by the escaped killer, Billy had installed a series of security "measures." A pitbull now stayed in the house. He'd ordered a steel front door and anchored it with a chain crisscrossing it on the inside. There were iron bars on all of the windows except for the one in the living room.

Long suspected of selling stolen goods, Billy denied it, saying it had never been proved. "I retired from all that stuff years ago," he explained, saying he was trying to set an example for his imprisoned son, Todd.

He blamed Legere for his son's troubles. He'd tried to warn his son about his newfound friend, telling him, "If Allan ever comes up with any ideas, stay clear of him. Don't do anything with him. Don't do nothing with him. I tried to warn my young lad and Scott. I tried to warn both of them."

"I knew Allan, but I should have known him a little bit better. I should've known he was too smart for them. He went behind my back. This man is dangerous. My young lad, I hammered it into him fifty times. Legere sucked him in a little at a time. He's smart that way. He's a professional at that game."

He said Legere told them: " 'Come on, we're going to run in, we're going to run in, we're going to grab a money box and we're going to run out. That's it.' Well, that wasn't it. Legere went in there, he didn't go in there for no money box. He went in there because he wanted to hurt somebody."

Matchett said he heard about the Glendenning murder on the radio and decided to talk the teenagers into turning themselves in. "The young lads didn't have the intiative to go down and pull something like that. If they hada robbed the Royal Bank, I'd be clapping them on the back. They woulda went to jail. I'd of respected them. To go to jail for this kind of crime, I would never go for something like that."

His hatred for Legere was palpable. "Legere's a rat. He proved that in court by testifying against them lads. They pleaded guilty. It don't mean he had to testify against them."

"Allan, he's about the person I'd be most scared of in my lifetime. I figured he'd come here. Account of Todd, account of Scott, he would love to take me down a notch. By killing me."

Matchett believed he'd tried at least once. "I came up the stairs, seen someone at the window. Went back down. I got my rifle. Back up again. The rifle was already loaded. I couldn't get the bolt ahead. The bolt locked on me. So I just took the gun, pointed it at him and he jumped over and ran. I waited. And the chance I got to get him, I missed. For what he done to my son, I would of killed him."

## FOURTEEN

# Capture

JANE Meredith hurried down Prince William Street in Saint John, 170 miles to the south of the Miramichi. It was a few minutes before 11:00 a.m. on Thursday, November 23, and she had to unlock the door to the Piper's Pub where she worked as a barmaid.

A man wearing a parka, woodsman's pants, and heavy boots stood waiting outside. Clean-shaven, with medium-length black hair sprinkled with gray, he held a plastic shopping bag in one hand. Once inside, he ordered a beer and sat at a corner table by the door next to a video machine. Although not a "regular," he was a good tipper and friendly. "Just your everyday person after a beer," she would recall later.

Around noon, a policeman walked in, but the man ignored him. Later, barmaid Judy Cook came over to play a video game and the man wished her good luck. A pub employee asked the stranger where he came from.

"Ottawa."

"What have you got in your bag?"

"A gun," he replied, then laughed. Everyone else laughed too.

He kept drinking, downing a beer an hour. When a car broke down on the street outside during the supper hour, the man went out, stopped the traffic, then expertly helped the driver fix his bad battery and restart the car before going back to Piper's. In the confusion, he lost his glasses, but someone spotted them in the washroom and gave them to the barmaid. She remembered how happy he was to get them back. "You don't have any idea how many I've broken or lost," he said with a grateful smile.

After drinking a few more glasses of beer and playing some pool, he left the pub at 9:45 p.m., just as the weather turned to snow. Left behind on the table was a signed, handwritten letter, twenty pages long. The handwriting was small and cramped, angling slightly to the right. It was later given to police.

Saint John taxi driver Ron Gomke looked at the growing snowstorm and smiled – perfect weather for picking up fares. The 21-year-old former mall security guard had just started driving cab three weeks earlier. He liked the work. At just under six feet tall and weighing more than two hundred pounds, he preferred the informal dress of a cabbie to the uniform required by Burns Security.

When he heard a man yell, Gomke stopped and looked back. The man trudged through the snow, jumped in on the front passenger side and said he wanted to go to Moncton, 110 miles to the north.

Excited by the promise of a big fare, Gomke called the dispatcher at ABC Taxi. "Car 20. Party going to Moncton. What's the fare?"

"One hundred dollars," said the dispatcher. "And get it up front."

The man dug into his pockets while Gomke stared out the window at the snow.

"We're going to Moncton," the man said suddenly.

Gomke turned. There was a rifle in the man's lap, and it was pointed at the cabbie.

"This is a sawed-off .308. Tell them you've received the fare and do it in the calmest manner you can," the man ordered. His voice sounded eerie, relaxed. As they drove off, the passenger turned to Gomke.

"I'm the one they're looking for," he said. "I'm Allan Legere."

†

[This section based on a letter by Allan Legere.]

*"Idiots!" thought Legere as he tried to figure out what to do next.*

*The entire province, the entire country, was looking for him.* RCMP *in camouflaged suits were hiding behind bushes all over the Miramichi waiting for him, dozens of them. They even had a damned helicopter with a heat-seeking device on it sweeping the woods.*

*Cops! They never were too bright. They'd been looking for months, trying to catch Allan Legere. TheAllan Legere. Trying to pin four more murders on him. His picture was everywhere, yet there he'd sat for the entire day, less than three hours away, in a Saint John bar having a drink.*

*The letter he'd left behind was his life story.*

*When he started it, he thought he had lots of paper, seventeen pages, but there was so much to say, so many lies to set straight, that he'd had to tear three pages out of a Miramichi telephone book to finish. One was a page with a phone company advertisement on it saying "Anybody with a backyard, or a front yard, call our repair service to locate cables before you do any digging." The other two pages were the French listings for government services — tourism, health and justice.*

*Justice!*

*Look at those numbers! The judges, the Crown prosecutors like Ferguson, the guy who put him away in 1987 for the killing of that old man.*

*What did they know about justice! Sure, he was there, but he didn't do it. It was the other two guys, Matchett and Curtis. It was supposed to be a nice, clean robbery, then those two teenage punks flipped out and started beating on the old man and his wife. It wasn't his fault. He couldn't control them. He didn't kill anyone.*

*They didn't care. None of them. They'd been trying to nail him for years. They tried to bury him alive in solitary confinement at the prison in Renous. Allowed out for just one hour a day.*

*He had no chance of justice. They'd left him no choice but to escape. The letter explained everything ...*

"We're betting you'll take off today," a guard said as Robert Hazlett and Robert Winters escorted me out that morning, heading to the hospital in Moncton. I just laughed, but thought to myself, 'If they expect me too, I may as well do it now.'

"I wish I could leave these prisons and somebody would just let me go," I said to Hazlett.

"You never know," he replied, "but maybe someday they just may let you take off."

I was better prepared than he thought. A year earlier, I convinced a guard to bring me some solder and paste to fix my TV. I used the stuff to make a key for my cuffs. I'd been to the doctor several times since and could have 'left' any time, but the time wasn't right. I didn't want to hurt anybody, but I had to get out.

The prison is a human warehouse, a place to stick people and forget about them. The guards are either castoffs from other prisons forced to leave because they were hated or misbehaved, or locals they hired who know nothing except what they learned during a 10 month course.

Some of the women were actually grocery store checkout girls before coming here. They're just trying to keep everything under wraps, nice and quiet. Never mind the beatings and guys who slash their wrists, the mental and physical torture. And the public wonders why ex-cons go nuts on the street? Torment a dog and call it bad, and it will live up to its name, and worse.

Getting away from them in Moncton was easy. Once in the bathroom I was out of the cuffs in seconds. I came out waving a telescopic TV antenna. I was by Winters so fast he didn't have time to hit me with the mace. I was running so fast I ran into a woman coming in the hospital door.

Sweezey was driving the van and he jumped out and came after me, cursing and yelling. I got mad, stopped and told him to fuck off, and he did. All with a harmless TV aerial. Now the RCMP have the public incited, saying I had a weapon. It's open season on me. Yeah, well, give a dog a bad name and he'll have to eventually live up to it.

It's a terrible mess. It started in 1986 when I got mixed up with two persons in that botched job and the police and RCMP railroaded me with circumstantial evidence, lies and paid liars.

Okay, if you take my life, I'll fight.

As I was racing through the parking lot, I spotted a car at the gate. The woman in the car was speaking through the window to the attendent in the booth. I yanked her door open.

"I just escaped from jail and I'm doing life," I yelled at her. "Get out or get over."

Instead of getting out, she said something stupid to the guy, something like, "This guy just escaped from jail." He made a grab for me, so I yelled at the woman again, "Get out or get over." She got over. I jumped in and took off towards Mountain Road.

"Let me out. Let me out," she kept saying. Make up your mind, will you. I told her to shut up and I'd let her off in a minute. When I did stop, she didn't just jump out, she insisted I wait while she took a small, plastic container from the back seat. A bird cage.

"Tell the CBC I shouldn't have to do life for something my two co-accused did in 1986 beating," I told her.

The 1986 case was only a safe theft. We thought they were gone. We didn't know the car was in the garage. Read the testimony of 62-year-old Mary Glendenning, the wife. She pointed out her attackers as Todd Matchett and Scott Curtis by size. She said Curtis beat her husband and Matchett used the gun to sexually assault her. She said the bigger guy was in the porch as a lookout. Even the judge and prosecutors said it. There was no proof I ever touched either victim on June 21, 1986. None.

I only had to go in because those two idiots were taking so long. I decided to go and see if they could steal a safe without a fuss. By the time I got there, Matchett and Curtis were already fighting and pushing with the victims. I had no disguise or gloves, so I didn't want to break it up. I did stop Scott Curtis from kicking the old man as he tried to run to the road.

It was Matchett who found out the safe was upstairs. I went up to try to open it. The people were not in any pain I could see. Of course, I couldn't see if Matchett and Curtis were giving them a little punch or kick. They were the ones who took the old people upstairs and started beating on them to open up the safe.

"Leave them alone," I yelled. "They won't open it. Just take the safe and throw it downstairs. I'll get the car down the road."

By the time I got back, Curtis and Matchett were on the front step. "I think the old fellow ain't breathing," Curtis said. I rushed past him and found the old fellow with a gag so tight you could barely put your fingers in it. I wiggled it looser and pushed it off his mouth. He was still breathing when I left, like he was sleeping.

It was Todd's father, Billy Matchett, who squealed on me. He didn't care about anything but his fat ass. He called RCMP Sgt. Mason Johnston. And it was Johnston who told the jury I'd talked to him and told him things only someone who was there could know. I told him nothing, but he told the jury I did. It got me convicted and got him a promotion. All for jailing the notorious Allan Legere.

They are painting me in a corner, the RCMP, the justice department shit faces. And although I'm doing life for a murder I didn't commit. It may turn out that all have to make a last stand.

And the RCMP *did* get my $13,100 share of the Glendenning money when they searched for it just after I was arrested. Whoever found it, kept it. I've looked – it isn't there. It would have taken a dog to find it. Maybe the dogmaster fixed up his house. I hope he chokes on it, the pig.

The RCMP even took hairs from vehicles of mine they seized and planted them to get me. It's easy to do and juries always believe the pigs. Just watch, they'll probably use hair from my cell to do the same thing at these latest murders.

What these bastards the RCMP, local pigs and CBC are doing is causing an uproar and telling people to hate me because of these latest crimes, saying I did them. This includes all the assholes who work for local newspaper publisher David Cadogan of Newcastle. He's had a vendetta for me ever since his home burnt and he blamed me. He even went around telling people I used to visit that they shouldn't be around me.

The pigs should go out and find whoever really did those crimes. It wasn't me.

Yes, I lost my glasses in Chatham this summer, but I did not even know a robbery and murder had occurred across the street from where I was trying to steal food, or else I would never have ventured nearby. If I was to rob a store, I would have stocked up on food, wouldn't you?

There was a robbery at the Flam place back in the 1970s. Maybe this was a repeat. The cops don't care. They want people to fear me. It's easier to blame me. Blaming me, rather than go looking for other people, saves money.

Mason Johnston wasn't the only one who helped put me away for the Glendenning thing. The lawyers were in on it too. I had things I wanted to say and Crown prosecutor Fred Ferguson said if I did, he'd read an anonymous letter I was supposed to have written telling them about the last murder Earl Lewis of Chatham did. He knew Earl would be stupid enough to believe it and try to kill me inside the penitentiary.

I've tried to tell people what they did to me.

When I spoke to my lawyer, David Hughes, in August 1988 he admitted Judge David Russell was at a party at his house a week before my April 1988 appeal. And Russell claims not to know me, yet he too is from Newcastle.

Hughes didn't tell me until after my trial that he once worked for the justice department and his father is a retired provincial appeal court judge. And he refused to use juror prejudice as a grounds for appeal of my murder conviction. Why? Either because he didn't want to admit he messed up, or he wanted me convicted.

On Nov. 7, 1986 – just before the Glendenning trial in Newcastle in January – I was stabbed by Scott Curtis while in the Dorchester Penitentiary. This happened only hours after Hughes visited me there and visited Curtis along with lawyer Bill Fenton, who represented Todd Matchett. Fenton was once a law partner of Hughes.

The meeting was about a two-page confession Curtis gave me. It said only he and Matchett beat the Glendennings. When I contacted Hughes, he said he would be down to see the confession, plus speak to Curtis. But when I arrived at the Dorchester visiting room to see Hughes, he'd brought along his old buddy Fenton to speak to Curtis first.

I was stabbed that night. Curtis couldn't tell the court he and Matchett did the beating, and still help Matchett, so he had to silence me.

And look at my trial. All or most of the jurors knew my criminal reputation. I told Hughes and wrote it on his jury list. I said I knew Allen Austin and Wally Jimmo. Ms. O'Donnell and Jimmo have relatives near Black River, which is near the crime scene. O'Donnell lives not far away in Napan. Gary Williston knew me well. And that's four of the twelve.

Yet Hughes never questioned one of them for prejudice. He was working hand in hand with some pros. Crown prosecutor Fred Ferguson has hated me for years and always tried to get me off the streets. He even tried to have me committed in 1976, but psychiatrists came to court and said I was okay.

In October 1988, I even sent registered letters to four jurors asking them to step forward to admit knowing about my bad reputation. Not one would respond.

My trial should never have been held in Newcastle. Ferguson told the judge I would get a fair trial. Fair! There were crowds of 500 people yelling for me to be hanged when I was charged in 1986. The retired police chief of Chatham, Dan Allen, said I could get a fair trial. Yet he'd been after me for 18 years. He's the one who told me when I got out of prison in 1985 I'd never make it on the Miramichi because of my reputation.

The CBC had *Miramichi Leader* editor Rick MacLean on the radio on Oct. 22, 1989 saying Allan Legere's name was like the boogie man and there was a mystique about him going back 20 years. So how could Ferguson and Allen get away with keeping my trial in their area and say it could be fair? They've been after me for years. They decided if I wouldn't join their ranks and squeal on others, then they had to get rid of me. I despise them and their counterparts.

What the RCMP, the justice department and my lawyer did was take my life. Sure, I deserved time for involvement in the Black River case, but I never did the violence and never told the others to do it. Yes, I was part of it, but I was not even in the house when Curtis and Matchett beat and tied up those old people. You can lead a horse to water, but you can't make it drink.

And the cops know Curtis and Matchett stabbed a Saint John man in April 1986, but won't pursue it because they're doing life and don't want to waste the money. The RCMP's Rick Daigle of Crime Stoppers knows. That TIPS program of theirs is a farce. If it costs money or time, the cops won't do anything.

This all started long before the Glendenning thing anyway. It's always been like this.

In October 1971, I moved back to Chatham from Ontario where I'd worked as a machinist. But I'd been raised in Chatham Head and people never let you forget it. Once back, I got work at the nearby Acadia mill, but I was laid off a few times in 1972 and got involved with some guys dealing in stolen goods. When I went to court on a charge, the judge gave me 22 months in jail – and the only other charge I'd had was shoplifting in 1967. And on the shoplifting charge I'd got 18 months, which was reduced to six months on appeal.

When I got out of jail in December 1972, a union guy helped me get back on working at the mill, but I was forced to do manual labor. I was one of only two machinists listed at the mill, but some Lynch guy got my job, even though he had no experience.

In early 1973, my five-year-old son was sexually molested. The police knew who did it, but did nothing. If that was A. Legere, the boom would have been lowered by those assholes without a doubt.

In 1974, they tried to pin the stabbing of Beatrice Redmond of Chatham Head on me, the one where the woman was stabbed more than 50 times just after leaving church. The RCMP spent so much time harrassing me and my buddies that the real killer got away.

In 1975, my mother's house was burned down. A Crown prosecutor knew who was responsible, yet did nothing. I've been persecuted without stop and jailed for the thefts and fights I've done. But for others, it's turn a blind eye …

On Aug. 19, 1982 I was shot in the back and nothing was done. A police tactical squad showed up at my door that morning talking about a break and entry. Cpl. Ross Hickey came in – after he passed his firearm to another officer – and asked if I had been involved in.

"No," I said. He left a few minutes later and told the guys outside to leave. But then another policeman, a Mr. Hart, apparently whispered in Hickey's ear about jewelry found four streets away from my trailer in the trailer park.

"Perhaps you should come to the station and speak to the sergeant," Hickey yelled out.

"Am I under arrest?" I yelled back.

"No."

"Then get your man off my property."

When Hickey told me his men were losing patience and he would give me 15 minutes before tear gas was fired in, I bolted out the rear window. I was shot in the back a few streets away.

Isn't it odd, at the trial the judge said the tape recorder wasn't working, so the steno would transcribe the proceedings. Sure, it's so much easier to delete and change later.

The judge asked Hickey why I wasn't arrested before I was shot? "At that time, there wasn't enough evidence," he said. Today, no doubt, that court record has disappeared, thanks to Moncton Police Chief Greg Cohoon, the bastard. When Cohoon was with Newcastle RCMP around 1973, he always tried to get me to be one of his informers, along with Cpl. James Carrol, now with Sydney, Nova Scotia police.

The first lawyer I hired in the shooting case quit to take a job with the justice department as a prosecutor. The guy I hired to sue the police quit too. It turns out he and the director of public prosecutions for the province once worked for the same law firm.

They all lie.

It was only recently revealed in the investigation of my escape – and Cohoon was part of that investigation – that I also escaped in January 1987 just after the Glendenning trial. I was being led into the Moncton Detention Center by two sheriffs with the justice department – one a moonlighting Moncton cop.

When I got out of the sheriff's car I passed the cop my leg irons and handcuffs and ran. I'd have made it, but I'd just been out of hospital for a month and was very weak. Even at that I might have made it, but my shoes slipped on the snow-packed ground.

Nobody reported it. That's why no one thought I was an escape risk in 1989.

Well, that wasn't the only time. In July 1987 I nearly did it again. I was being moved from Renous to Dorchester for a court appearance in Moncton – the trial of co-accused Scott Curtis for stabbing me. At Dorchester, I was caught with a homemade plastic handcuff key made from a toothbrush and a piece of wire. The guards – Kaye and Cormier – knew about it, so did their boss. Judge Miller at the trial knew too because Curtis's lawyer asked if I'd tried to escape or been caught with escape tools.

Nobody reported that either. Liars. Well, walk a mile in my shoes, then tell me how you feel.

The courts should have ordered a new trial for me in the Glendenning case. I was convicted of murder just because I happened to be helping in a crime where a murder took place, even though I didn't do it. That's called constructive murder. And the Supreme Court has struck down the sections of the law dealing with that, saying they were unconstitutional. Section 213(d) was struck down on Dec. 3, 1987. Section 213(a) on June 9, 1988.

The New Brunswick Court of Appeal knew that. I didn't appeal my murder conviction until April 1988. The court didn't announce its decision until August. Then it refused my appeal. Judges Ryan, Angers said the decision throwing out 213(d) didn't apply to me because I'd been convicted under 213(a). But by August, 213(a) had been thrown out too. I told them that in registered letters sent before their decision came down, but got no reply.

I told the Supreme Court what happened. I sent registered letters to judges Antonio Larmer (sic), Gerald Laforrest (sic) and William McIntyre (sic). I explained about the injustices done to me by the provincial justice department, the prejudiced appeal court, the RCMP – who paid and coerced witnesses to testify against me, Chatham police Dan Allen and Crown prosecutor Fred Ferguson of

Newcastle who told the judge I could get a fair trial in Newcastle, my lawyer – David Hughes – who didn't ask the
jurors about knowing of my bad reputation.

I never got any reply from the judges. I know why. After
my escape, the justice department, RCMP, Ferguson, all of
them, swayed the appeal court and Supreme Court not to
hear my appeal unless I turn myself in. They said I had to
surrender by October or they wouldn't consider my case.

Right.

In January 1989, I had my hearing asking the Supreme
Court to let me present my case. By the summer I still had
no reply. It should have been automatic. My trial used sections 213(d) and 213(a). What were they waiting for? Cases
worse than mine had been sent back for a new trial.

I know what was going on. They didn't want me to get a
new trial or a chance of being free again. It was the rich
people and influential locals, people on the Miramichi and
in Moncton, people in the RCMP and justice department.
The Supreme Court is taking instructions from the provincial justice department and RCMP.

I warned them what would happen.

In 1989, I sent registered letters to a CBC-TV reporter and
a magazine editor in Halifax. I told them what was going
on. I said the shit would hit the fan one of these days. I
wrote to New Brunswick Premier Frank McKenna and told
him too. I warned him that if they insisted on railroading
me, that one day the shit would hit the fan severely. But
nobody could be bothered. My case got too deep into government corruption. It's like the Mafia or worse. I told
them all, yet they don't listen.

Look at the Bible, Revelations 12:9 – "And the great
dragon was cast out, that old serpent, Now is come salva-
tion, and strength, and the kingdom of our God, and the
power of his Christ: for the accuser of our brethern is cast
down, which accused them before our God day and night.
And they overcame him by the blood of the Lamb, and by
the word of their testimony; and they loved not their lives

unto the death. Therefore rejoice, ye heavens, and ye that dwell in them. Woe to the inhabiters of the earth and of the sea! for the devil is come down unto you, having great wrath, because he knoweth that he hath but a short time. And when the dragon saw that he was cast unto the earth, he persecuted the woman which brought forth the man child."

Uncanny. The devil cannot do zip without God's okay.

I am being forced to fight for my life.

· †

Ron Gomke looked into the calm blue eyes staring at him. Oh my God, he thought. The man the tabloids were calling the "Madman of the Miramichi" was here. In Saint John. In his cab.

"If your dispatcher sends anyone," Allan Legere warned, "the moment the cruiser pulls us over, it's over for you." He didn't want to hurt him, Legere explained. "I'll let you go if everything goes smooth. I want to go to Chatham, stay in a motel until six o'clock, then I want to go the airport and hijack a plane to Iran."

Gomke quickly agreed. He struggled to stay calm, to keep the car on the slippery road, and listen to the Legere's non-stop conversation.

The cabbie's father had died a few years before and Gomke prayed silently to him. I'm going to meet you soon Dad. I'm going to meet you soon.

"Those cops," Legere snorted. "You have to laugh. They thought they were so close. They're so easy to elude. I lived in the woods, made friends with the chipmunks and squirrels. Hell, they ate right out of my hand."

Gomke nodded. Whatever you say.

"It was getting colder. I couldn't stay in the woods, I had to keep moving." Legere talked about the murdered women, denied killing them or the priest. Sure, he'd met the priest back in the early eighties when he went to his house. He'd told him it's not right to gamble, not right to have bingos in a church hall. "The priest didn't like that. Chased me out of his house."

Gomke tried to focus on the road. Blowing snow forced him to creep along the highway at about forty miles an hour, following a truck. In his rearview mirror, he could see the blinking hazard lights of a car struggling to keep up. Impatient, Legere ordered Gomke to pass the truck and drive the sixty mile an hour speed limit.

A few miles from downtown Moncton, the cab spun out of control. Cursing, Legere grabbed at the wheel and yelled at Gomke not to ditch the car. Nevertheless, the car plowed into a snowbank.

"You've done it," Legere snarled. "You really screwed up now." He ordered Gomke out of the car. They had to climb out passenger's side because the left side of the car was jammed into the snow. Hiding his gun, Legere forced Gomke to follow him to the side of the road.

Just before midnight, Michelle Mercer was driving home to Prince Edward Island. She was tired from a long drive to Montreal and the struggle to keep her Japanese car on the road. She was thinking about pulling over for the night and waiting out the storm in a motel when her lights caught a man waving his arms by the side of the road. She spotted a taxi in the ditch and another man. She pulled over.

The smaller man shoved the bigger one into the back seat, then tried to squeeze in beside him, but there was so much luggage there he couldn't fit.

"There's room in the front seat," Mercer suggested, noting there was something odd about the two men. The clean-shaven man sitting next to her asked where she was going. When she said only as far as the next motel, he grew agitated.

Minutes later, the smaller, more slender man said he had lost his teeth. He insisted they turn around and go back to the cab so he could find them. She couldn't go back, Mercer explained, but she would drop them off and they could catch a drive back with a passing car.

There's something wrong here, she thought, suddenly anxious to get the men out of her car. She decided to identify herself, hoping that would prevent the men from trying anything. She told the man sitting next to her she was a member of the RCMP.

The smaller man's calm voice filled the car. "Please do as I say. I'm the one they're looking for. I'm Allan Legere." There was a rifle, its barrel sawed off, pointing at her.

Legere now insisted she turn around so he could get his lost teeth, but just before they got there, he discovered them in a coat pocket. He ordered Mercer to turn again and head towards Moncton.

The roads were getting worse. They were barely past a truck stop when the car started to slide out of control. Furious, Legere order Mercer to be more careful. He couldn't handle three hostages, he warned. If he had to grab another driver, he'd have to get rid of one or both of them.

Drive to Moncton, he demanded. Mercer did as she was told, but somehow lost her way and ended up heading back the way they'd came, westbound on the Trans-Canada.

"You're screwing around," Legere shouted. Now he wanted to go to Chatham.

Legere seemed confused, unable to make up his mind. At one point, he pulled out marijuana joint and started smoking it, but threw it out the window when Mercer objected. He fluffed her hair, said he liked her and wouldn't hurt her. Minutes later he threatened to kill her if she didn't do what he said.

Once again he denied killing the priest. Sure, he had broken into a home, but only later had he discovered that it belonged to a priest. He claimed he'd discovered money and pornographic magazines while in the house. He'd met Father Smith the once, when he'd told him holding bingos in a church hall was a sin. He'd been living in a tent for months, but the weather was getting too cold for that. He had just returned from Montreal. He had to go there to buy a pair of glasses, he explained.

"Where were you in Montreal?" Mercer asked.

Legere laughed. "I can't tell you that, you're a cop."

He was no killer, he told her. He'd never even killed an animal. The squirrels became his friends while he was hiding. In an effort to convince her, he demonstrated some of the noises he claimed he'd made when talking to them.

He had to get to Chatham so he could hijack an airplane to Iran. He could have gone to Florida the day before, but lacked the necessary identification. Mercer suggested he go to the Moncton airport and hijack a plane there.

He couldn't do that, he explained, there were security problems. He talked about going to the United States, or maybe Edmundston, a small city in northern New Brunswick a few miles from the Québec and U.S. borders. Maybe if he had more money, he could go to there.

Mercer offered him her bank card and car if he let them go. Legere liked the idea and once more told Mercer to turn around. They started west once more, towards Edmundston.

On the outskirts of Sussex, a town between Saint John and Moncton, Mercer told Legere she needed gas. They pulled into an Irving gas station and restaurant on the Trans-Canada Highway.

Twenty-four-year-old Joy Levesque was working the overnight shift when she noticed Mercer's car pull up to the pumps at 1:50 a.m. "They pulled in and just sat there for fifteen minutes," she remembered. "I thought maybe they couldn't read the big sign that says self-serve. I told my brother to go out and tell the guy to move to pump four because pump one had been froze up all night. But by the time he got to the door, we could see the numbers rolling on pump one."

Legere had grabbed the car keys and some money from Mercer, stuffed his gun in a plastic bag and jumped out to pump $15 of gas. He walked into the store and dropped a twenty dollar bill on the counter.

"Boy," Levesque said, "You must have the magic touch. That pump hasn't been working all night." He just looked at her, didn't say anything and headed to the door without waiting for the change. She was about to yell after him about the money when the car took off. "I thought maybe the man and woman had been having an argument and the car was going to stop before it got to the highway. The woman was going awful fast. That's when I began to worry. The car was just fish-tailing." The man turned and disappeared behind a row of parked tractor-trailers.

Minutes before Mercer had turned to Gomke as Legere went into the store.

"I've got a spare set of keys. Do you want to go for it?" she asked.

"Will he let us go?" Gomke replied. Mercer said she didn't think so, there was no other chance.

"Then go for it, we've got nothing to lose."

Mercer started the car and took off just as Legere charged out the gas station door.

"Slow down, slow down," Gomke pleaded.

"Are you with him?" she shot back.

No, he said. She was just driving too fast. They might end up in the ditch, and Legere would catch them.

Following Gomke's directions, Mercer headed for the Sussex RCMP detachment. The office was closed, but there was a phone box outside the front door for emergencies. Mercer gave her badge number and described what had happened.

Within minutes, police cruisers roared up to the gas station. Joy Levesque was still inside. "I was sitting there doing some paper work and then I see these policemen outside the door asking me something through the glass. I nodded yes, thinking they were asking me if everything was okay. But they must have been asking if he was hiding in here. They came in with rifles drawn."

Police searched the area, but came away empty-handed..
In the excitement, one officer's rifle went off accidentally
and damaged the garage floor. Levesque, who lived nearby
and had only started working at the store about two months
earlier, didn't wish to wake up the store's manager when
there had been no robbery. She waited until morning to let
him know what had happened.

In the meantime, the RCMP issued a province-wide alert.
Roadblocks were set up. Allan Legere wasn't getting away
this time, dammit. But where was he?

Truck driver Brian Golding had been on his way from
Montreal to Halifax when he stopped at the truck stop near
Sussex to clean his windshield.

As he walked over to the office to buy a snack, he noticed
a man pumping gas into a Japanese compact. The next time
he noticed the man he was running out of the building,
chasing after a car roaring out of the parking lot. The man
then turned and spotted Golding standing next to the
orange Mack truck with the words *Fastrax, A Division of
Day & Ross Inc., Hartland, N.B* on the driver's door.

"Come on," the man yelled, "Let's get out of here."
Golding didn't move. Then the man pulled out a gun and
pointed it at him. "I'm Allan Legere, let's get out of here."

"I didn't believe him at first," Golding would recall.
"His appearance was different from what I was used to seeing in the paper and I could smell that he had been drinking." In fact, the trucker, with his light-brown moustache
and shoulder-length curly hair, looked more like the "real"
Allan Legere than the man yelling at him. Still, there was
no mistaking the gun, so Golding did as he was told and got
the orange Mack truck moving. "Where to?" he asked.

"Moncton," Legere replied. Once on the road, Legere
kept insisting they speed up.

"I was doing my best to get the truck going," Golding
remembered, "but the roads were bad and I had a heavy
load." Finally, Legere took his foot and jammed it on top of

Golding's, forcing the gas pedal towards the floor. "I know this truck can go faster than this," Legere snapped.

At this point, Golding lost his temper and told Legere that if he wanted to drive the truck, he damn well could. Legere calmed down and started talking, telling Golding about the manhunt, how the police were calling him the prime suspect in four murders on the Miramichi.

"You guilty?" Golding asked.

"It doesn't matter if I did it or not," he replied. "The cops will frame me anyway." At one point during the drive, Legere pulled out a bullet for the .308 rifle and showed it to Golding. "If this hits you," he warned, "you don't walk away from it."

He took Golding's wallet, removed the identification papers, then returning it without taking the approximately $20 in the billfold.

"He told me he was 41. I was 24. I asked him if he thought he could pass for 24."

As they approached Moncton, Golding spotted a sign indicating a set of weigh scales for trucks was open. As he signalled to turn in, Legere exploded. Jamming the gun into Golding's leg, he warned: "Don't stop. I can feel the devil coming up inside me."

As they drove by, Golding noticed the scale operator had his back turned to the highway and was talking to another trucker, so he didn't notice them slip past.

Once on Route 126, the secondary highway connecting Moncton with Newcastle, Legere seemed to relax again. He started to talk more, describing what had happened in the past few hours.

"He said he had taken the train to Saint John and that he drank at a bar there. He said he took a cab, but it went off the road. And then he flagged a lady cop down." He described himself as a survivor and talked about how he hid from the police.

"As we were driving along he asked me to open the window. It was a power window and the control was on my side. He said he hadn't slept in a couple of days and he wanted to stay awake." Despite the open window, Legere grew silent. Golding waited a few minutes, then looked over.

"He had kinda nodded off. He had the gun on his lap pointed toward me. I wasn't sure if I should grab the gun, since it was pointed at me. I thought I might end up shooting myself." Instead, Golding shouted Legere's name, waking him up.

They had reached Rogersville, about twenty-five miles south of Newcastle. By then it was almost 5:00 a.m. November 24. Legere said he wanted to be at CFB Chatham at six because there was a commercial flight boarding then, but he didn't want to arrive early. Golding pointed to the time and asked what they should do, suggesting at the same time that they pull over for a while. Legere agreed.

Golding asked him where he was planning to go. Iran, Legere replied. When Golding asked what kind of plane was in Chatham and Legere said a four-engine propeller aircraft, the trucker said he doubted it could make such a trip. At that point, Legere asked if driving a truck was difficult.

"I told him if we dropped the trailer, it would be easier to drive." Legere agreed to have the truck taken down a dirt road where he and Golding unhitched the trailer. By the time they had finished, however, Legere had changed his mind. Forget about waiting for a while. Keep heading north towards Newcastle.

About four miles south of Newcastle, Legere ordered Golding to pull a left on Route 118, a side road running along the Miramichi River. He didn't know that another trucker had spotted Golding's tractor-trailer going down a road not normally used by such trucks. Suspicious, the trucker had called police on his CB.

RCMP Corporals Terry Barter and Gary Lutwick were part of a team of officers manning a road block on Route 126 near Newcastle that morning. When the call came saying a truck had been spotted on the South Barnaby Road, the two men sped off in a four-wheel drive. "I got on the radio to make sure this was the right road," Barter said, "and was told it was not, that the road we wanted was up ahead a bit further. We were just about to turn around when we saw a set of headlights." Barter flipped on the blue and red police lights to indicate he wanted the truck to pull over, but the driver ignored him.

Golding saw the police and asked Legere what to do.

"Keep driving."

The police stayed right behind the truck, struggling to make out the licence number, which was obscured by snow. After about a half-mile, Golding turned to Legere and told him he didn't think he could keep going.

"Okay," said Legere, indicating he could pull over. As the truck driver got the truck stopped, Legere looked into the mirror to see what the police were doing. Golding yanked open the door and jumped. "It's him. It's him," he shouted as he ran back towards the police. "He's got a gun."

Barter, who was armed with an M-16 rifle, was taking no chances. He grabbed Golding and searched him. Then, convinced the man they wanted was still in the truck, Barter ordered Golding to stay back. Barter approached the truck from the passenger side while Lutwick took the driver's side.

"Get out of the truck," Lutwick yelled. "Get out of the truck. I want to see your hands on the door."

The hands appeared, then disappeared. A metal object with a leather strap was thrown out the window and clattered onto the frozen pavement.

"Get out of the truck," Lutwick shouted again.

"It's all right. I'm okay. You got me," Legere said, climbing down.

Barter leaped from the other side of the truck to help cover him. "Shut up and get down, you cocksucker," the officer yelled. Frightened, Legere hit the ground, sprawling spread-eagle on the pavement. Lutwick approached warily, stopping when he was about twenty feet away, then moving closer when he realized Barter was covering him.

"I'm okay," Legere said. "I'm giving up."

Barter ran to the police truck to get a pair of handcuffs. Lutwick stood over Legere.

"At that point, he made a movement," Lutwick recalled. "I put my foot on the back of his neck and pushed him to the ground. I told him not to move."

Barter came running up with the cuffs. As he bent down to put them on, Legere pulled his arms in under his body and started to push himself up. Barter lashed out with his foot, kicking the prisoner on the right cheek.

"Stay down," Barter screamed. Legere flopped back onto the pavement and froze, too frightened to move.

Once the cuffs were on, Barter ran back to the four-wheel drive and called the dispatcher to say he had a suspect in custody.

"Is it Allan Legere?" the dispatcher's voice squawked over the radio.

"You got me," Legere shouted in response. "I'm Allan Legere."

## FIFTEEN

# In Custody

WHEN word came over the radio that Emergency Response Team members Barter and Lutwick had captured Legere, a second group of officers rushed from the road block to the truck.

When Const. Ken MacPhee arrived at the truck, Legere was on his back with his hands behind him. The RCMP officer, who had only joined the hunt two days before after being called in from Sackville, New Brunswick, grabbed a set of leg shackles out of his car and locked them on Legere.

Legere was "hyper" at this point, talking non-stop. Four times he told MacPhee that he could have shot police officers, but didn't. He claimed he'd let Michelle Mercer go after kidnapping her. He complained about being kicked unnecessarily in the face and demanded the return of his dentures.

When Cpl. Luc Bolduc arrived and dropped into the front seat of the car, Legere started to curse at him, mistaking him for the officer who had kicked him. "You're the cocksucker that kicked me in the face," Legere yelled. "Man-to-man you wouldn't have done it, I'll tell you. Fuckin' prick." Legere demanded to know his name, so Bolduc told him.

Furious, Legere looked out the window at the officers

standing around the car. "Look at them, they're laughing. It's no fucking wonder I hate you guys so much."

At 5:45 a.m., Legere was driven to the RCMP building in Newcastle, about six miles away. Sitting in the back seat, separated from the RCMP by a plastic barrier, he kept up his fusillade of conversation. They would never have caught him but for winter, he claimed. He'd tried to leave the country, but couldn't get over the border.

"I had no money, no birth certificate, nowhere to go. If I had had a birth certificate, I'd have been long gone and you would never have seen me again." Over and over he talked about being in Saint John and lacking a birth certificate.

"I didn't know what to do. I was thinking about turning myself in."

He described grabbing the cabbie and cop, twisting the story as he did so. "Me and my luck, an RCMP female officer got stuck behind me." He talked about kidnapping the truck driver, about the number of times he could have killed police officers or their dogs. He said he'd only been able to escape because a guard gave him the solder to make the key.

At one point he looked at Bolduc, "Man, you kick as bad as me. Man, why did you kick me in the face like that?"

"Nobody kicked you in the face," Bolduc answered.

"Well," Legere demanded, "I want to see a doctor and this will all come out in court." Bolduc promised he could see one after they got to the detachment in Newcastle.

Legere wanted the handcuffs removed, but Bolduc refused. "We're not in a situation where we can loosen your handcuffs there. Just sit still; the more you move the worse it gets. We'll get to the detachment in a few minutes and we'll loose them up for you."

They arrived at the detachment at 6:04 a.m. and drove into the garage at the back of the building. Legere was stripped and given a blanket. A search of his clothing turned up a used train ticket for a one-way trip from

Montreal to Saint John. He'd come back from Montreal to Saint John on that ticket, Legere volunteered.

Officers still at the scene where he had been arrested, began gathering evidence. RCMP Corporal Ron Godin picked up the sawed off .308 Browning rifle Legere has thrown from the truck. It was loaded and cocked. There were another five shells in the clip.

Prosecutor Fred Ferguson was sleeping at the Wharf Inn in Newcastle, just a few hundred yards from the home of the murdered Daughney sisters and about a half-mile from the rectory of Father Smith. Shortly after 6:00 a.m. his phone rang.

Several blocks away, RCMP Const. Kevin Mole was running down the hall of the Journey's End motel, his cellular phone jammed to his ear, his jacket half-on, plans for a trip to Fredericton forgotten. "Get up. Get up," he yelled at Ferguson. "If you don't, you're going to miss the biggest story in the eastern half of North America."

"Where?" Ferguson shouted back, pulling on his pants.

"South Nelson."

"Is he alive?"

"You bet."

Ferguson arrived at the RCMP station at seven o'clock. It was still dark. As he jumped out of his car he was met by Rick MacLean of the *Miramichi Leader*. They grabbed each other in a bear hug, pounding each other on the back.

"You don't know how I feel," Ferguson said before turning and rushing into the building.

Sgt. Mason Johnston was already inside, having arrived at the detachment at about 6:00 a.m., just minutes ahead of Legere. He found the side door locked. Mystified by the speed with which reporters had managed to get there, he was forced to spend about ten minutes outside telling reporters they had to go through proper channels to find out if Allan Legere was indeed there. Cars were jamming both sides of the road as people strained to get a look at New Brunswick's most notorious criminal.

Johnston knew officers Mole and Ron Charlebois, a ten-year veteran of the force, had been assigned to question Legere when he was caught. He simply wanted to look at him.

"Come here you short little fucker, I want to talk to you," Legere shouted when he spotted him.

Johnston was stunned. He'd known Legere for twenty years, but hardly recognized this man in front of him. "He had lost a lot of weight. He didn't have his beard. His hair was short, his nose more pronounced than it is now because his face was thin and sallow. If I was walking down the street and he was on the sidewalk across from me, I probably wouldn't have recognized him. I think the only reason that I would have recognized him if I met him face on and was able to look at him directly."

Legere had a complaint.

"What are you talking about?" Johnston asked.

"They didn't have to do that to me," Legere said, motioning towards his face. "I didn't shoot anybody. I could have shot people at the scene where they got me."

"What are you talking about?"

"The fuckin' French frog, Bolduc, kicked me in the face." Johnston noticed swelling under Legere's right eye. The area was a bluish-black colour. Johnston promised to get him a doctor. Legere wanted the cuffs removed.

"Look," Johnston explained, "Kevin will be down here in a minute and we will take the cuffs off." He turned to leave.

"By the way, Mason, why didn't the police officer report shooting his gun at me?" Legere taunted.

"What are you talking about?"

"The night they nearly had me, the police dog was so close he came up and sniffed my ass. I just turned around and gave him a swat and told him to fuck off, and the dog did." Legere laughed.

"How come the police officer didn't report that he fired shots. I could have killed the police officer that night, but I didn't. I just fired a shot in the air." Legere kept talking, as if he didn't want Johnston to leave. "I got myself in an awful mess this time."

Johnston said nothing.

The female cop, Legere added, he liked her, she was a nice person, smart.

"Why did you come back to the area?" Johnston asked.

Legere looked at him. "Well, I only had $900. I had no money left."

"Well, why did you leave?"

Legere smiled. "Well, last week, it was getting cold."

"Where were you?"

"Look, I was in the woods all this time." Legere described living with the squirrels, taming them, learning how to talk to them.

Johnston interrupted. "Well, if you hadn't escaped, you wouldn't be in all this problem right now."

Legere ignored him. He kept talking about the prison guards and how stupid they were. He described his escape in Moncton and how police searched for him in the west end when he was in the east end. He claimed he had jumped a train, but hurt a foot, thought he'd broken it when it was momentarily jammed between the couplings connecting two cars.

"Oh, you jumped a train. It must have been you down in Truro," Johnston said, referring to the May 7 attack on Max Ramsay, the man who was beaten and had his car stolen.

"No, that wasn't me down in Truro. I read about that in the paper," Legere replied. He did manage, however, to return to Newcastle within days of escaping, he claimed. He hitchhiked north on Route 126 and stopped in the French village of Rogersville for a chicken dinner.

"You mean you survived all this time living in the woods?" Johnston said, clearly skeptical.

"Yes, when the weather was nice. It wasn't difficult. It

was lonely at times. I probably ate better than you did. You know, I read in the paper where they all, everybody says I'm this great woodsman," Legere said and laughed. "I don't know nothing about the woods."

Growing excited, the tempo of his speech accelerating, he started to describe his months on the loose yet again. He described how he cooked meals, making a fire during the day so police couldn't spot it. He'd seen helicopters overhead at times.

"Do you mean to tell me that you spent all this time alone?" Johnston asked.

"Yes."

"You didn't have dealings with anyone?"

"No."

"Well, that's hard to believe."

"So help me God, Mason," Legere insisted. "I only came in contact with two people the whole time I was out. I saw a fellow fishing up behind the golf course up between the Kelly Road there. I saw him, I think he saw me. I was walking across the bridge in Newcastle once. I saw a guy, I met a guy. I thought the guy might have recognized me. I thought about going back and throwing him over the bridge because the guy said, 'Hi Al' or 'Hi pal.'"

Legere described being on the train to Montreal the night police boarded it. Yes, they had checked him for the tell-tale tattoos. "He asked me to roll up the wrong arm. I thought I was caught for sure."

Kevin Mole arrived at the Newcastle office. A fourteen-year veteran of the RCMP, he had been stationed on the Miramichi in the early 1980s and been back many times as part of his work as an investigator. He dropped his briefcase in the interview room, then telephoned Nina Flam to tell her it was over. Fears of another attack had haunted her since May. "She was very fearful of telling anyone in an official capacity who she thought might be responsible for fear it would get out and her daughters would be in jeopardy."

Then Mole picked up some plastic exhibit bags, a pair of surgical gloves and a pair of first-aid scissors. He walked to the cell area where Legere was being held. Mason Johnston and Ron Charlebois were there too.

"Well," said Mole when he spotted Legere, "what happened to your hair?"

"Shave and a haircut in Montreal, $22," Legere answered with a smile. "Jeez, you're fat," he teased.

"Well, you don't look so good yourself. I would never have recognized you, you're so thin." Legere was barefoot, shackled and naked except for a brown wool blanket. He was so thin, in fact, that his face seemed longer than normal.

Mole removed Legere's handcuffs, then asked Charlebois the time. It was 6:47. Noting that, Mole sat down on the right-hand corner of the bed next to Legere and read him the standard police caution and informed him of his rights under the Charter.

"I'm arresting you for the murder of Annie Flam. It is my duty to inform you that you have the right to retain and instruct counsel without delay. Do you understand?"

"Yeah," Legere replied.

"You need not say anything. You have nothing to hope from any promise or favour and nothing to fear from any threat, whether or not you say anything. Anything you do say may be used as evidence. Do you understand?"

"Yeah."

"You must understand that anything said to you previously should not influence you or make you feel compelled to say anything at this time. Whatever you felt influenced or compelled to say earlier, you're not obliged to repeat, nor are you obliged to say anything further, but whatever you do say may be given in evidence. Do you understand what has been said to you?"

"Yeah, yeah."

Const. MacPhee entered the cell area and and handed
Mason Johnston a handwritten form drafted by Fred Ferguson, it began, "I —— do consent to give hair samples."

Mole asked Legere to stand up and told him they
required hair samples. At this point Johnston passed him
the handwritten form, but Mole only glanced at it and
handed it back, seemingly without realizing what it was.
He didn't think he needed permission anyway. He remembered the problems they'd run into when taking hair from
Legere in June 1986 and their concerns then about following the law as spelled out in the *Alderton* case. This time,
however, there was no lag between the time they arrested
Legere and the time when they demanded the hair samples.
They could say the seizure of the hair was part of the arrest.

"You know the routine," Mole said to Legere.

"You know how I feel about that," Legere answered.
"I'm not consenting."

"I'm going to have to take the hair, Allan. Do you want
to help me?"

"I'm not helping you. You do what you have to do, but
I'm not helping you."

There was no comb because most of the evidence material had been taken to the Major Crime Unit office near
Chatham, so Mole plucked hairs from the top of Legere's
head instead.

Mole had collected hair before, but noticed that taking
hair from Legere was "like taking it from a corpse, it just
came right out. It was very easy to come out and there was
no flinch, or anything."

Legere ignored Mole as the RCMP officer took his
samples and talked to Johnston instead, describing how he
had used a series of five camps and stayed in a different one
each night, moving only at night. He mentioned Billy
Matchett. "Too bad that Billy's house burnt," he chuckled.

With a pair of blunt scissors, Mole proceeded to cut hair
from Legere's head and place it in an evidence bag. He asked
Legere to stand, then plucked and cut hairs from his pubic

area, putting these in a separate bag. He sealed the bag, signed his name, noted the date, time and place where the hair was taken and the file number – 89-548.

It was the first time Mole had seen Legere fully undressed. "I was surprised at how very thin he was from the waist down. He was very muscular. His upper body is very well developed, but his legs and his waist are very, very small, almost disproportionate to his body. He has a very, very narrow waist, very thin legs. The clump of hair in the genital area was very sparse around the legs, as if it had been worn away or that he had gone a long time without underwear. I noticed that his hair was very, very light brown colour, which surprised me. I expected Legere's pubic hair to be similar to his head hair and I've always known Legere to have dark hair."

Mole wanted to get Legere out of the cell and into the more controlled surroundings of the interview room, but first he had to wait until someone brought the prisoner a pair of coveralls.

While they waited, Legere talked about a night he was chased and nearly caught, how he'd been forced to drop the beer he was carrying, which angered him. He joked that despite the helicopters and four-wheel drive trucks hunting for him, he'd read the papers regularly, had them "delivered" to him. His meals were "the best, steak and lobster."

He recounted the scene on the train to Montreal the night Father Smith's body was found. How he had tried to pretend he was with the man sleeping in the seat beside him, how the police had insisted he show them his identification papers anyway. He replayed the moment when he had been ordered to roll up his sleeve, trying to convince police that he was with the person asleep next to him on the train. The police officers demanding he stand up and roll up his sleeve.

"Oh fuck, they got me now," he'd thought. "Boy, I thought I was caught." He lifted an arm in the air to demonstrate. "I brought it up a little bit and the policeman said more. I brought it up a little bit more."

As he had done in June 1986 after Johnston had arrested him for the murder of John Glendenning, Legere insisted on showing off his strength. He wanted to lift the officer over his head once more. "Come here," he motioned to Johnston. He grabbed the officer under the arms, but could barely lift him off the ground.

"Jesus Christ, Mason, you've put on a lot of weight."

"I weigh less now than in '86, Allan," Johnston replied, unable to get over just how much strength and weight Legere had lost during the seven months he was at large.

Finally, just before 8:00 a.m., Mole, Charlebois and Legere headed to the interview room at the front of the building. Inside the windowless, eight-by-ten foot room was a table with three chairs, a telephone book and a reel-to-reel tape recorder.

Legere repeated the story about being chased and exchanging gun fire with a police officer. "He shot at me first and I bet you didn't get a report of that," he charged, pointing his finger. "I could have shot him, but I didn't. I just shot over his head, I shot in the air."

They talked for about a half-hour before Legere would let Mole turn on the tape recorder. Charlebois – who was struck by the way Legere talked to the officers in the detachment as if they were old friends – was there to take notes. It was a tough job. "Normally, when you speak with him," Mole said of Legere, "he doesn't want you to take notes and he stops you from doing it, he distracts you."

Once the tape recorder was turned on, Mole repeated the Charter and police cautions, changing the routine slightly to fit the occasion – "I am investigating you for the murder of Annie Flam, Linda Daughney, Donna Daughney and Reverend James Smith."

Immediately, Legere grew wary, cautious about what he was saying. Two hours later police were to discover that the machine hadn't been recording.

At about 9:30, while Legere was eating a breakfast of bacon and eggs, Mole left the interview room to find some Kleenex. Legere said he had to blow his nose. Mole wanted to ensure police kept the material for analysis. Finding a fresh roll of toilet paper still in its wrapper, he brought it and an empty green metal waste-paper can back with him.

He met Dr. Roy Cole, who was waiting to examine Legere, standing at the interview room door. As Mole stood by the door, Cole, wearing a mask and surgical gloves, checked Legere, and pronounced him fit.

At 10:15, Legere demanded that Mole explain why a request he had made for a lawyer had been ignored.

"I don't know what you're talking about," Mole replied.

"I asked the fuckin' cop this morning to get me a fuckin' lawyer, you know, talk to a lawyer," Legere snarled.

"If you request it," Mole replied, "if you want to speak with a lawyer, then we'll make one available to you."

They looked through a list of local lawyers in the telephone book, but Legere said he didn't want any of them because he considered them a bunch of flunkies, part of the group out to get him. He asked Mole for advice on which lawyer would be a good one.

"That's an area that I haven't been working around too much," Mole replied. "Depends on the lawyer you get. Every lawyer is a quality lawyer."

Legere was dubious. "People around here, lawyers around here, they're all together." Forgetting for the moment his demand to call a lawyer, he began to talk about how he was being persecuted, how no one was willing to help him.

Eventually, Mole interrupted, anxious to get the conversation back on track.

"I'm telling you something right now, now that you're in jail, I don't think they're going to look for anyone else. You follow me."

"Yeah, I know," Legere replied. "Unless they have an accomplice, or something like that."

Thirty minutes later, Legere brought up the matter of a lawyer again. "Don't you think it's goddamned high time you get me a lawyer?"

Charlebois replied, "Oh sure, if you want a lawyer, you can have a lawyer."

"Yeah, but who?"

Legere warned the officers they were making a big mistake by not getting him one. He insisted on finding one in Fredericton, a two-hour drive away. He didn't want any flunky lawyer either, they had to ensure he had the best. That was the law. There was no telephone book for that city in the building, so Charlebois arranged for a fax of the list of lawyers from the Fredericton Yellow Pages.

"You have an opportunity right now, before this thing gets too haywire," Mole said while they waited. "The people who want to write books, these people are looking for things for themselves, you've got the opportunity right now to give your version of what happened."

Legere wasn't interested. "What I'd like to know, what I'd fuckin' like to know, is how many charges am I being charged with?"

Mole left the room again around 11:20 to take out the waste container containing the used Kleenex and remains of the breakfast. There was blood on some of the used tissues, so Mole sealed them in a plastic evidence bag.

The list of lawyers arrived around noon. Mole then rhymed off the list of charges for him: escaping lawful custody, forcible confinement, possibly assault, abduction of the people on the ride from Saint John and four counts of murder.

"That many, eh," Legere answered, before turning to the phone. The officers left the room. At 2:15, Legere was taken for fingerprinting, then returned to his cell fifteen minutes later.

Throughout the day, Mole was struck by Legere's mood and how talkative he was. "He seemed quite happy to see us, and whenever he talked about eluding the police or comments that were made in the media, he had a real glint in his eye. He was really excited about that."

While Kevin Mole and Ron Charlebois were questioning Legere in the interview room, Mason Johnston turned his attention to ensuring police collected whatever material they could for DNA analysis. He ordered the purchase of a new bed sheet. Minutes before Legere left the interview room to be fingerprinted and photographed, Johnston took the sheet and a new portable toilet to the cell where Legere would be held after he was questioned. He fitted the new sheet on the mattress, hoping it might allow them to get further hair samples. He then shut off the toilet, bailed out the water, using a rag to soak up the remaining water, then put an "out of order" sign on the toilet. The plan was to save for analysis any hair which stuck to the new sheet and any urine or feces Legere would leave in the toilet.

When Legere returned to the cell, Johnston asked him if he'd called a lawyer.

"Well, I made a phone call," Legere replied, "but nobody around here will want to represent me.

"Kevin isn't bullshittin' you," Johnston said. "You should get hold of a lawyer." The telephone outside the cell area rang, and Legere was taken to it. He hung up after a short conversation. "He doesn't want to handle my case."

"Well," Johnston replied, "call somebody else."

"I don't know who to call."

"What about your previous counsel, David Hughes?" Hughes had defended Legere in the 1987 Glendenning murder trial.

Legere started to swear. He wouldn't take Hughes even if he could get him. When additional calls failed to scare up a lawyer by about 4:00 p.m., Johnston called Hughes, then passed the phone to Legere once the lawyer was on the line and left the office so the two could talk privately.

Once outside, Johnston called Mole over and pointed at the portable toilet because Legere had urinated in it. Mole took the toilet away. When Legere returned, Johnston said the plumbing had been fixed. The use of a clean sheet on the mattress, however, had failed. The number of hairs found which, by their colour, were clearly not Legere's meant the cell area had not been clean enough for the idea to work.

After dusk, RCMP Supt. Al Rivard went outside to speak with the more than twenty reporters, cameramen and photographers on hand. He was carrying a photograph of Legere and the sketch of the suspected accomplice. He told the reporters they were, in fact, the same man. Chatham police chief Dan Allen had been right.

Legere was supposed to be taken to Renous prison at seven o'clock, but it wasn't until just before 10:00 p.m. that the metal door at the rear of the Newcastle detachment opened.

A dozen members of the ERT squad had their rifles at the ready. Guarding against a Jack Ruby-like attempt to kill Legere, two officers walked on either side of the prisoner as they escorted him through the glare of television lights and flashing cameras to a waiting car. Legere was now wearing green prison fatigues, rubber boots, and sunglasses. He was handcuffed to a body chain and there were leg irons around his ankles.

"Coward," someone yelled.

"Allan Legere," a reporter called out, "what do you have to say to the people of the Miramichi?"

"Fuck you," was the reply.

It had been a day of celebrating for the Miramichi. The snowstorm ended before dawn and the sun had shone brightly. People who had refused to talk to reporters before, gladly appeared in front of cameras and microphones.

Ron, the juror from the Glendenning case of 1987, got a call from his brother at 6:15. He dressed and drove straight to the RCMP detachment. "There was a lot of traffic around, so I didn't stop. I came home and sat around for half an hour and listened to the radio. I went back again and it was still about the same thing going on. But I knew they had him then. It was just like a weight taken off you. It just felt so good. It felt like we weren't being threatened no more."

Premier Frank McKenna was notified of Legere's arrest almost immediately. He was overjoyed and relieved. "I always believed the RCMP would get him."

Billy Matchett hadn't slept. He listened on his scanner to the news of the capture. Matchett thought of going to South Nelson just to see for himself, but changed his mind and called three or four friends he thought should know.

At Hôtel Dieu Hospital in Chatham, the capture was announced over the PA system, prompting a spontaneous coffee-and-donut-party in the cafeteria. The executive director, Bob Stewart, paid the tab. "It was much the same feeling that you have on Christmas Eve," he said. "There was just so much relief and happiness through the place that it was catching. Staff were coming in and patting each other on the back and giving hugs."

Sixty-six-year-old Mary Phallen, a life-long resident of Newcastle, spent hours talking to friends and relatives. "My phone never stopped ringing this morning, different people from places all around the country. My granddaughter called me and told me they'd got Legere. I didn't even know it yet."

At radio station CFAN in Newcastle, a woman from Saint John phoned just moments after she had contacted her elderly mother, who lived on the Miramichi. Her mother, suffering from insomnia since the killing of Annie Flam, was often able only to doze off fitfully until daybreak. No longer, her daughter told a worker at the station. She described how she'd awakened her: "Mom, wake up so you can sleep."

Newcastle police chief Dan Newton predicted the region would be changed forever by what had happened. "It will give us all some peace of mind. At the same time, it has put us on guard in our daily lives."

A Newcastle businessman tried to sum up the local reaction. "The comment I got from most of the people I talked to today was, 'It's too bad they picked him up alive,' because there will always be fear that he's going to escape again. He's done it before. He's a very intelligent man and he can do it again."

Local Liberal member of Parliament Maurice Dionne stood up in the House of Commons that day to compliment the police. "For the past six months, the people of the Miramichi have gone through hell ... All the victims were gentle and good people who had never hurt anyone ... I want to take this opportunity to applaud and thank most sincerely, all the brave and courageous men and women who put their lives on the line to bring this awful nightmare to a successful conclusion ... I alway want to congratulate the people of the Miramichi for their stoicism in the face of this nightmare."

The *Miramichi Leader* published a twenty-page special edition, the first one in recent memory. It featured photos and news from the day, plus twenty-two advertisements from businesses congratulating the police. It sold out.

Fred Ferguson was circumspect when asked if he had ever been worried about himself and his family. "Somebody who was in my position probably couldn't feel anything else but fear and trepidation. I feel very good today. This is the first day of the rest of my life." He didn't mention that he'd asked his wife to send flowers to three of the RCMP officers he felt had been especially helpful during the entire hunt. Ferguson later joked to Kevin Mole, one of the three men who received them, that he'd stopped by the officer's motel room just to see what kind of flower basket could cost $75.

New Brunswick's Solicitor General, Conrad Landry, suggested the hunt was not quite over. "We're not letting our guards down. Police feel quite certain that he had an accomplice or accomplices and until these people are apprehended, there'll be no party for a little while yet. But I think the people will sleep a lot better tonight than they have in a long time."

There was a total of $73,620 in the special fund the day Legere was caught. Crime Stoppers had paid out an undisclosed amount for a description of Legere that led to a police sketch, said Jim Lavers, the president of the Miramichi branch of Crime Stoppers.

At the RCMP detachment, policemen slapped and hugged each other. They'd worked hard, more than anyone except their families and other policemen would ever know.

United Church minister Edward Scott of Newcastle felt elated too. "This morning when I woke up, it was just euphoria. And I sat in the kitchen and just drank it in along with my coffee. Christmas has come a month early. It's great to see people smiling again. I have a sense of profound thanksgiving. Webster can't really provide the words in his dictionary to describe my feelings. My heart began to pound like a four-year-old after encountering Santa Claus for the first time."

At 8:45 on November 24, the bells of St. Michael's Basilica in Chatham rang out. Normally, they're rung only for weddings and weekend masses, but associate pastor Don Melanson decided he'd use the bells to call parishioners to the nine o'clock mass. Some people called to find out who was getting married at such an hour. Father Leon Creamer, the basilica's pastor, replied that it was a way of rejoicing.

That afternoon, Father Vincent Donovan spoke to about two hundred people who gathered at St. Mary's Roman Catholic church in Newcastle. "The Almighty has done great things for us. He has showed us the power of His arm. And we are here to thank Him for that wonderful deed. Our Miramichi area will never be the same again. This is part of our history. It is up to us to make this a better place to live. Vengeance is mine, saith the Lord. We can't do much about vengeance in our hearts, but it's what we do with those feelings. If He can make something out of nothing, then surely,

He can turn good from evil. We are here to transform the evil that has touched our lives with something positive. Even though our doors may be locked, our hearts will be open. Our hearts will be open to one another."

That same afternoon, the RCMP and local police held a news conference in the main auditorium of the Newcastle town hall. The smaller room next door had been used on previous occasions, but it was far too small for the crush of reporters, now numbering more than twenty-four.

The reporters and cameramen were as excited as police. Many had done nothing but cover the story for more than a month, practically setting up residence in Newcastle. The news release handed to them by police was, for once, detailed, giving a blow-by-blow account of Legere's capture. RCMP Supt. Al Rivard told them he wasn't surprised that Legere had given up without a fight. "There are certain aspects of Allan Legere that would lead me to believe that he would give up. I always considered him to be somewhat of a coward because of the victims we are alleging he is a suspect in." The syntax was garbled, but everyone would use the quote anyway.

Rivard played down the idea that Legere may have had help with the attacks. "Allan Legere lost some thirty-five to forty pounds and has cut his hair. What I am suggesting to you is that I am somewhat satisfied that this composite [sketch] and this picture of Allan Legere are one and the same."

As for charges, he added, "we don't have any deadlines at all. I have asked my investigators to make sure they do their investigation thoroughly and completely and take all the time they need." In fact, he had wanted charges to be filed quickly, and tried unsuccessfully to pressure the prosecutors into it. They flatly refused, saying there was no rush since Legere was already in prison and they weren't ready. In interviews over the following months, Rivard first said charges would be laid in the New Year, then in a few months, then in June. Finally, he stopped giving interviews.

Allan Legere ignored the celebrations. He was more concerned about the loss of the television from his cell at the
Atlantic Insititution in Renous. A few days after his capture, he contacted Mason Johnston and spent about fifteen
minutes trying to convince him to return the set which police had confiscated November 22. Legere didn't know police had opened the back of the set and discovered a cache of
metal "bits" which had been fashioned into handcuff keys.
Johnston played along, promising to talk to the prosecutors
about getting back the TV and some letters.

"It's only fucking junk, but the junk is good to me,"
Legere said finally, satisfied that Johnston would do what
he promised. Then he mentioned the coverage his case was
receiving. "Holy fuck, Mason, I was going to say read the
Saint John paper, where do all these fucking, these fellows
writing books about serial killers and all this – holy fuck,
ever weird, eh? Keep notes? I'm the kind of guy, if I was
going to send a message to the media, I'd write it the day I
left, or before or shortly after. Wouldn't be a fucking diary,
that's for goddamn sure."

"No, everybody's trying to figure it out, aren't they?"
Johnston replied.

"Ahh, they're looking too far in the fucking straw,"
Legere said. "They're trying to make me something I'm
not, but they're trying to too, eh? They're trying to make it
into something big. Bullshit, eh?"


In late November, Legere was taken to Moncton for a court
appearance related to his escape.

Everything would have been different, if the courts had
only treated him differently, he told the officers escorting
him. He didn't know they were recording what he was saying.

"You know, I'll tell you the funny part of it is, if they
would of let me get out in about ten years time before I run
away, you know. Like, you know, give me another trial.

Give me a half decent sentence. I would of did ten, twelve years okay.

"I would of did a lot, a lot better for mankind than I did now, cause I would a talked to a lot of young people and I know I could of changed a lot of minds, eh? And that way there I woulda been more beneficial.

"But they were after my throat so bad. There's a lot, there was a lot of rich people that, that were pressuring the government. Then they pressured the prosecutor and the prosecutor took a vendetta. The little faggot."

"Magnum Fred?" asked one of the guards, referring to the nickname Fred Ferguson picked up while working with the Moncton police force one summer during law school.

"Fuck, I don't like that cunt," Legere snarled. "If I woulda seen Fred Ferguson, boys, in my travels, I can't say I wouldn't did nothing. Honest to God. Well, actually, I, I, I, ah, I, ah, I got his number, but I didn't find his address, eh? His address wasn't in the book, just his number.

"And I tell ya, I tell ya, I'll be honest, I don't care now. But what I was gonna do, I was gonna go over to Robert Martin, the judge. Hold the three of them hostages. Gonna, gonna call Fred over, say it's something important. I was gonna get Dave Cadogan, the newspaper guy, to come over and I was gonna hold them hostage and shoot them – one every half-hour – unless I went to Iran. McKenna, you know, I sent you a letter and told you, so it's no surprise to you. I was gonna do that there and I, I just stopped in time. Just stopped in fucking time."

# PART THREE

## SIXTEEN

# A Sense of Theatre

ONE week before Allan Legere's trial on charges of escaping, then kidnapping and assaulting Peggy Olive on May 3, 1989, chance handed police a crucial piece of evidence related to the murder of Father James Smith. On August 7, 1990 near the communities of Matapedia, Québec, and Campbellton, New Brunswick, CN bridge inspectors Richard Walker and Serge Delarosbil discovered an NBTel (telephone company) calling card and a VISA card partially buried in dirt near a railway bridge. The name on the cards was *James V. Smith*. Had the cards fallen a few feet farther, they would have disappeared into the river thirty feet below.

That afternoon, Walker called the number on the calling card and asked for Father Smith. At the Chatham Head rectory, the startled priest who answered the call explained that Father Smith had been murdered nine months previous. Notified about the discovery, RCMP rushed to the bridge and began a search. At about 5:00 p.m., an officer crawling on his hands and knees scratching through gravel spotted another credit card, this one an American Express card, and it too belonged to Father Smith. Discovery of the cards helped police place the killer of the priest on the train running between Bathurst and Montreal. Investigators were stunned by their luck. To RCMP Sgt. Vince

Poissonnier, the man overseeing the Legere investigation, it was more than luck. "If you weren't a believer in God before, you became one after that."

Legere's escape trial began on August 13, 1990 in Moncton. Police dressed in flak jackets surrounded the rear entrance of the nineteen-storey Assumption building in the city's downtown. Police dogs patrolled nearby railroad tracks. Yellow police tape kept back reporters, cameramen and the curious public.

A few minutes before nine o'clock that morning, a dark blue sheriff's sedan arrived, followed by the grey truck belonging to the RCMP Emergency Response Team. The rear passenger door on the right side opened and a sheriff's deputy slid out, followed by Allan Legere, then another another deputy. They were all chained together. In addition, Legere's legs were shackled, he was handcuffed and the cuffs were fastened to a body belt. Legere's hair was cut short and parted in the middle, but he'd grown a moustache since his recapture.

"Coward," yelled someone in the crowd. "Murderer," shouted another.

Legere was escorted to the third-floor lockup. On the ground floor, only one of four elevators was working. Police had shut off the others. A lineup of people, including prospective jury members, snaked down the hall. Purses were emptied, everyone was searched with a metal detector.

When Legere was brought to the second-floor courtroom he was flanked by two plainclothes RCMP officers, members of the ERT team which had hunted him through the Miramichi woods. A black box encasing the lock on his handcuffs was unlocked, then the handcuffs. His leg shackles were removed and the chain passed through a bolt in the floor in the prisoner's box. It was the same room in which Legere had slashed his wrists seven years before during a break-and-enter trial. Legere spotted CBC reporter André Veniot sitting in the front row a few feet away.

"CBC is hard up for news, André. Good thing I came back, huh?"

Legere pleaded not guilty to escape and kidnapping. Asked for his plea on the charge of assaulting Olive with a weapon, he replied emphatically, "That, I'm not guilty of."

Jury selection took the entire day. "I didn't expect this," said one woman who was excused after she claimed she was so nervous she was sick. A young man begged to be rejected saying he feared Legere might retaliate against him somehow. Legere nodded and used a series of hand signals to let his lawyer, David Hughes, know if he approved of a prospective juror or not. Eight women and four men were eventually chosen.

Crown prosecutor Tony Allman began calling his witnesses the next day. Their stories were already known to most people – the case had prompted enormous publicity, and, in an unusual move, Legere had insisted months earlier at his preliminary hearing that the testimony be made public.

The guards recounted Legere's escape. Peggy Olive, her voice quavering at times, described how Legere had taken over her car near the hospital parking lot.

Hughes seemed to be just going through the motions as he questioned them. When he asked warden Donald Wheaton which inmates inside the prison had started threatening his client since his recapture, the judge interrupted, calling the question irrelevant.

"My client has instructed me to bring this information out," Hughes replied.

At one point, a group of five teenagers attempted to raise a sign which read *Stand. Courage Allan.* A sheriff's deputy removed the sign. One of the five, Donald Guimond, later claimed he was strip searched before being thrown out of the building. "Legere escaped for a reason you know," he told reporters. "He was being badly treated. And prison won't help him. It'll only make him worse."

On the third day of the trial, Legere testified from his

prisoner's box. "I couldn't take the pressure any longer. I was the bum boy, stuck in segregation. No sunlight, no nothing." He'd been cooped up in his cell twenty-three hours a day for three years. He was frustrated about how long it took to appeal the Glendenning murder conviction and angry that Todd Matchett and Scott Curtis were allowed to mingle with other prisoners when he wasn't. "I was having to do double jeopardy. Not only was I doing life, but in segregation you can't mingle with the general population."

Claiming he had made the makeshift keys in 1988 and could have escaped at any time, he blamed his escape on lax guards. "If they didn't care if I went, why should I? If that's the way you want it, I'm going to leave." He described guard Robert Hazlett as a "nice old guy." Fellow guard Robert Winters was "too fat" to chase him and driver Douglas Sweezey "would run at the drop of a hat."

He denied "kidnapping" Peggy Olive. "Illegal confinement, maybe," he allowed. As for his weapon, it was a piece of tinfoil. He said he'd apologized to Olive the day before, on August 12, explaining that "she sort of got caught in the middle of the sandwich." He was the only defence witness.

The next day, August 14, after six hours of deliberation, the jury found Legere guilty of escaping, kidnapping and assault. He was sentenced to nine years in prison, to be served at the same time as his life sentence.

This brief trial also marked the first public appearance of a group of women vowing to fight for justice for Allan Legere. Caroline Norwood was a 51-year-old newspaper editor and councillor from the Digby area of Nova Scotia. She was married and the mother of six children. She sat in the courtroom with Lois Gaunce and Gaunce's daughter, Cindy, of the Sussex area.

Norwood described Legere as another Donald Marshall, referring to the Nova Scotia Micmac Indian who had spent eleven years behind bars for a murder he didn't commit. She said she was helping Legere write his autobiography.

As Legere was escorted out of the Assumption building, the three women held up a sign containing a big red heart and the words *Allan, we love you.*

"What a farce," Legere shouted when asked about the trial. "Sorry to Peggy Olive."

Caroline Norwood and Lois Gaunce are the two women closest to Allan Legere. Norwood, in fact, left her family to become engaged to him. Gaunce describes herself as happily married. She is the mother of three boys, aged 11 to 21, and a 17-year-old daughter. She says she views Legere as a brother, although she says he once proposed to her and always calls her Lynn, as if to emphasize their "special connection." She considers Legere "smart and funny. He makes you feel welcome and comfortable."

To this day, both women are devoted to him, convinced he's innocent, the victim of a conspiracy.

Cases of women who fall in love with men accused and convicted of murder are not as unusual as some might think. Ted Bundy, executed in Florida in 1989, murdered dozens of women, yet during his trial a row of admiring females sat near him. Bundy, in fact, married one of them and fathered a child. Angelo Buono, one half of the "Hillside Strangler" team that killed ten women, married one of his former wives while in prison. Kenneth Bianchi, the other half of the killing duo, convinced love-sick Veronica Lynn Compton to stage a copycat killing to try to prove he was innocent. Compton is serving a life sentence for attempted murder. Bianchi later married another woman while in prison. John Wayne Gacy of Chicago, convicted of killing thirty-three young men, has a fan club of adoring lonely women who proclaim his innocence.

In his study of serial killers, *Hunting Humans*, Elliott Leyton writes, "During their trials, they will almost certainly be surrounded by admiring women who press their affections upon the killer, radiating him little but admiration and love."

He warns of the danger people who associate with such killers risk. "There is a pitfall which entraps researchers and readers alike when venturing into this kind of territory. I refer to the propensity ... to become so emotionally involved with the killers as to minimize, or even entirely forget the evil these men have done."

Such relationships follow a pattern: involvement beginning after the person has become well-known; denial of their guilt; and isolation from family and friends, which increases the killer's control over the woman.

In her 1991 book *Women Who Love Men Who Kill* (Simon & Schuster) Sheila Isenberg describes the killers and the women who fall for them. The men usually received little education before they committed murder. "Many had miserable childhoods. The men are often handsome and well built ... usually intense and charismatic."

The women are overwhelmed by that charm and manage to deny the brutal crimes their men have committed, Isenberg says. "When it comes to the murder itself, an element of unreality creeps in. None will say her lover has the capacity to kill. Although the evidence is there, although the facts are known, not a single woman believes that her man really did it – even though he stands convicted. They put the crime aside when thinking about the men they love."

Isolation soon follows, Isenberg adds. "Women who love killers, if they tell the truth about their lives, are often ostracized by acquaintances, and even by friends and family. This makes the women, alienated to start with for many reasons, feel increasingly estranged; they begin to identify more and more with their murderer/lovers."

The identification extends to the murderer's legal problems. "A woman assumes her man's life, his identity; she does his time with him. He's committed the crime but she shares the imprisonment. His legal battle becomes her struggle, his friends and family become her closest allies."

Gaunce and Norwood began to write to Allan Legere

long before his trial. In fact, Gaunce said she started feeling sorry for Legere after his 1987 conviction for the murder of John Glendenning, an injustice, she said, that had left him to take the rap for Todd Matchett and Scott Curtis. Part of her sympathy arises from the circumstance surrounding the death of her brother, Carl Nodwell. He was killed in 1978 in a drunken brawl. The jury acquitted the man accused of killing him. Today Gaunce's home in Lower Millstream near Sussex, New Brunswick is filled with photographs of her brother. Her mother, who gets around in a makeshift wheelchair, has never forgotten the trial and verdict. "This is my son," she says, holding up a photograph of him. "He was murdered."

The injustice Lois Gaunce felt she saw at that trial, she transferred to Legere. "I used to think the justice system was the law and whatever it does is right and it would never make mistakes until this happened to my brother."

She has a collection of Legere's paintings. A Mother's Day picture depicts two cardinals and two baby birds. Another is of a princess walking on a rainbow emanating from a fiery sun. The woman is holding balloons and is beside a unicorn. An inscription at the bottom, surrounded by starbursts, reads: "The universe unfolded, 'twas an awesome sight, I wish I may, I wish I might, Ahoy there, let it be bright, my name after all is Light."

Legere continues to send cartoons to Gaunce's four children on their birthdays – mostly of Bart Simpson and dragons. One shows Bart Simpson stealing from a cookie jar. "The perfect crime," reads the caption underneath.

Legere and Gaunce don't talk about the murders. "I've never really asked Allan about the murders. Eventually we'll probably discuss them but I made up my mind before I ever wrote to him that I'm not going to continually interrogate him. He's got enough people doing that and if I'm going to be his friend, it will be a friend with no conditions.

"To me he's part of the family now. I have a few snapshots of him that he had sent to me and I got reproductions done. Cindy [Gaunce's daughter] has one in her photo album with the family pictures. I mean, my kids feel real good towards him." Her husband, a trucker, says he remains neutral about the entire affair.

Gaunce insists she has a realistic perception of Legere. "I'm not saying that if you did make him mad, he wouldn't punch you. But I don't think he'd hit a woman. I don't think he's the monster they're making him out to be. I mean, I'm not saying Allan's any saint. He's a hellcat, no way around it. And hellcats get blamed for things they don't do."

Caroline Norwood began to write to Allan Legere in May 1990 and first met him, according to Legere, on August 13 during his trial in Moncton on escape charges. Apparently, their romance blossomed quickly. Legere claims that he received a letter from Norwood on October 19 in which she vowed she was ready to leave her husband, Laforest, to marry him. The letter says: "You can tell your friends that I plan to marry you as soon as we are divorced from our so-called mates. I consider you my husband more than the fellow I was legally married to … absolutely nothing is going to deter me from getting a divorce and becoming your wife. I love you, Caroline." Another letter from Norwood, which Legere said he received on October 29, was full of encouraging words and promises: "Don't sit and fret and worry. What will be, will be … the die was cast many months ago and nothing will ever change between us … I have to unravel things at my own pace and I know you will wait a few weeks for things to be organized. I love you and yes, I will marry you … love Caroline."

Norwood says a curiosity to see the "real" Allan Legere prompted her first letter to him. "It seemed to me the press had created a picture of him that didn't seem exactly accurate, like putting *convicted killer* every time they wrote about him. " She wondered why since he wasn't the person who had done the actual killing of John Glendenning.

She wrote to Legere. "I said, 'Did you ever stop to think

how people would think of you if they didn't keep referring to you as this killer, killer, killer? And would it change the way people thought about you?'"

By the fall of 1990 Norwood, a municipal councillor for Brier Island in Digby County in southwestern Nova Scotia, had left her husband of thirty years, her six children and a job as editor of the local weekly newspaper, to become Legere's fiancée and spokesperson. She reportedly moved to Bathurst, about fifty miles north of Newcastle, so she could be closer to him. "People fall in love with people all the time, in and out of jail. I'm not questioning it. I'm not asking why. I'm just accepting it for what it is, I'm not looking for any deep psychological reasons. He said one time that if you look for good in people, that's what you'll find and perhaps that is what I did. I just went on that premise one hundred per cent, that it was good, and that is what I found."

Once in love with Legere, Norwood accepted his version of his life without question and defended him at every opportunity. During an hour-long interview with Dave Crase of CHSJ Television, Norwood repeatedly cited Legere's record as proof of his non-violent nature. "There really isn't a great history of violence in his record at all. He has convictions for common assault, fighting in a club, sentences of three months, four months or a fine. Resisting arrest. There again, the sentence was three months. Just the average stuff that happens on any weekend in any town in New Brunswick. This man is not this brutal killer. I don't know where they find this. Gentle is the word I would use."

In an effort to describe the way Legere had been persecuted throughout his life, she read an excerpt from the autobiography she said he was working on. It dealt with his first arrest, in July 1964 when he was sixteen:

"I was living in Chatham Head and on one summer night I walked to Newcastle to see the circus in town. It was next door to the curling club. As I passed a car I spotted an open beer sitting atop the dash of the car. I reached in and took a mouthful and was returning it when two burly men, one, he's got the name, of Nelson, now deceased, Nelson-Miramichi, and another man of Chatham. They grabbed me and one held while the other punched my face repeatedly, then called the Newcastle police. Sgt. Jim Lawn [name has been changed] came with a paddy wagon and took me to jail. My nose was pouring blood. I was under age or bordering at 16 and assaulted with bodily harm. Neither man was charged with having open liquor in the car. The judge fined me $15. Both of the men were members of the curling club, I was from Chatham Head. Chatham Head, case closed. I was held in jail until court a few days later, no doctor summoned."

When she finished reading it, Norwood told Crase, "That was his first brush with the law. It tells you something, doesn't it?"

She explained away Legere's 1987 murder conviction, portraying him as a victim of a legal technicality. "He didn't take part in the beatings. He didn't hurt anybody. He didn't lay a hand on the people." Asked who could have killed the four people murdered while he was at large, she replied, "The woods are full of people. It could be the guy running the furniture store, the Baptist minister or the Catholic priest."

Norwood also attacked the media on his behalf. "There were some seventy-three stories printed in the major newspapers in '89 about Allan Legere and in just about everyone he's called the killer or mass murderer. Where's the presumption of innocence?"

She questioned the motives of the police. "They have to come up with someone and since they built this image of this man as a killer, who better to charge. This man has been treated extremely unjustly, unfairly. He's been made a scapegoat."

She insisted Legere would win a stay of proceedings in the four murder charges and there would be an inquiry into the way the case was handled. Legere would get his appeal granted by the Supreme Court and one day would be free.

"I think this whole situation is just a blip in his life and the best part of his life is yet to come when he can contribute to humanity through his artwork and through his writing help guide other people in their lives to live better."

Legere's engagement to Norwood left her isolated. She was ostracized by people who could not accept what she was doing, able to see her fiancé only rarely, and then under tight security. In March 1991 they cancelled the marriage, but not before prison officials began an internal investigation of an unauthorized open visit the two had that reportedly resulted in a "sexually compromising position." Legere explained the decision to call off the marriage – which would have required both of them to get divorces first – in a letter to a Moncton newspaper. "It's not an easy road, for sure, i.e. being involved with an incarcerated person, especially with my terrible name." Besides, Norwood's husband Laforest had a heart operation in late 1990 "and is forever pining away, as in lonely."

Laforest wrote his own letter to a Halifax newspaper saying, "It is my good fortune that Allan Joseph Legere shall never marry Caroline B. Norwood. I think Caroline and I have solved or dissolved that situation."

Worries about the way Legere was being treated, and his mental well-being, however, kept bringing her back, she explained. "[Allan] is so resigned to everything, that's why I jumped in. I tried not to for the sake of my family. My husband will probably rage and scream again, but that's all right."

Allan Legere's romantic entanglements were far from the minds of the more than five hundred people who jammed into Father James Smith's church on November 19, 1990. They braved freezing rain and slippery roads to attend a memorial mass marking the first anniversary of the murder of their priest.

In his homily, Bishop Edward Troy tried to help people come to terms with what had happened and what they were feeling. "In this mass, we seek to be healed of our pain and give thanks for the ministry of our brother priest. The whole Miramichi, the entire province, the whole country was horror struck by the last in the series of killings."

Looking down from the podium, he saw members of the Smith family sitting near the front. "We come to pray for your comfort and our own comfort," he told them. He described Father Smith as a priest people remembered as a comforter of the sick. "We knew him and loved him with all his virtues and his faults. Perhaps each of us has a story to tell of how he touched our lives and brought in a ray of sunshine."

Pray for an early end to the mystery of the murders, Troy urged, and for justice to be done so the hearts of everyone might rest easy again.


As Troy was speaking, the RCMP in Newcastle were announcing plans for a news conference the next morning at the town hall in Newcastle.

At 11:00 a.m. on November 20 about twenty journalists and cameramen jammed into a corner of the auditorium. RCMP Sgt. Ernie Munden, flanked by RCMP Insp. Al Hutchinson of Fredericton and RCMP Supt. Al Rivard of Moncton, read a statement.

Munden confirmed what everyone suspected. Just four days short of the anniversary of the capture of Allan Legere, the RCMP were finally laying charges – four counts of first-degree murder. Legere would appear on December 5 to answer to the charges.

"This has been a difficult time in the history of the Miramichi," said Munden, reading the statement. "We wish to acknowledge the patience and understanding displayed by the community and most media representatives. These have been lengthy and complex investigations, complicated in part by new procedures in forensic laboratory testing. All evidence will be presented in court and cannot be discussed, so that the accused maintains his right to a fair and impartial hearing."

After the reading of the statement, the questions poured in. Was the use of DNA fingerprinting the reason it had taken so long to lay the charged? Although Hutchinson offered no comment, Rivard said it was the forensic testing in the RCMP lab in Ottawa which held had things up. The case against Legere could be called a test case because it involved procedures never before used in Canada, he explained. "This type of testing is relatively new. I believe it is the first in Canada." He pointed out it had been used successfully in cases in Great Britain and the United States.

Was there any reason for laying the charges almost exactly a year after Legere's capture? No, Rivard replied. "The investigation is complete and the tests have been completed and that's why the charges are being laid now."

Who would be the Crown prosecutors? Would Fred Ferguson do it a second time? No. Tony Allman of Moncton would lead the team. Ferguson's colleague, Jack Walsh of Douglastown, would also be involved.

Ferguson, for his part, had thought the job was his and had started to read up on DNA fingerprinting. He was furious when Bob Murray, the director of public prosecutions, told him the case was being assigned to another prosecutor because of the threats Legere had made to kill Ferguson. Murray was worried it might look like Ferguson was out for revenge, not justice. The naming of Allman was doubly galling for Ferguson, since the two often clashed when they met at provincial meetings. Ferguson considered Allman too much of a "company man," a little too loyal, too willing to toe the line when it came to orders from Fredericton. (Those doubts would turn into admiration as the trial proceeded.)

At the media conference, reporters wanted to know if there'd be any other charges laid. Well, Rivard answered, the police and prosecutors were discussing charges related to the kidnapping of the truck driver and police officer.

How much had the investigation cost? The total hadn't been tabulated, Rivard replied. "But it was very, very expensive." There were at least a hundred officers involved in the hunt alone, Munden added.

Would the trial be held in Newcastle? We don't know, said Hutchinson.

And was Legere a suspect in the attacks on Morrissy Doran and the Russells in Newcastle now that the case against the man charged with the crimes had fallen apart for lack of evidence? Yes, Hutchinson said.

Fog masked the arrival of the police car as it glided up to the side door of the Newcastle courthouse at 7:45 a.m. on December 5. The car doors popped open and Allan Legere was whisked up a short set of stone stairs into the building. Despite the attempt to avoid onlookers, reporters, cameramen and a few of the curious were already waiting in the dark and cold as Legere was escorted inside for his 9:30 court appearance.

Minutes afterwards, RCMP blocked off two of the three lanes of traffic running past the side door, part of an unprecedented cordon of security surrounding the sandstone building. Police also guarded the front door.

Inside, security was tight. Anyone wishing to climb the stairs to the main courtroom on the second floor first had to empty their pockets. Women's purses were checked, and everyone had to submit to a body search by an RCMP officer using a portable metal detector.

An artist hired by CBC Television to do drawings of the proceedings spent more than a half-hour trying to convince RCMP officers that the small knife he had with him was needed so he could sharpen the coloured pencils he planned to use. Finally, the officers relented and allowed him to take along the inch-long blade, but the detachable handle had to be left behind.

At 9:33, Allan Legere entered the courtroom, wearing plastic-rimmed glasses and looking fit under a dark blue sports coat. His hair was once again its customary length, reaching just past the collar. He was escorted to a special prisoner's box, which had been placed on the slightly raised platform to the left of the judge in an area normally reserved for jurors. RCMP officers stood next to him as the shackles on his legs were fastened to the floor. His hand free of handcuffs, he leaned forward and dangled his hands over the side of the box. He smiled at Norwood, who sat alongside his mother, Louise. The two women talked quietly, occasionally laughing in hushed tones.

There were about twenty-five people sitting in the benches on the main floor of the courtroom. Most were journalists. The tight security apparently had scared away most spectators.

Sitting at the Crown prosecutors table were Tony Allman and Jack Walsh. The two men could hardly have been more different. Walsh, a 38-year-old Miramichi native, was a hard-driving, meticulous lawyer who found it difficult to relax before a trial. Over six feet tall, with dark hair and wire-rimmed glasses, Walsh's interests included country and western music and spending time at his cabin in the woods. He had been practising law since 1977 and only became a Crown prosecutor in 1987. Married to a local girl, he had two daughters whose crayon drawings decorated the walls and door of his Newcastle office. Allman, on the other hand, was born in Stoke-on-Trent in the English Midlands in 1944 and had been educated at Oxford. He had met a New Brunswick woman studying in England, fell in love and moved to the province. He was named a Crown prosecutor in Moncton in 1983 after years in private practice. Married with a daughter and two sons, he remained an anglophile and especially loved the British programs airing on PBS. Nevertheless, he felt at home in Canada and considered hockey the best team sport ever invented.

Provincial Court Judge Drew Stymiest entered at 9:37 and the four charges of first-degree murder were read aloud. Allman stood up and announced he planned to use a rarely

used section of the criminal code called a preferred indictment. It would allow the Crown to avoid the preliminary
hearing normally held to decide if there is enough evidence
to warrant a trial.

Legere, who had been standing during the reading of the
charges and was about to sit down, froze at the announcement. He looked at his lawyer, Weldon Furlotte. Stymiest
announced a brief recess. Furlotte, wearing wire-rimmed
glasses, his long gray hair combed forward over his forehead, rushed over to Legere and the two men began talking
in hushed but earnest tones.

This case was the biggest of Furlotte's brief legal career.
Although born in Montreal, he and his family had moved to
Campbellton in northern New Brunswick where he grew
up to become an electrician with Canadian National Rail-
ways. In 1977, living in Moncton and tired of his job after
twenty-two years, Furlotte decided to become a lawyer. He
arranged to work a four-to-twelve evening shift so he could
attend day classes at Mount Allison University, about
thirty miles southeast of Moncton near the Nova Scotia
border. He did that for four years, then at age 38, he was
granted a leave of absence in 1981 to go to law school. Based
in Moncton, Furlotte was defending Allan Legere after
David Hughes, who had defended Legere in the Glendenning murder case, decided to bow out, citing previous com-
mitments. Hughes said he was too busy to set aside six to
nine months to handle the case. It was Hughes who recommended Furlotte to Legere.

Legere and Furlotte were just finishing their whispered
conversation in the Newcastle courtroom when Mr. Justice
David Dickson of the Court of Queen's Bench in Fredericton walked in at 9:42. A big man, more than six feet tall, he
looked younger than his 71 years as he took his seat behind
the bench looking down on the lawyers. Appointed to
the bench in 1964, he had been the last judge in New
Brunswick to sentence anyone to death, which he had done

in a case in the early seventies involving two men convicted of killing two Moncton police officers. (The sentence was later commuted to life when Parliament abolished the death penalty.) He had been chosen for the case because of his enviable track record in murder cases, twenty cases without a single successful appeal. Also, as a semi-retired judge he had the time to hear the lengthy case.

With the recess over, Dickson adjusted his glasses and demanded to see the necessary forms and the signature of the province's attorney general, which is required to permit the preferred indictment process. Satisfied, he began the formalities.

"Where's Mr. Legere?" he demanded. Legere raised his hand.

Dickson ordered court clerk Shelley Williams to read the charges. She began with the murder of Annie Flam. Legere was asked for his plea.

"I'll not enter a plea until I have a preliminary hearing," he replied, an edge in his voice.

"Write down not guilty," Dickson instructed.

Williams read the charges in the killings of the Daughney sisters.

"I'll not enter a plea until I have a preliminary hearing," Legere replied.

Dickson interrupted. Did Legere understand his refusal meant an automatic plea of not guilty?

"I agree with Mr. Legere," Furlotte answered.

Frowning, Dickson turned to Legere and asked him if he understood what was happening.

"I understand."

Williams read the final indictment, for the murder of Father James Smith.

"I'll not enter a plea until I have a preliminary hearing."

Dickson eyed the indictment. Normally, the list of witnesses is typed on the back, he said, turning towards Allman. The prosecutor explained there were two reasons why that was not done: there wasn't enough room on the legal-size sheet of paper; also, the Crown had three cardboard boxes of material to give to Furlotte and the list was included there.

"I think you should prepare that list as soon as you possibly can," Dickson insisted. And copies should be forwarded to the court and Furlotte.

Eager to press on, the judge suggested Furlotte consider attempting to have the trial moved to another part of the province. Caught off-guard, Furlotte agreed, but said he had not been able to go through the "evidence" related to such a request.

"Evidence has nothing to do with it," Dickson interrupted. "You want the case tried in Newcastle, or somewhere else?"

"No way would I consider a trial in Newcastle," Furlotte replied. Flustered, he started to plead for more preparation time, suggesting the trial could take five or six months.

Dickson cut him off. Naturally, the trial should be moved, he said. As for a lengthy trial, well, he didn't think so. The only question remaining was where to hold the trial. English facilities in Saint John and Woodstock were too far away and would only add to the expense for witnesses travelling from the Miramichi. Moncton wouldn't work.

"Twenty-five years ago, the government unfortunately made a decision to construct courthouses in shopping malls. Moncton may have a good courtroom, but it has no jury room." It would therefore have to be held in his own area, Fredericton, preferably in January, he said. "How about January 14?"

Furlotte, as well as Crown prosecutors Allman and Jack Walsh, were stunned by the suggestion. Legere attempted to interrupt, holding up his right hand and calling out "Your Honour." Furlotte jumped to his feet to protest, his face red with anger.

"It might be necessary to allow for preliminary motions," the judge allowed, attempting to cut off Furlotte before he could speak.

Furlotte ignored him. "I expect it would take me four to five months without any preliminary motions. There is a mass, a mass of evidence to go through. I had to give up my practice just to be prepared."

Dickson was unimpressed. There could be no question of delaying the trial for five or six months.

"Then I don't want any part of it," Furlotte shot back, still standing. He demanded the judge let him drop the case. When Dickson refused, Furlotte again demanded a delay. "When I'm ready for a trial, set a date. The Crown and police had a year. I can't compete with a whole police force."

"Does that mean you have other trials?" Dickson shot back.

"I have six scheduled by the end of February," replied Furlotte.

"That doesn't have a thing to do with it," retorted Dickson, coldly.

Still Furlotte refused to budge. He had to interview every witness, he said, go over the testimony of the police. "If you're not going to give the defence enough time to prepare for trial, you may as well hang him right now."

"Hang him right now?" Dickson responded. "Is that what you're suggesting to me? What sort of language is that?"

Furlotte sat down before answering. "I just happened to be upset. I think [Legere] deserves better than that."

Dickson softened his stance, too. No one lawyer could handle such a case alone. He would be prepared to back Furlotte if he insisted on calling in a second lawyer.

Up to this point, prosecutors Allman and Walsh had sat by silently, listening to the two men. Now Allman stood up. Furlotte's concerns had merit, he offered. "There are approximately two hundred witnesses. They come from all parts of Canada and the United States." He suggested a two- or three-month delay before beginning the trial.

Dickson curtly rejected the idea. "I'm going to set the date of Monday, February 4, at 10:00 a.m. That's two months. The accused is remanded until that time."

Legere interrupted. "Can I not speak at all?" Dickson suggested Furlotte speak to his client.

Ignoring his lawyer, Legere stared straight at the judge. "I'd rather speak to you, if you don't mind." It took police a year to prepare the DNA evidence, he argued. "Furlotte don't have a clue about DNA. How do you expect him to defend me? They know what they're doing. They're going to convict me and you're letting them do it."

Not waiting for Dickson to respond, Legere turned to his left and spoke directly to the reporters frantically scribbling down what he was saying. "They know what they're doing, don't you goddamn well worry."

Determined to regain control, Dickson ordered the lawyers to meet him in his chambers. Legere demanded he be allowed in as well, but Dickson refused.

Incensed, Legere strained at his shackles. "Don't expect me to go along with it, because I'm not," he shouted at the judge. "You can drag me in and drag me out. They can't give me another day. I don't give a fuck."

Dickson was considerably more cooperative when court resumed at 12:32 p.m.. He had reviewed twenty-two items with the lawyers, he explained. "We discussed the administration of the trial, schedule of witnesses and presentation of evidence, possible courtrooms that might be used in Fredericton, disclosure of the Crown's case to the defence counsel and so on. We discussed the programming of the trial." Given the number of witnesses and the likelihood of it being a long trial, it would start officially on February 4, but the calling of witnesses would not begin until early April – at the earliest.

As Legere left the courtroom, he looked over at Caroline Norwood and mouthed the words "Home, with her," while glancing at his mother. Junior high school students on their lunch break shouted at Legere as he was whisked out the side exit and into a waiting police car. Legere ignored them.

Lois Gaunce strained to catch his attention. She wanted reporters to know that she didn't believe Legere had done anything wrong. "I'm convinced he didn't do anything. I never believed he did it. He was framed by the justice system and the RCMP. They are covering up a lot of their garbage."

Legere sat in the back seat of one car, officers on either side of him, two more in the front seat. A second car pulled up in front of the vehicle and another eased in behind, then they all headed towards the Atlantic Institution. It was about 1:00 p.m.

At about 2:00 p.m. that same day, police officers were called to a Chatham home. Inside, they found the body of a 27-year-old man. He had been shot. The next afternoon, a 39-nine year old acquaintance was charged with the killing. It was the ninth killing in the Miramichi area, population 50,000, in nineteen months.

In a December 22, 1990 letter to *The Times-Transcript* daily newspaper in Moncton, Allan Legere announced he was going on a hunger strike in January to protest what he called the "biased" behaviour of Mr. Justice David Dickson, the judge handling his murder case. He also complained about the media coverage of his case, accusing reporters and politicians of suggesting he was guilty before he had been properly tried. Legere arrived at court on February 4, 1991 to listen to lawyers hash out the details of when his trial would begin. Dickson said he would begin hearing arguments as to the admissibility of evidence on April 22. Legere, meanwhile, told reporters he had stopped eating all solid foods on January 12 and had been living on little more than tea with a bit of milk ever since. His fiancée, Caroline Norwood, said he looked "surprisingly well" considering the fact that he had lost eleven and one-half pounds during his hunger strike. She attributed his continued good health to his "strong personality." Prison officials said they had continued to give Legere a tray of food at each meal and did not bother to to check to see if any of it was missing when they returned to pick it up later.

Allan Legere's court battles continued on April 20, 1991 when he appeared before the New Brunswick Court of Appeal to ask that the book *Terror: Murder and Panic in New Brunswick* be banned. The book, written by Rick MacLean and André Veniot and published in paperback by McClelland and Stewart, had been on sale for almost a year, but Legere was determined to appeal an earlier decision that had allowed it to be sold. Arguing the appeal himself, Legere insisted the book linked his name to the four murders committed in 1989 while he was on the run, thereby making it impossible for anyone to come to any conclusion other than that he was the killer. The court agreed by a 2-1 vote. Judge J.A. Angers, for one, said the book, which had already sold more than 35,000 copies, violated Legere's right to a fair trial. Judge A.J. Hoyt disagreed. "Perhaps the jury selection process would be lengthened by the book's continued distribution," he said, "but that in itself is not sufficient reason to prohibit its distribution." McClelland and Stewart subsequently withdrew the book from distribution and sale in New Brunswick. Legere had his ban.

Six weeks of *voir dire* hearings began at the Burton courthouse outside Fredericton on April 22. Used to decide if certain evidence can be entered at the trial, nothing can be reported from a *voir dire*. As a result, few reporters were there to cover any of it.

The courthouse site was no stranger to history. Since the early 1800s, it had witnessed everything from slave-whipping to hot-tempered political debates where speakers clubbed each other. In 1816, the courthouse property was the site of New Brunswick's first official hanging, when a young man, convicted of stealing a loaf of bread, was dropped from a willow tree near the river. The original courthouse, which burned in 1979, was the site of New

Brunswick's last witchcraft trial, held in the 1960s. A beautiful teenage female "witch" and an older male "witch" were taken to court after a diary revealed that a skull had been stolen from a grave for a satanic ritual. The oddly rectangular hill on which the courthouse sits is thought to be a sacred Indian burial ground. During the 1940s, construction workers raising the courthouse to install a foundation unearthed Indian remains wrapped in moose hides.

The courthouse brought back especially fond memories for Mr. Justice David Dickson. "Twenty-six years ago I think I tried one of the first jury trials I presided over on this very spot. Not in this courthouse because the original courthouse which stood here for many years was burned shortly after that, but the old courthouse used to be here. It was a murder trial that involved a 14-year-old youth.

"The judge's bench was down at that end and you looked up-river, sort of. The town crier was an old fellow, 94-years-old, who lived in Oromocto. I remember that because at the opening of the trial I said it must be the first time in history that the age of the court crier is exactly twice the age of the presiding judges, plus seven years. I think he was 93, so you can figure out my age at the time. I was a boy judge."

The *voir dire* featured lengthy arguments between Furlotte and Dickson about the defence counsel's need for more time to prepare, as well as blow-by-blow accounts of Legere's capture, and a heated and highly technical cross-examination of defence witness Dr. William Shields by Jack Walsh, the prosecutor assigned to present the DNA section of the Crown's case.

Shields, a zoology professor at New York State University in Syracuse, had recently published the book *Inbreeding and the Evolution of Sex*. Defence lawyer Weldon Furlotte was counting on Shields to weaken the potent DNA evidence the Crown planned to introduce by showing that the close-knit Miramichi region – what Toronto writer

Bronwyn Drainie called the "Ozarks of Canada" – was, in fact, "genetically inbred." The expression is used by scientists to describe a region with an unusually high incidence of intermarriage, as opposed to incest. A genetically in-bred area has a greater number of people with similar DNA than "normal." Furlotte was attacking, therefore, the heart of the Crown's DNA case. If he could show many people on the Miramichi had DNA like that found at the murder scenes, he could argue his client was just one of *many* people who might have been the killer.

Walsh understood what was at stake and he had spent months preparing. His cross-examination of Shields was "vintage" Walsh, combining his relentless devotion to mastering the details of a case with a dogged determination to make his point while questioning a witness. He quickly attacked Shields' credentials, suggesting the zoologist knew little about human population genetics. Shields told Walsh his definition of what constituted an expert in that field was poor.

Walsh said he was surprised Shields had failed to read the testimony of the Crown's star witness, Dr. Kenneth Kidd, before taking the stand. Kidd, a geneticist from Yale University, is considered a world expert on DNA fingerprinting. Shields retorted that Walsh clearly had no understanding of the way science works – he had looked at Kidd's data, what the man had said about it in court didn't matter.

Walsh and Shields battled over the statistical approach used by the RCMP to determine if the DNA uncovered at two of the murder scenes was Legere's. Shields said his calculations showed it was possible it was not. Walsh, in turn, accused the scientist of using unreasonable figures derived from shoddy research.

As the *voir dire* session wound down, Judge Dickson took notice of the scientist's background and attempted to lighten the mood with a quick question. "Did you know Woody Hayes of Ohio State University?"

"I certainly did," Shields replied.

"His sister married Dick Larkin, who was the freshman football coach. Did you know him too?"

"I didn't know Larkin," Shields answered. "I knew Woody Hayes."

"Larkin told me once fifty-seven years ago that I had a great future as a world class high-jumper. I was going to say that if you ever went to a homecoming there that you might pass the word along that his forecast was a miserable failure."

Shields promised he would.

The scientist was in anything but a friendly mood, however, when he left the stand. Word later filtered back to the prosecutors that Shields was so furious about the way he had been treated by Walsh that he threatened not to return for the actual trial. On the prosecution side there was concern Walsh had been too hard on Shields and had tipped his hand in advance of the trial.

The *voir dire* ended about a week later with co-counsel Michael Ryan, a Fredericton lawyer and son of an appeal court judge, informing Dickson that he would need time to prepare a pair of pre-trial motions. He planned to ask for a stay of proceedings that would put the trial on hold, perhaps permanently. He would argue publicity surrounding the case had utterly ruined Legere's chances for a fair trial. Ryan also wanted the four murder charges against Legere tried in four separate trials. Dickson agreed to hear the motions by the end of July.

Ryan, however, didn't get a chance to argue the two motions before Dickson. In late July, Legere relayed a message through Lois Gaunce that, even though his trial was set to begin August 26, he now wanted Ryan replaced. Contacted by a reporter on the evening of July 24 and asked if he had been fired, Ryan would say little. "I don't know. Have I [been fired]?" he responded. "I'm sorry, but I'm not in a situation where I can say anything."

Furlotte refused to comment.

Legere, for his part, had long felt that Ryan wasn't

working hard enough on his case. In a scathing seven-page
letter dated July 2, Legere levelled a long list of complaints
at Ryan, occasionally underlining points he wanted to
emphasize.

> "Weldon brought info about polls, cost, etc, and since
> this is an integral part of the two motions you are sup-
> posedly preparing (ie: "severance of charges" & "stay of
> proceedings") I distinctly asked your secretary to make
> sure that you contact me, today or tonight. To date, no
> call. I called your home tonight, you are absent. The last
> time I saw you, was at our last 2 court dates June 6 & 7,
> 91. I'm not calling and coaxing you anymore. If you are
> not interested in my case, as it seems, kindly notify the
> judge & legal aid, because I am having it hard enough,
> without having to chase a lawyer, and I don't like being
> lied to."

Legere also wrote to Dickson about Ryan, accusing Ryan of
shoddy work and demanding to know why the judge had
refused Furlotte's request for a delay so he could better prepare. "If nothing is done to ensure that my trial defense is
'sound and fair,' I will do everything in my power to have
this investigated," he said.

The story about Legere claiming he had dumped Ryan
appeared on page one of the Moncton daily *The Times-
Transcript* July 25, along with one quoting yet another
Legere letter. This one complained about a federal government decision to deport three South Americans convicted
of attempting to break Colombian drug-runners out of a
New Brunswick jail.

"May I change my address to Columbia?" Legere wrote.
"I'll go on the next plane! You'll save a mint, and I'll not
miss Canada (this part) any more than N.B. will miss me!
And I promise – never to return!!!"

Pleased by the coverage, Legere wrote a letter dated July
26 to James Foster, the reporter who did the Ryan story. In

it, he denied suggestions he was a difficult client who went around firing lawyers. "It's *not* the case, as Weldon Furlotte knows. I actually liked Mr. Ryan. But now, I wouldn't hire him for a traffic ticket. He should take up beach combing. When I see the inept, sleazy ways of some lawyers, I could scream and say to myself, if I would have only been brought up in better surroundings & the opportunities for college, I'd certainly would prefer 'that' lifestyle to this. Unless we are all fated."

# SEVENTEEN

# Pieces of the Jigsaw

As Allan Legere's trial date of August 26 drew closer, the New Brunswick justice department began its hunt for a jury. They mailed letters to 510 people, ten times the usual number and a legal record for the province.

Since no courthouse in New Brunswick could hold all the prospective jurors, officials booked the auditorium in the high school in the town of Oromocto, about five miles southeast of Fredericton. It was just four hundred yards from an RCMP detachment, making it doubly attractive.

While many of those receiving the letters scrambled for excuses to avoid showing up August 26, contractors struggled to turn the auditorium into a courtroom. They built a judge's bench and jury box on the stage. They screwed a metal ring into the floorboards so Legere's leg irons could be bolted to it. Flags borrowed from the provincial government were draped behind the bench. Police swept through the school, looking for potential escape routes, checking doors and roping off a route through the halls for prospective jurors to use.

Security teams selected rooms for the judge, prosecutors, and Legere and his lawyer. Dickson would spend his breaks surrounded by drums, horns and a piano in the music room. The prosecutors were given a classroom, complete with rows of desks and a blackboard. Legere was assigned a narrow dressing room next to the stage and exit door. Workers stripped the room, carting away a wall of mirrors, a bank of make-up lights, soap dispensers – anything Legere might be able to fashion into a weapon. A ring identical to the one in the makeshift courtroom was bolted to the floor.

At night, Legere would be held in the basement of the Fredericton jail, in a cell normally reserved to punish prisoners. It was seven feet wide by ten feet long with concrete floors and walls, no windows, a sink and a toilet. There were two TV cameras trained on him at all times and another in the hallway. A guard would be posted outside the cell all night to watch Legere through the bars. A mattress was brought in for the star prisoner. Normally, prisoners sent there had to sleep on the concrete floor.

A week before the jury selection began, Judge Dickson arrived for an inspection of the auditorium. A stickler for decorum, he nodded his approval when he spotted a photograph of the Queen hanging on a wall, but ordered the drapes pulled across an eight-foot mural of an eagle that workers, thinking it provided an ideal backdrop, had left exposed.

Monday, August 26, 1991. It was the kind of day that heralded the end of summer, a mixture of cloud and sun, with a chilly breeze blowing in the morning.

Police arrived at dawn to search Oromocto High School one more time. By 8:30 a.m. the parking lot at the front of the high school was jammed with cars. It was registration day for students, and parents, unaware that the school was the site of the jury selection for the Legere trial, filled the parking spaces usually set aside for the media. The reporters parked on the lawn, then staked out the front and back of the building. The wailing of a siren broke the morning stillness. People turned to look, thinking perhaps it was a signal to mark Allan Legere's arrival, but it was only an alarm sounding at the fire station down the street.

At 9:20 a.m., an unmarked brown-and-beige Suburban four by four rounded the corner at high speed. Allan Legere was in the rear seat, his faced pressed against the window. The truck sped to the back door of the school, braking about a foot from the entrance nearest the stage. The side door of the truck opened and Legere, his hair pulled back in a pony tail, climbed out clumsily, shackles around his wrists and ankles. He was wearing a white shirt and blue jeans held up by red, white and blue suspenders.

"Need a new judge," Legere muttered to the crowd of reporters as he was hustled inside.

The 325-seat auditorium was situated in the centre of the school and police refused to let anyone near it unless escorted by a guard. Everyone had to empty their pockets and walk through airport-style metal detectors. Handbags were searched.

Despite the contractor's best efforts, the auditorium still looked like a theatre. Yellow police tape normally used at crime scenes cordoned off the centre section of seats for prospective jurors. Wires criss-crossed the stage floor. A video camera was mounted above the stage on the left wall. Black and red velvet drapes framed Judge Dickson's bench and high-backed padded chair in the centre of the stage. The three prosecutors – Tony Allman, Jack Walsh and Graham Sleeth – sat on blue plastic chairs at a folding table on the left, while Legere's lawyer, Weldon Furlotte, sat at another on the judge's right, three empty chairs beside him. The court stenographer squeezed into a one-piece student's desk on Dickson's left. Some prospective jurors read books. One woman had brought along her three-year-old daughter, who kept pulling at the police tape.

Two Mounties led Legere to a table and bench near Furlotte. Legere was wearing a blue blazer at this point, but quickly removed it while being chained to the floor. He folded the jacket neatly and put it aside, then put on his wire-rimmed glasses and reached for a glass of water. Court clerk Gerald Pugh read out the four charges. "Not guilty," Legere said four times.

Dickson, wearing the threadbare judge's robes once used by his father, had gone white-water rafting in Maine the week before and was suffering from a bad cold. He apologized for his hoarse voice before outlining the events leading up to the trial – the decision to move it from Newcastle, the six-week *voir dire* held in the spring. The trial, he predicted, would be a long one. Prosecutors, after all, planned to call 243 witnesses.

Only 180 prospective jurors were in the auditorium. Some couldn't be found, others cited financial hardship. Thirty-four no longer lived in the area, twenty-six had young children, seven had criminal records. Some were sick; six were dead.

Dickson tried to lighten the mood. "Quite naturally, the deceased people aren't here. If any of them are here, would they please shout out? We'd like to know what prescription they're taking?" There were a few giggles.

During a short recess before the selection began, Furlotte visited Dickson in his room and said he would challenge every potential juror as to their feelings about Legere. Furlotte showed the judge the questions he planned to ask. Dickson thought some went too far. He wrote down a list of his own: Had they formed an opinion about the case? Did they follow it in the news? Could they resist pressures from family and friends? Had they read the book *Terror* by MacLean and Veniot?

Prospective jurors were called to the stage four at a time. Thirty-two people were questioned the first day, none were chosen. Nineteen were excused, including the wife of an RCMP officer, a woman who was a friend of one of the victims and a number of people who would have lost their unemployment insurance benefits had they been picked. Throughout the day, Furlotte stumbled over the questions the judge had written for him, questions he said he could barely read. He kept trying to ask people if they thought his client was guilty, only to be cut off each time by the judge, who said the only issue was whether or not they could be fair. Allman jumped up to protest whenever Furlotte reworded one of the judge's questions.

Legere's only comment came while Furlotte was questioning a man. "If he's not allowed to tell his opinion, how are you going to know if he thinks I'm guilty or not?"

The law allowed Furlotte to reject up to twenty potential jurors without saying why. He used four of the those challenges the first day. The Crown, for its part, turned down one gum-chewing man who couldn't hear the questions. A mini-jury of two people chosen from the spectators judged five others biased. Two were set aside complaining of shortness of breath.

"I wish you'd pass it on to the lawyers," Dickson quipped.

Eager to get the time-consuming selection over with, the judge took to cajoling people. When Harold Sappier, a New Brunswick Indian, took the stand, Dickson did his best to persuade him to serve. "Mr. Sappier, you've got nothing to do but sit in court and listen to this thing, I can tell from the look of you."

"I have other things to do," Sappier replied, taken aback.

"You've got no excuse, you say?"

"No."

"Good, let's sit you down in the back row then." Minutes later, however, after Furlotte had questioned and accepted him as a juror, Allman stood him aside, meaning they would use him only if they couldn't find twelve others.

As the day progressed, a pattern seemed to develop in Furlotte's choices. Briefly discussing each candidate with Legere, he would reject any young woman. One of the women clasped her hands to her chest when rejected, looked up and let out a sigh heard through the auditorium. "Oh thank you, thank you," she exclaimed, to laughter from the crowd. Even Legere laughed.

By late in the afternoon of the second day, eleven jurors had been selected. Only one more was required for the trial proper to begin. The court clerk called out the next four names, starting with a Mr. Cunningham, but no one stood up.

"Anyone know where he might be?" demanded Dickson, impatient to finish. "Mr. Cunningham would be the next person selected as a juror and if he's absented himself without reason, it puts him in a rather difficult position." No one identified himself as Mr. Cunningham.

Giving up, Dickson called out the next name on the list – Jeffrey Moorcraft. A slim, dark-haired man answered, and the Crown and defence quickly asked him their standard set of questions. They seemed satisfied with his replies.

"Thank you, Mr. Porter," said Dickson.

"Moorcraft," the man said, correcting him. With Moorcraft, the one hundred and fiftieth person questioned, the trial of Allan Legere had a duly constituted jury. The six-man, six-woman jury ranged in age from mid-thirties to mid-sixties and included housewives, civil servants, and a man who ran a janitorial service.

Dickson warned them against discussing the case with strangers. "If you do anything that's out of the way and frustrate the whole trial, you and I are going to look like awful asses."

Allan Legere appeared downcast over the selections. "Some of them are okay, but seven have formed an opinion about me, so I can't be presumed innocent."

After the prisoner, lawyers and jurors left, workers proceeded to tear down the temporary courtroom, accompanied by the blaring heavy-metal sounds of *Back in Black* by Australian rock band AC-DC. "It's rock and roll time," joked an RCMP sergeant.

The running battle between Mr. Justice David Dickson and Weldon Furlotte continued during the first week of testimony at the trial. The judge dismissed requests from the lawyer to split the case into four trials and refused to allow him more time to prepare. At one point, disgusted with the way things were going, Furlotte threw his arms in the air and threatened to quit. "For once, I would like to have the court make a decision in *my* favor," he snapped at Dickson.

"For *once?*" the judge shot back. "*You* changed the venue."

"*You* told me to change the venue," Furlotte snarled back.

Legere controlled his own defence. Against Furlotte's advice, he had hired lawyer Bill Kearney to help with the case. A former Crown prosecutor from Fredericton, Kearney had been fired after being charged with a series of sex offences involving young girls. A judge ruled, however, that the provincial government had ruined Kearney's chances for a fair trial by firing him and threw out the case.

Hunched over a white binder, pen in hand, Legere kept forwarding a steady stream of notes to his lawyers, telling them what to ask.

The controversy swirling around the defence was in sharp contrast to the picture presented by the Crown. In his opening remarks, prosecutor Tony Allman calmly promised he would present a complex jigsaw puzzle of circumstantial evidence – including DNA evidence – that, once properly assembled, would reveal the face of a killer.

The defence almost immediately telegraphed its plan for attacking the DNA evidence, even though the Crown was weeks away from introducing it. "Have you heard rumours," Furlotte asked Chatham police officer Willis Dickson, "that you might be Allan Legere's half brother?" No, the officer replied. Furlotte wanted to suggest that there were a number of Miramichiers related in some way to Legere. The lawyer appeared determined to argue that genetic in-breeding had created a pool of people with similar DNA on the Miramichi, thereby making accurate DNA fingerprinting impossible.

The Crown planned to look at each case in turn, beginning with the May 1989 murder of Annie Flam. A police video took jurors through what was left of the Flam home – the store on the first floor, up the stairs to a bedroom where the roof had collapsed on the blackened remains of Annie Flam.

On the morning of September 4, the day before Nina Flam was to testify, Allan Legere jumped up and, straining against the ankle chains bolted to the floor, shouted at the judge. "I have six jurors over there who've formed an opinion on my guilt and one that admitted reading *Terror*, which is now banned by the New Brunswick Court of Appeal. These six shouldn't be on the panel because I have to prove to them I'm innocent. And also, I feel that because of some of your decisions, you should dismiss yourself from the case." After a twenty-five minute delay during which the judge ordered the jury out of the room, the trial resumed with Legere once more in the prisoner's box quietly writing notes and drawing pictures. Judge Dickson was also drawing. A portrait painter whose works had been shown in the Beaverbrook Art Gallery in Fredericton, he interpolated drawings of some of the witnesses with his trial notes.

Despite warnings from the judge not to harass her, there were TV crews waiting in the cemetery next to the Burton courthouse the morning of September 5 when Nina Flam and RCMP officer Kevin Mole arrived. Newspaper photographer Harry Mullin of the *Telegraph Journal* saw the scrum of cameramen run towards Flam's car but decided not to join them. It just didn't feel like the right thing to do, he said.

The packed courtroom fell silent as Flam walked in holding on to Mole's arm. Dickson had warned everyone not to turn and stare at her.

Mole led the small woman in the powder blue pant suit past the spectators towards the front of the court. Spectators had expected to see an old and frail woman take the stand, not this compact, sturdy figure. About five feet tall, with curly, grey hair and glasses, Nina Flam let go of Mole's arm in the aisle and continued on alone to the witness box, limping slightly from the skin grafts she'd required after the 1989 fire.

As she sat quietly in the witness box, looking down at her hands, Judge Dickson rolled his chair closer to her. "Mrs. Flam," he said softly, "I've never met you. You moved out of the hospital room at the Chalmer's hospital. You were in the burn unit. I took over your room, but not for the same reason. I got thrown off a camel crossing the Great Thar desert in India and had to have some plastic surgery."

He smiled. She smiled back.

He then apologized for the delay that morning. After being driven to the courthouse by Kevin Mole, Flam had spent more than an hour sitting with him in a nearby office waiting to testify. During that time, the prosecutors asked Dickson to exclude spectators from the courtroom. Flam wasn't afraid of appearing in public, but she might be a better witness in private, Walsh said. Fellow prosecutor Graham Sleeth said reporters could buy a copy of the transcript after the trial.

This move infuriated Weldon Furlotte, who proceeded to criticize the prosecutors for not warning him about the request until that morning. Arguing that Legere deserved a public trial and that Nina Flam was a valuable witness for the defence, he suggested she be shielded with a screen if necessary, rather than have her testimony delivered in private. Tipped the day before, reporters for the CBC and the Fredericton *Daily Gleaner* had lawyers there to argue against being excluded. Dickson sided with them.

As Walsh began to gently question Flam, Mole stood at the back of the courtroom where she could see him. He'd first met her in the hospital the day after the attack in May 1989. She'd whispered her story to him through an oxygen mask, pausing often to cough up mucus from her smoke-damaged lungs. Two years of preparing her for this moment had turned him into a friend.

Jurors and spectators fought back tears as the 63-year-old woman described in a strong, clear voice being raped and beaten by a masked attacker. She said he was slight, with light coloured pubic hair.

There was a fifteen-minute break after she testified. Before she returned to the courtroom for the cross-examination, Dickson had a warning for Furlotte. "Surely, Mr. Furlotte, you don't intend to harass this witness," he said uneasily. "I don't have to tell you it would make a most unfavourable impression on any jury."

Furlotte assured the judge he would go easy on her, but first he wanted some advice. "Sometime during the cross-examination of Mrs. Flam, I would like her to view the pubic hair of Mr. Legere. Either we could ask the witness to come over and Mr. Legere could just pull his pants down, not to show his privates, but just to show the pubic hair, or we could have police officers cut some pubic hair off Mr. Legere this morning and bring it over in a container."

Spectators gasped. Walsh buried his face in his hands and shook his head. Dickson was enraged. "I'm not going to get into a sordid business of exposing one's private parts in a courtroom. That's utter nonsense."

Furlotte wasn't ready to give up. He said the colour of Legere's pubic hair could prove he wasn't the attacker. "I don't think pubic hair is that private a part. At least, it's got nothing to do with the testicles. It's just hair in that general area."

Walsh protested. "We take strong exception to any kind of hair lineup." Besides, it would be impossible to reproduce the conditions under which Nina Flam had seen it.

Dickson cut off the discussion. Then, before allowing the jury and Nina to return to the room, he warned Furlotte not to mention that police had used hypnosis when questioning her because such evidence is generally considered inadmissible in Canadian courts.

Referring to the more than one hundred pages of statements she'd given police, Furlotte told Nina Flam that her description of the attacker really didn't match Legere. Not only that, she'd said the voice of her assailant sounded more like a neighbour's than Legere's. "Did some people, be they police officers, try to convince you it may have been Allan Legere? You told the police officer that the individual was not as big as Allan Legere?" Furlotte asked.

"I don't recall," Nina Flam replied, looking confused. "I don't know Allan Legere. I didn't know Allan Legere."

Furlotte asked Legere to stand. "You can see Mr. Legere in court today," he said, motioning towards his client. "Do you still feel that individual who attacked you is smaller than Mr. Legere? Can you see him?"

Legere stared at Nina Flam; she wouldn't look at him.

"I don't know," she said, hanging her head.

Furlotte turned to the question about the colour of Legere's pubic hair. "When you say light brown, do you mean something the colour of my hair – light blonde, blonde-gray?"

Dickson interrupted. "We may have to put you in as an exhibit."

"Well, sometimes, I think I'd be better off there, My Lord," Furlotte replied.

Nina Flam seemed angry and close to tears. "Just light. That's all I know. Not black, not brown. I don't have a colour chart." Walsh objected, saying Furlotte was distorting police statements and badgering the witness.

Nina Flam spent a wearying two hours on the stand. There were increasingly long pauses between Furlotte's questions. Finally, Dickson interrupted him. "You'd help the jury a lot more if you let them go to lunch."

Furlotte protested. "If you're going to keep downplaying my competence ..."

"The jury can assess that for themselves," Dickson retorted.

Minutes later, with Legere scowling openly, Furlotte

completed his cross-examination. Mole led Nina out of the courtroom. Obeying the judge's order, the spectators stared straight ahead. Dickson warned reporters not to jam television cameras in her face, in fact, he didn't want to see her on TV at all. The request was ignored. Later that evening, Flam appeared on regional and national newscasts, shown as she entered and left the building.

Reports on Flam's testimony set off a storm of protest from angry readers and viewers. Letters to the editor of the *Telegraph Journal* complained about the paper's "lurid" reporting, while Carol Adams of CBC-TV faced complaints for saying "the attacker put his penis in Nina Flam's mouth." The problems of reporting such evidence became the focus of a CBC Radio story produced for the weekly current events program *Maritime Magazine*, airing across the Maritimes.

Two weeks into the trial, Judge David Dickson was called by an official of the provincial justice department who told him there was a problem with the mileage charges being presented by juror Jeffrey Moorcraft. The figures were too high. Moorcraft was living in the "wrong" county — York, about one hour's drive from Burton, in Queen's County — and should not be permitted to continue to serve on the jury, the official told Dickson. The judge checked the law, however, and since Moorcraft had been living in Queen's County at the time of his selection, he would be permitted to stay.

On September 11, as the trial shifted to the murders of the Daughney sisters, Legere abruptly fired Bill Kearney. Furlotte announced the firing before the jury came in, saying Legere didn't think Kearney was working hard enough. Legere said the former prosecutor had devoted only ten hours one weekend to reading the Flam files and had yet to meet with him. Legere also had doubts about Kearney's loyalty to his cause.

With Kearney sitting beside him, Furlotte said he'd warned Legere earlier that it was "almost suicidal" to hire a lawyer facing sex charges.

Kearney, for his part, appeared dumbfounded. He'd been recommended by David Hughes, who had represented him in the sex case and had once represented Legere. True, the silver-haired lawyer hadn't asked a single question so far in the trial and always seemed deep in thought, slumped far back in his chair, eyes closed, chewing on an arm of his glasses. He was, he said, listening intensely to the testimony. "The comments I was hearing from my friend [Furlotte] was that everybody's burnt out," he explained to Dickson, his hands trembling. "We had a great discussion that you had to pace yourself. My mind has been fully addressed to the case at all times of the day. I have never refused to meet Mr. Legere at any time."

Dickson decided to appoint Kearney an *amicus curiae*, Latin for "friend of the court." He would remain seated next to Furlotte, observe the proceedings and be ready to help when asked.

"I don't want him on my case, Your Honour," Legere yelled. "He had access to my files and everything."

Dickson's face reddened. "I've reached about the end of my tether and it may come very soon that the accused will be excluded and have to listen to what we're doing on a loudspeaker," he warned. "I'm going to remain in charge of this trial. I'm not going to tolerate practices that I've never tolerated before." What the spectators didn't know was that Legere had sent a note to Dickson saying he wanted to fire Furlotte, too. Determined not to let Legere defend himself, the judge had kept Kearney in court as a back up.

Since Kearney sat nearest to the prisoner's box, Legere was forced to continue using him to pass notes to Furlotte.

On Friday, September 13, the jury was given a day off to permit Weldon Furlotte's arguments for a stay of proceedings, a move which would have brought the trial to an abrupt end. Observers considered Furlotte's motion a waste of time, so the courtroom was practically empty except for Legere, his lawyer, Dickson, the Crown prosecutors, two RCMP officers and a couple of reporters who dropped in briefly. Furlotte talked for five hours and submitted hundreds of newspaper clippings, plus numerous quotes from the book *Terror: Murder and Panic in New Brunswick* as part of his argument that pre-trial publicity had ruined Legere's chances of a fair trial. He also mentioned a form letter he said he had mailed to 721 lawyers around the province during the winter of 1991. He had asked the lawyers if they thought Legere could get a fair trial, given the advance publicity his case had received. Furlotte had received fewer than ten responses, none agreed with the lawyer's premise. As expected, Dickson dismissed the poll, calling it "ridiculous." A few days later he announced he was refusing the request to put the trial on hold.

Two weeks after Allan Legere announced his wish to fire lawyer Bill Kearney, Weldon Furlotte, with the jury out of the room, offered his own complaints about Kearney. Legere wants him moved somewhere else in the courtroom, or thrown out altogether, Furlotte said. "He's hellbound and determined that he does not want Mr. Kearney assisting me. Mr. Legere feels that with Mr. Kearney sitting here, it makes him look bad in front of the jury. There's nothing Mr. Kearney can do for the court. Have him sit up with the clerk or something." Otherwise, he warned, his client might grow desperate and act up in front of the jury.

Dickson reacted angrily to what he regarded as a threat. "The trial isn't for the accused. The trial is for our society." He suggested Furlotte and Kearney change seats so Furlotte would be closer to Legere.

"What do you want him there for?" Legere demanded. "What are you, old buddies or something? Jesus Christ, I asked you in July for a [second] lawyer and you weren't that horny about getting me a lawyer."

Turning to Kearney, he sneered, "Let him go downtown and play with somebody. He's as useless as tits on a bull." He implied that Kearney was in touch with the Crown. "I don't trust him and I don't trust you," he said, glaring at Tony Allman.

Dickson scolded Furlotte for failing to mention his concerns about Kearney when he was hired. "I got the impression you were most happy to have Mr. Kearney here."

He said he'd rule on Furlotte's request later and called the jury back into the room. Jurors barely noticed that afternoon when Bill Kearney started sitting among the spectators.

On Monday, September 30, the jurors watched witness Morley Thompson as he flipped through pages 48, 49, 50, and 51 of a blue ledger. The Montreal pawnbroker was a huge man who barely fit into the witness stand. Holding the ledger about an inch from his thick glasses, he compared his handwritten entries from November 20, 1989 with pieces of jewelry sealed in plastic evidence bags.

One by one, Graham Sleeth handed him the items, which included a pendant with an Egyptian figure on it and a distinctive ring with a large red stone. Thompson identified each of them.

As he did so, Furlotte protested, saying there was nothing to connect the jewelry to Legere. The pawnbroker didn't even have a signature from the man who had called himself Fernand Savoie that could be compared to Legere's handwriting. Earlier, Furlotte had hinted at a set-up – that somehow the jewelry from the Daughney home and from their bodies had been planted by police in Montreal. He said police hadn't itemized the jewelry in the overturned jewelry box at the Daughney residence. And what, he wondered, happened to the jewelry recovered during the autopsies?

Crown prosecutor Fred Ferguson, a major nemesis of Allan Legere (*J.K.R. Walls*)

Lawyer David Hughes, Q.C., has acted on Legere's behalf on more than one occasion.

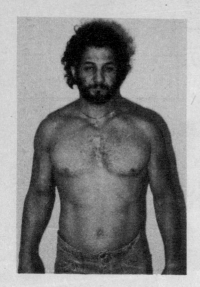

Allan Legere at the time of his arrest for the John Glendenning murder in June, 1986.

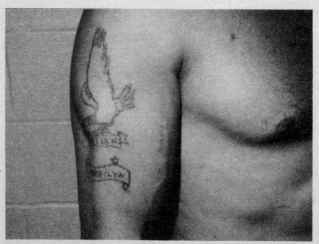

The eagle tattoo on Legere's right bicep that police claimed they did not see early in the morning of November 17, 1989.

Court of Queen's Bench Judge David Dickson presided over Legere's controversial 1991 trial for the Miramichi murders. (*David Russell, Justice, Court of Queen's Bench, Fredericton*)

In defending Allan Legere, Weldon Furlotte tried to show that his client was the victim of mistaken identity.

Key Players in the prosecution of Allan Legere (left to right): Dr. George Carmody, Crown prosecutor Jack Walsh, Dr. John Bowen, Crown prosecutors Tony Allman and Graham Sleeth, Dr. Kenneth Kidd.

They stood by "their" man: Lois Gaunce (left) and Caroline Norwood.

RCMP Sgt. Vincent Poissonnier (*André Veniot*)

RCMP Cpl. Kevin Mole (*RCMP photo*)

Sgt. Robert Kennedy, RCMP Identification Section (*RCMP photo*)

# DNA Identification

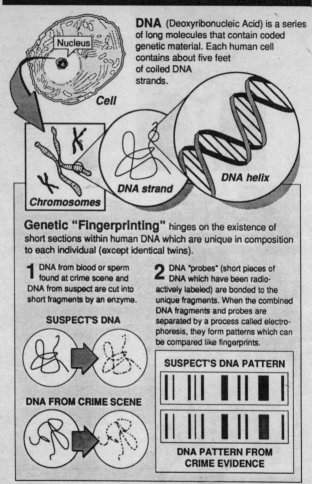

**DNA** (Deoxyribonucleic Acid) is a series of long molecules that contain coded genetic material. Each human cell contains about five feet of coiled DNA strands.

Nucleus

Cell

Chromosomes

DNA strand

DNA helix

**Genetic "Fingerprinting"** hinges on the existence of short sections within human DNA which are unique in composition to each individual (except identical twins).

**1** DNA from blood or sperm found at crime scene and DNA from suspect are cut into short fragments by an enzyme.

**2** DNA "probes" (short pieces of DNA which have been radioactively labeled) are bonded to the unique fragments. When the combined DNA fragments and probes are separated by a process called electrophoresis, they form patterns which can be compared like fingerprints.

**SUSPECT'S DNA**

**DNA FROM CRIME SCENE**

**SUSPECT'S DNA PATTERN**

**DNA PATTERN FROM CRIME EVIDENCE**

Sources: Cellmark Diagnostics; The Almanac of Science and Technology; *Scientific American*

The artistry of Allan Legere: (top) a seascape Legere drew in the early days of his 1991 trial; (below) a Christmas card he drew in 1991. (*Photo: Harry Mullin*)

November 2, 1991: Allan Legere is led into the courthouse in Burton, N.B. One day later he was found guilty in the first-degree murders of four New Brunswick residents. (*Canapress/Andrew Vaughan*)

Sleeth reminded Dickson that the Crown would be calling two hotel chambermaids from Montreal who would identify Legere as the man calling himself Savoie.

"Good enough," Dickson said.

For his part, Thompson remembered buying the jewelry from a man called Fernand Savoie, but little else. "He wasn't too tall, wasn't too heavy," said Thompson, sounding meek under the questioning from the baritone-voiced prosecutor. "No, uh, I don't see that person in the courtroom today."

Two weeks earlier, a police video of the Daughney household had been shown to the jury. One "scene" showed an upturned jewelry box on the second-floor landing. Also presented were photographs of the sisters' bodies. One female juror cried after glancing at these photographs and refused to look at them again. Furlotte had tried unsuccessfully to have some photographs excluded from evidence, saying the victims should have been washed. The blood made their injuries look worse and would only prejudice the jury against Legere, he argued.

RCMP Sgt. Wayne Lock described examining the sisters' bodies with a laser in a Halifax laboratory. Using a wand similar to a flashlight, scientists wearing orange-filtered goggles shone the laser over every inch of the bodies and found small semen stains. The semen on Donna's stomach and Linda's thigh was invisible to the naked eye, but glowed under the laser, said Lock, who helped develop the procedure. Swabs were taken and stored at $-20°$ C for DNA testing.

Outside, the fall weather was sunny and warm. Legere complained about the heat and jurors fanned themselves with aerial photographs of the Daughney sisters' neighbourhood. The courtroom was equipped with an air-conditioning system, but it was so noisy the jury couldn't hear what witnesses were saying. As a result, it was turned on briefly each morning to try to cool the room, then shut off for the trial.

Two body builders told the court that Legere had "expressed a physical attraction" for Donna Daughney at a Newcastle fitness club in 1985 and 1986. Dickson ruled against allowing them to say that Legere had talked about "chewing Donna's ass off" and that she was "built for comfort." Allman, however, wanted to get these comments and other like them in court, saying "sex is one of the mainsprings of criminal activity."

This infuriated Legere, who shouted, "The only thing you haven't done is prop the bodies up there. You have nothing else."

Furlotte had threatened to ask every male witness in the trial whether or not he'd ever made sexist comments about women.

"I'm not a human rights commission," Dickson had ruled. "We're not going to waste the time of the jury."

Meanwhile, advertisements for Legere's paintings were appearing on the local cable TV channel, placed there by the ever-devoted Lois Gaunce. At the courthouse, the media were under tight restrictions imposed by Dickson. Cameras were now banned from the courthouse grounds after a TV cameraman had ignored his request and taken pictures of Nina Flam.

Also banned were any photographs of the jurors and the court artist was criticized for doing what Dickson deemed "poor sketches" of the jurors. However, after two TV producers met with the judge, he relaxed the restrictions a little: TV crews would now be allowed to shoot near the courthouse on Tuesday and Thursday mornings, but they had to leave when the jurors arrived.

Testimony also came from Mary Geikie and her daughters, Kellie and Deborah. Friends of the Daughneys, the Geikies had wept when a police officer had laid out several items of jewelry on their kitchen table a few months after the murders and asked them if they recognized any of the pieces. Mary told the court there was no mistaking the gold ring with the large red stone. Donna had owned one "just like it" and she'd never seen another. "It's identical." She said the sisters often wore several rings and earrings when they went out and described Linda as a "jewelry freak."

Kellie Geikie burst into tears as she examined the ring with the red stone. "I know in my heart that's Donna's ring. We used to joke about it – that when she died, I wanted it," said the 22-year-old woman.

Joanne Johnson, a second cousin of the Daughney sisters, said Donna had inherited the ring from an aunt. Donna's best friend, Diana Wetmore of Saint John, said Donna used to get many compliments about the ring.

Furlotte questioned their ability to remember the jewelry.

"I love rings," Kellie Geikie replied. "Every chance I get, I compare them to ones I wear."

Chatham resident Mary Susan Gregan told the court she recognized her diamond ring and pendant among the exhibits. They had been stolen a week after Legere escaped, she said.

During the cross-examination of two truck drivers who had seen a man near the Daughney home the night of the murders, Furlotte suggested the person they saw was not, in fact, Allan Legere. Perhaps it was Allard Vienneau, the 30-year-old Newcastle-area man later charged with beating Morrissey Doran of Newcastle on September 30, 1989 and Sonny and Evangeline Russell, also of Newcastle, the next night, he said.

Aware that Furlotte had represented Vienneau (charges against him were eventually dropped) and appeared to be on the verge of implicating him in the double murder, Dickson warned the lawyer to drop it. "You realize you're using up your brownie points. We're wandering very far afield," the judge said.

"Can I hire you for a lawyer?" Allan Legere asked, a smirk creasing his face.

At that Dickson ordered Legere removed from the court and told the guards to set up a video camera to enable

Legere to watch the proceedings on closed-circuit TV from his holding cell.

"You're just a prejudiced old fart anyways," Legere snarled. "You should have been off the bench ten years ago. I don't want the camera. You take it home."

"Up yours," he screamed as he was led away.

Dickson explained the expulsion to the jurors. "You've seen some evidence of the accused's character – unsavoury exclamations and efforts made to intimidate witnesses. I've tried to turn a blind eye to it. I haven't been looking for trouble." Legere could return the next day, if he promised to behave. Legere's removal set in motion a pattern. As the trial progressed and Legere would explode occasionally, a letter of apology would be sent from the accused to the judge after the outburst.

In late September, as the weather turned cooler, a blonde with a penchant for skin-tight jeans and spiked heels started to attend the trial. She was dismissed as another "squirrel," a term coined by reporters to describe Legere's "groupies" and prompted by his claim that he'd tamed squirrels while living in the woods. She began to sit with Legere supporter Lois Gaunce and eventually to meet with her in the parking lot each morning, they would whisper to each other during testimony and go outside to smoke during recesses.

One day a woman at the trial overheard the blonde tell Gaunce that she had a relative on the jury. The woman went to the RCMP, who had also heard from court officials that the blonde was dropping off juror Jeff Moorcraft in the parking lot of a nearby grocery store each morning and meeting him there each night. Fearing a mistrial, RCMP Sgt. Vince Poissonnier, the officer in charge of the police investigation into the four murders committed on the Miramichi while Legere was at large, warned the Crown prosecutors and ordered his men to watch the two women.

On September 25, both police and the prosecutors

noticed that the blonde was sitting with someone else, a short woman with red hair. The woman was the wife of a juror. Later that day, despite a driving rain which forced dedicated smokers to sneak a puff in the no-smoking foyer and flick their ashes out the door, the blonde and Gaunce met outside. The next morning they sat together again and were joined by Caroline Norwood.

Poissonnier asked for a meeting with his superiors and Bob Murray, long-time director of public prosecutions for the province. It was a tense meeting at RCMP headquarters in Fredericton attended by Poissonnier, Murray, RCMP Sgt. Mason Johnston, the three Crown prosecutors involved in the Legere case, and RCMP Inspectors Rod Smith and Mike Connolly. Poissonnier, an outspoken twenty-year veteran of the force know for his taste in Italian silk suits, pricey wines and high-powered motorcycles, wanted permission for a risky full-scale surveillance of the blonde. He suspected a conspiracy to influence a juror, but knew his superiors were nervous about this unorthodox procedure. Police surveillance, they feared, could be interpreted as tampering with the jury, which would force a new trial. The officers discussed the situation for ninety minutes, weighing the risks of causing a mistrial against the need to know if their suspicions were right. Finally, Bob Murray spoke up. "We have no choice," he said. Everyone agreed.

They needed a code name for the surveillance. It had to begin with the letter "J" because New Brunswick is designated as J Division by the RCMP. "Call it Operation Jobless," Poissonnier said, "because if I fuck up, I'll be out of a job." To be on the safe side, police were assigned to watch only Lois Gaunce at first. The surveillance team included an officer who, with his shoulder length hair and moustache, looked like a regular from a local tavern. Another, in golf jacket and polyester slacks, could have passed for a husband out grocery shopping. They followed Gaunce home several times and on Friday, September 27, to Renous where she met with Legere. On September 30, police photographed Gaunce and the blonde having lunch at the Pizza Delight restaurant at a nearby mall. Poissonnier decided to have the blonde and juror followed, too. That night, the couple met as usual in the grocery store parking lot, stopped at Fredericton liquor store, then drove to a home in the nearby village of Nackawic.

By October 1 RCMP had determined that the blonde was Pamela Kellar. Originally from Saint John and the mother of four, she was now separated from her husband and children. While the reporters covering the trial knew nothing about the surveillance, at least one knew about the link between the blonde and Moorcraft. Rod Allen of the daily newspaper *The Times-Transcript* of Moncton had been watching the blonde during testimony, shifting seats in the courtroom when necessary so he could see her. Sometimes she sensed he was watching and would scowl openly when looking at him.

The day the Montreal pawnbroker was on the stand, Allen noticed juror Moorcraft was seemingly ignoring the crucial evidence and exchanging glances across the courtroom with the blonde. That night, Allen followed the blonde and spotted her meeting Moorcraft in the parking lot of a nearby grocery store.

In court the next day, Moorcraft slumped in his seat, and, by pressing his fingers to his lips, indicated to the blonde that he was bored and wanted a cigarette. She giggled. Allen wasn't sure what to do next. He approached Poissonnier, who asked him to pass on anything he might discover, something Allen's editors, concerned about editorial impartiality, advised him not to do.

Meanwhile, RCMP officer Ron Charlebois had been assigned to sit in front of Kellar and Gaunce and listen in on any conversation. As court ended that day, Dickson warned the jury not to discuss the case with anyone.

Kellar turned to Gaunce and Charlebois heard her whisper, "Is he psychic? He's psychic. What do they know, more than we do?"

On October 2, the women drove three miles to a roadside diner for lunch. An undercover policeman wearing a plaid jacket and hat walked in and sat nearby.

"They can't kick him off the jury," he heard Kellar say.

"I hope not," Gaunce replied.

"He's got to have someone going for him," Kellar added, referring to Allan Legere.

The conversation turned briefly to a recent murder in Sussex, then Gaunce mentioned the jewelry taken from the Daughney home and recovered in Montreal.

"That looks bad," Kellar said.

"That couldn't have been him," Gaunce replied. "You watch, New Brunswick will find out in twenty years that Legere is innocent. They'll see him in a different light."

At this time, members of the jury also were starting to worry about Moorcraft. The driver of the jury van heard two female jurors talking about Moorcraft's girlfriend and confronting him about it. "She should not be sitting with that black-hair lady," one told Moorcraft as they were being driven home one night. "She's a friend of Legere's." When Moorcraft ignored them, four jurors approached deputy sheriff Les Sears, the man overseeing jury security, and urged him to speak to the judge.

On October 2, the RCMP discussed what they'd learned with the prosecutors, who had to decide what to do next.

There was a fifteen-minute delay the following morning before the trial resumed. The jury was absent. The courtroom was cleared of spectators. Speaking before Judge Dickson, Tony Allman outlined the growing concerns about Moorcraft and the decision to have him watched. Poissonnier described Legere's relationship with Gaunce and Norwood, and the link with Kellar and Moorcraft, who had met each other six months earlier and were now living together.

After hearing Poissonnier for forty minutes, Dickson lost his patience. "How much further do you have to go with this?" he demanded of Allman. "To me, it's already apparent this juror can't continue at this point." Allman had Poissonnier skip ahead to the conversation in the restaurant. The prosecutor then emphasized that the RCMP had neither spoken to nor eavesdropped on Moorcraft, something which could be interpreted as jury tampering and cause a mistrial.

"Well, I certainly have heard enough here, plus my own observations from time to time, to convince myself an order should be made discharging that particular juror," Dickson declared before letting Furlotte cross-examine Poissonnier. "It's not a question of whether he is implicated. It would make a farce of the trial to continue like this."

Weldon Furlotte challenged Poissonnier. Had one of the jurors been asked to warn Moorcraft about talking to Kellar?

Angry at the insinuation, Poissonnier shot back. "Mr. Furlotte, I'm not allowed, entitled, or capable of knowing that."

Might Kellar have befriended other jurors' spouses, or used Moorcraft to pass on information to the jury?

"It's a possibility," Poissonnier allowed curtly.

Dickson interrupted. "The appearance itself is terrible. There's no way this juror could stay on."

Furlotte said he would call for a mistrial. "I'm deeply concerned that this may have contaminated the whole jury."

Dickson said he would consider the motion when it was made, but in the meantime, he was removing Moorcraft from the jury and banning Kellar and Gaunce from the courtroom. Norwood could continue to attend, but only if she sat at the back beside a sheriff. Reporters were told not to interview them at any time.

After a brief recess, spectators were allowed back in, but the jury remained in another room. Dickson ordered Pamela Kellar and Lois Gaunce to stand up. Four police officers moved into the aisle beside them. Dickson then told the women that they were forbidden to even set foot on the courthouse grounds.

"It doesn't matter," Lois Gaunce muttered. "This is a complete farce. I don't care if you're pleased to hear it or not. It's the truth." Pamela Kellar pursed her lips. The police escorted the women out.

"See ya, Allan," Gaunce shouted over her shoulder.

"Yup," Legere replied, not even bothering to look her way.

The judge then allowed the jury to return to the courtroom. Choosing his words carefully to avoid prejudicing the jury against Legere, Dickson told the jurors that Jeffrey Moorcraft was being expelled because his girlfriend was associating with a friend of Allan Legere's. All eyes turned to Moorcraft as Dickson said his name. (A few minutes earlier in the judge's chambers, Moorcraft had tried to convince Dickson that there was no reason he should be thrown out, saying he had done nothing wrong. Dickson had rejected his argument, saying for appearance's sake he had to go.)

"Mr. Moorcraft, I thank you," Dickson began. "I'm not quite sure if you're an unwitting victim here – perhaps. I don't hold any blame on you. Perhaps you've acted somewhat indiscreetly, but I think others have been responsible for drawing you into this. Sorry about that. Sorry you can't continue on the jury." At that, Moorcraft stood up and left the room without a word.

Dickson looked at Furlotte, then the jury. "I must say, with my knowledge of this whole matter, I can see no reason why the balance of the jury is compromised in any way. I can't see why we shouldn't continue."

During the lunch break, Dickson took the unusual step of inviting the reporters into his chambers to answer their questions about what had happened and what they could report. Rosaire L'Italien of Radio Canada asked if videotape of Kellar shouting at a cameraman outside the courthouse could be used since it wasn't really an interview. Dickson chuckled, but said no, and no drawings of her either. "I've been saying that if this trial is ever seen through to the conclusion, it will be one of the greatest judicial accomplishments ever," the judge added.

One more thing, was the reporter for the Fredericton *Daily Gleaner* in the group? he asked. He wasn't. "Well, you tell that *Daily Gleaner* guy to stop calling it a shotgun. It's a rifle," Dickson said of the weapon Legere was carrying when captured.

The trial resumed with RCMP officers Mason Johnston and Kevin Mole taking the stand. As had happened at the Glendenning trial in 1987, Johnston's notetaking abilities were questioned. Furlotte probed unsuccessfully for inconsistencies in the officer's account of his conversation with the Legere the day he was recaptured.

"He was talking a mile a minute, a real motormouth," Johnston said, as if to taunt Legere, who was glaring at him the entire time.

Mole described his encounter with Legere that same day, November 24, 1989. "He talked in profanities. He said he didn't know what all that talk was about an accomplice. He said that was bullshit and that he had stayed in the woods all summer." Legere had claimed he'd used a series of five sites in the the area around Chatham, staying at a different one each day. He had met only two people the entire time, a man fishing near the golf course and a man he passed while walking across the Morrissy Bridge.

During his cross-examination, Furlotte pulled out a pair of composite drawings done by police artists and showed them to Mole. "Does Mr. Legere look like either, neither or both?"

"I can see resemblances in both," Mole replied calmly.

Furlotte attempted to shake Mole's testimony about Legere's appearance when recaptured, wanting to know how the accused could have lost forty pounds in six months if he had been eating as well as he had claimed.

"That depends on what you're doing when you're eating," Mole answered.

As Mole was leaving the stand at the end of the day, Legere exploded. "This all makes good press, but I'm fuckin' sick of it," he yelled, clutching sheets of paper in one hand. "I endured eight hours of interrogation, I was kicked in the head, and they took my blood illegally."

Dickson waved for the court officers to get Legere out of the room.

"I met Mason Johnston in 1987!" Legere shouted as he was being hustled out. "He was instrumental in my getting a life sentence for a murder I didn't commit. And what about that juror they kicked off! He was on my side!"

On Tuesday, October 8, Allman turned to the crucial piece of physical evidence in the Father Smith murder case – a pair of boots.

The jury had already seen a police video of the scene. It had opened with a shot from the bottom of the parking lot looking up the small hill to the church and rectory. The mournful wail of a train whistle, sounding from somewhere in the distance and captured accidentally by the RCMP cameraman, had added to the sense of foreboding.

"Turn the volume down," Legere had shouted, shattering the moment.

No one could forget what they'd seen in that video – the pools of blood surrounding the chair in the kitchen, the large and bloody boot print left behind on a church bulletin as the killer walked through the room.

The court was told about two pairs of boots: a set of Greb Kodiak work boots found near the train station in Bathurst the day after Smith's murder; and a pair of Gorilla brand boots Legere was wearing when captured.

RCMP Sgt. Dan Chiasson testified that nicks and marks on the boots found in Bathurst matched the prints found in Smith's rectory. The killer had worn those boots.

RCMP Sgt. Robert Kennedy walked to the witness box carrying a clear plastic bag containing pink plaster casts of a pair of feet. An expert in the identification and matching of human feet and footwear, he described what he'd done in the first few hours after Legere was captured.

Handed the boots found in Bathurst, he'd been asked to make casts of Legere's feet to effect a comparison. Kennedy knew there was only one kind of material suitable for the job, a special foam used by some foot doctors. He called around, but couldn't find any inside the province. There was some available in Prince Edward island and the RCMP chartered a plane to pick it up.

After carefully mixing the foam to ensure there were no impurities, Kennedy explained to Allan Legere who he was and told him he was there to make moulds of his feet. He made three sets, each time asking Legere to stick his feet about halfway into a tray of the quick-drying foam. Later, he poured plaster into the impressions, producing an exact copy of Legere's feet. Ideally, the plaster feet could then be used to attempt to match the contours of Legere's feet to the boots which made the prints in Smith's home.

There were problems with the second and third sets of casts, where it appeared Legere had moved his feet slightly, distorting the impressions. As Kennedy examined the first set of casts, however, he noticed an odd reddish-brown mark in the heel of the left foot. It aligned perfectly with the tip of a nail protruding into the sole of the left boot worn by the killer.

Kennedy began a series of measurements and comparisons. A hole in one of the bread bags used by the killer to line his boots matched the nail mark on the plaster foot. A second hole slid neatly over the big toe. As well, he compared photographs of Legere's feet and the killer's boots.

In court, Kennedy drew the jury's attention to the outer edge of the foot. "You can see there is a predominant drop on the edge of the foot under the smallest toe, which is unusual. It is consistent with indentations and sweat marks found on the in-sole," he explained.

He showed a ten-minute video to help illustrate what he'd done. The final image was a shot done in ultra-violet light, which caused sweat stains and depressed areas in the in-soles to darken while leaving higher areas a bright green. The video showed Kennedy slowly lowering a cast of Legere's foot onto the in-sole of the killer's boot. It was a perfect fit.

In his cross-examination, Furlotte suggested the reddish-brown mark linking Legere's foot to the killer's could have been dirt in the foam, or something from the floor of the RCMP station where Legere was walking around barefoot after his capture.

No, Kennedy replied. He habitually wiped a subject's feet before working on them, and he always washed his materials thoroughly before using them. Whatever the spot was, it was on Legere's foot when he stuck it in the foam.

Furlotte asked Kennedy how he could be certain his measurements matched when they were sometimes off by as much as 6.6 per cent.

Accurate measurements are difficult to make on curved surfaces, Kennedy replied, which is why he didn't depend upon them in his work.

What about the computer system used to attempt to find a match based in the measurements, it hadn't worked perfectly either, had it?

No, Kennedy admitted. Again, that's why he didn't attach much importance to the measurements.

Allman had two more questions. "Mr. Furlotte suggested there might be one in two hundred people who could have left similar markings on the soles of the boots, but you said the statistic would be higher."

"Yes."

"How much higher?"

"I really couldn't give you a specific number," Kennedy replied.

The next witness was FBI Special Agent William Bodziak, author of a book on footwear evidence and an expert witness who had testified at thousands of trials since 1973. He confirmed Kennedy's findings. While he was unable to explain the reddish-brown spot on the left heel of the first cast, he was ready to offer his opinion about its meaning. "The exactness of the position in relation to the hole in the in-sole, and the fact that I have never seen a spot like this before, leads me to believe it is not a coincidence."

Furlotte wanted to know if members of the same family might have feet that look the same.

Similar perhaps, but not identical, Bodziak replied. "Even if you studied twins, which I have, you would find they have different feet. Their foot shape and characteristics are formed from a lifetime of different environmental and wear factors."

Pressed to come up with statistics, Bodziak said that wasn't possible.

Furlotte asked one more question. "Could someone have worn the Kodiak boots before or after Mr. Legere."

"That is possible," Bodziak admitted, "for a short time."

Tony Allman was pleased, confident he'd proved the boots placed Legere inside Smith's rectory. He was furious the next morning, however, when he picked up *The New Brunswick Telegraph Journal* and read the front page headline – "Legere's lawyer uncovers wrinkles in boot evidence." The story, by reporter Shaun Waters, suggested the evidence was inconclusive because of the lack of statistical support and quoted Bodziak as saying Legere was probably the person who wore the killer's boots, but he couldn't be sure.

Known for his even temper and unflappable demeanour, Allman uncharacteristically complained to Dickson the next day, saying the story was inaccurate. The judge said he'd read the story and didn't see anything wrong with it, but would take note of the complaint.

Waters cornered Allman after the proceedings and demanded to know what was wrong. Allman argued that Waters had misquoted Bodziak at one point, reporting that the FBI agent had said the odds that Legere had worn the killer's boots were "a bit" higher than one in two hundred

when the words should have been "a lot." Waters checked
his notes. He had misread his shorthand and conceded Allman was right. He stood his ground, however, when challenged about the use of the word "probably" to describe the
chances the boots had been Legere's. Allman insisted Bodziak had said "highly probable" and vowed to get a copy of
the transcript to prove it, even though *Times-Transcript*
reporter Rod Allen confirmed Waters' version.

Calming down quickly as he let off steam, Allman
reverted to form, eventually giving both reporters bear hugs
and acknowledging that he couldn't expect everything to
go his way each day.

On Thursday morning, October 10, Weldon Furlotte
appeared nervous as he prepared to to begin his *voir dire*
arguments for a mistrial based on the expulsion of juror Jeffrey Moorcraft the week before. He dug through a pile of
papers in front of him, spreading them out, turning them
over, reading them. People sitting in the courtroom began
to fidget. "It's just like that telephone commercial," said
Furlotte at one point, grinning sheepishly and attempting a
joke, "lost in the files."

Ready at last, he outlined the basis of his argument –
Allan Legere could not get a fair trial because the jury
would assume he had tried to influence Moorcraft. In addition, Judge Dickson had made the situation worse by mentioning that Legere's "girlfriend" Lois Gaunce had been
involved.

Furlotte asked Legere to explain what had happened.
"First of all, Your Honour," Legere began, "I'd like to verify
that Mrs. Gaunce is a happily married woman and not a
girlfriend of mine, just an acquaintance, just one of very few
who are not anti-Legere."

The first he had heard of Pamela Kellar was when
Gaunce visited him at the prison to talk about paintings.
She said she'd learned Kellar was a friend of Moorcraft's.

"Then I was told that Miss Kellar was being supplied

information from Mr. Moorcraft, in effect, what days the jurors were in my favor." He said he'd told Gaunce that was illegal and to be careful because prison authorities might be taping their conversation. He swore he told Furlotte about it the following Monday, September 30.

"I can't tell the court any more because I don't know any more. I have not given any messages back to Miss Kellar because I knew that something was going to blow up soon."

Asked by Furlotte what had happened to him since then, Legere angrily said that prison authorities had cut off his right to have visitors and make phone calls, even to his mother.

Tony Allman peppered Legere with questions about what was said during the meeting he had with Gaunce at the prison.

"Miss Gaunce is a supporter of yours, is she?

"I would say that, yes."

"Did you ever propose marriage to her?"

"I don't think I could propose marriage to her. Maybe joke around with her, that's about it."

Allman zeroed in. "Did you ever say, 'I think the best thing you could do is marry me really …'"

Legere attempted to interrupt. "Oh, ya," he said.

Allman ignored him and continued quoting: "'… so I could focus on you totally. See, I can't focus on you totally unless I do have you, because I focus on you totally.' Did you ever say that to her?"

Legere knew there was only one way the prosecutor could have learned about those words, but unwilling to give up, he attempted to bluff his way out.

"Yes, I did. Yes, I did. She just laughed me off and said, 'Now, Allan, don't get too serious now.' She's a very, very serious woman. She doesn't flirt. I do the flirting."

Allman pressed his attack. "When Miss Gaunce talked about the situation between Kellar and the juror, did she say to you that she could arrange for you to have a meeting with her. 'I could arrange that if you want that?'"

"No, I don't think it come out that way, Mr. Allman."

"Did you say to her, 'Ya, she could tell us what's going on?'"

"I don't recall saying that."

In fact, Legere knew he had said it, he knew that his conversation had been taped, and he knew Allman had the tape.

Allman pounded away, forcing Legere to come up with ever more fanciful explanations and memory lapses to disguise his instructions to Gaunce on how to use Kellar.

"Did you tell her, discussing the situation, that, 'it sounds good, eh? You know that sounds good to me, that sounds good. Keep it under your hat. It could mean something. I tell you that fuckin' much. Oh my God, we could get close to everybody.'"

"That was the time that I was talking to Mrs. Gaunce, on that Saturday?"

Allman's voice shot across the room: "I'm asking you! Do you think you said that to Mrs. Gaunce …"

"I may have," Legere admitted grudgingly.

Summing up, Weldon Furlotte struggled to put the best face on the fiasco and to ensure that the judge didn't think he'd had any part in it. He'd misunderstood Legere, he explained, his voice quavering at times. He thought Kellar was telling *everyone* what Moorcraft was saying, not just Gaunce. When he realized the truth, he was deeply upset. Still, there was no proof Legere had done anything wrong. There had to be a mistrial because the incident would inevitably prejudice the jury against his client.

Dickson refused the motion. The trial would continue. It was time for the Crown to introduce the long-awaited DNA evidence.

## EIGHTEEN

# DNA on Trial

The story of DNA fingerprinting began on November 21, 1983 in the small village of Narborough, near the city of Leicester in England's midlands.

On that day 15-year-old Lynda Mann left a friend's home at 7:30 p.m. The next morning, a hospital employee found her body sprawled on grass near a clump of trees. Naked from the waist down, she had been raped, beaten and strangled. One hundred and fifty police officers were assigned to the case, but by the following August they'd hit a dead end.

At Leicester University, 34-year-old geneticist Alec Jeffreys was working on a project studying DNA – deoxyribonucleic acid. Called the building block of life, DNA carries the genetic instructions passed on to children from their parents. It determines everything, from the colour of a person's hair to the size of their feet. Most of the DNA information is the same for everyone, since everyone has a head, two legs and two arms. Certain parts differ widely, however, and these were what interested Jeffreys. He was looking for ways to spot those differences.

He took DNA from human blood cells, broke it up with chemicals, put it into tiny channels of Jello-like gel and zapped it with electricity, separating the bits into patterns.

That done, he added radioactive chemicals called probes which stuck to the DNA. When X-rayed, the photographs showed unique patterns of sooty black bands against a white background – autorads. Looking like a fuzzy version of the bar codes on packages of food at a grocery store, they were called DNA fingerprints.

Jeffreys published his findings in March 1985 and made a bold claim: like a fingerprint, a person's DNA is unique and could be used to identify someone.

The Narborough killer struck again in 1986. The body of 15-year-old Dawn Ashworth was found. Like Mann, she was naked from the waist down and had been raped and strangled. In January 1987, no closer to solving either murder, police put Jeffrey's DNA fingerprinting theory to the test. They asked all local men between 17 and 34 without alibis to provide blood and saliva samples. By May, they'd tested nearly four thousand men.

A 27-year-old baker with a history of flashing paid a fellow worker to take his place for the test. The ploy worked until the baker bragged about it in a pub. On September 19, 1987 police arrested baker Colin Pitchfork for the murder of Dawn Ashworth. He was later jailed for life.

The case caught the attention of the district attorney in Orlando, Florida. Police had a suspect and twenty-three rape victims, but no proof. In 1988, they used DNA fingerprinting to convict the suspect on charges of sexual battery, armed burglary, and aggravated battery, making it the first such case in North America.

The same year, DNA fingerprinting had its introduction in Canada, albeit with different results than in the U.S. Charges were dropped against an Alberta man accused of seven rapes when DNA testing proved he was innocent. Later that year in Ottawa, DNA helped convict a handyman accused of raping a 68-year-old woman in her home. The judge accepted the new science, saying it was no different than fingerprint, blood and fibre evidence, which had been used for years. It was the first conviction based on DNA evidence in Canadian legal history.

The first Canadian murder conviction using DNA

involved Claude Bourguignon, an Ottawa man charged with raping and killing his two-year-old nephew. The judge admitted the DNA evidence, but refused the use of the accompanying statistics. Despite that, the jury found Bourguignon guilty.

The legal future of DNA fingerprinting seemed more secure. District attorneys across the United States scrambled to use it. Some defendants quickly pleaded guilty when told DNA evidence was to be used against them. In 1989, however, a double murder case against Joseph Castro of New York unravelled when experts attacked the DNA evidence, citing bad lab work. The evidence was ruled inadmissible. Castro was eventually convicted of first-degree murder without it, but the case renewed the scientific debate over the accuracy of DNA fingerprinting.

A stinging article in the June 1989 issue of the respected scientific journal *Nature* questioned DNA testing done by laboratories for police, saying higher standards were demanded for strep throat tests. A second attack, published in *Scientific American* in May 1990, challenged the theory behind DNA fingerprinting, the testing procedures, and the ability of judges and lawyers to understand the results.

Sitting in the Burton courthouse on the morning of Tuesday, October 15, Crown prosecutor Jack Walsh was all too familiar with the scientific debate and how it might affect his chances of convicting Allan Legere. He was tired of the arguments, the endless hours of poking holes in his own case, then devising ways to plug them. He had spent two years and travelled thousands of miles in Canada and the United States, speaking with university professors, FBI agents and RCMP scientists, preparing for the moment when he would call his first expert witness to the stand and begin the job of trying to convince a jury that it should believe in DNA. That moment had come.

Walsh began by giving the jury a lesson in the basics of DNA. The teacher was Dr. John Waye, a slim, dark-haired assistant biology professor at McMaster University in Hamilton, Ontario. He was the first of what police called their "kid scientists" because they all looked so young.

Taking the entire afternoon of October 15, and using a series of charts and models, Waye explained the intricacies of DNA – the chemical chain which contains forty-six strands called chromosomes, twenty-three from the mother and twenty-three from the father. The entire DNA strand is found in every cell in the human body, from the hair on the head to body fluids like semen.

The basics explained, Waye delved into the process used in DNA fingerprinting: tearing open a cell with chemicals, splitting the DNA with more chemicals to produce manageable bits, then using electricity and X-rays to produce the fuzzy lines used to compare a suspect's DNA with material found at a crime scene. If the X-ray photographs don't match, the police have the wrong person, Waye emphasized. If they match, however, a second test is done, then a third. If the DNA still matches, scientists believe the police have the right person.

As the jurors struggled gamely to understand the increasingly technical explanation, Waye explained how statistics produced by population geneticists are used in DNA fingerprinting to estimate the chances of a match.

Researchers look at the amount of difference in the DNA of various ethnic groups, Waye said. That's essential for DNA fingerprinting. He used a rape case as an example. If the odds are only one in thirty that semen found on the victim came from a suspect, the test is probably useless because in a town with 3,000 men, as many as one hundred might have matching DNA. If the odds are one in ten million, however, the chances of anyone *but* the suspect being the rapist are remote.

Walsh asked Waye what things might spoil a DNA sample, making it impossible to test.

Strong acids would do it. So would dirt, because it contains bacteria, Waye responded.

What about heat and smoke? Walsh asked.

It would depend on things like the amount of heat and length of exposure, Waye answered. "What I can say is that heat and smoke won't change the *pattern* on the finding. It can't make DNA that is not compatible appear to be compatible."

Furlotte, not surprisingly, homed in on the scientific controversy over DNA fingerprinting.

"Do all scientists think it is reliable?" he asked Waye.

"Scientists are by nature argumentative people. They don't accept anything at face value," Waye replied calmly. "There were some papers opposing DNA analysis in the beginning, but the dispute has died down considerably."

Furlotte wanted to know more about population genetics and its use in DNA fingerprinting. "Do you know whether there are more opponents than proponents?"

"In my opinion, the number of opponents was always small," Waye replied. He described a conference on genetics he had attended just the week before in Washington, D.C. "There were a thousand geneticists in one room discussing nothing but population figures. Maybe the opponents couldn't use the microphones. Maybe they were shy. I don't know. But I know I didn't hear any opposition."

Couldn't genetic similarities in a family cause a rare DNA pattern to become more common? Furlotte asked.

"There is a greater probability of finding a match if people are related," Waye admitted. "A genetic pattern that might appear one in a million times in the general population could appear one in one thousand times if the samples belong to two brothers. If the results were that close, you could bleed the whole family to get the truth."

"So the patterns are always going to be more common in a family member?"

No, Waye responded. "Once you go beyond the immediate siblings, that likelihood changes. If you were talking, say, cousins, the numbers would get closer to the general population."

Furlotte challenged the value of the Hardy-Weinburg formula. Quickly dubbed the Hardy-Hamburger formula by reporters frustrated by its complexity, this statistical approach makes a series of assumptions: no new people come into a community, no one leaves, and breeding occurs freely and without selection.

True, those assumptions aren't realistic, Waye allowed, but like many systems used in science, it's close enough that the mathematics works.

Furlotte asked Waye about data bases — information gathered in DNA testing of groups to try to find out how common certain genetic patterns are. In-breeding, he suggested, might distort those attempts.

"You would have to look at a region or community of individuals where nobody wanted to leave and nobody wanted to come in," Waye replied. "It would have to be a place where people married their sisters, their brothers, or their uncles and the practice had gone on for generations."

"Sounds like the Miramichi," Legere shouted from the prisoner's box.

Ignoring the remark, Waye described the research he had heard the week before in Washington. "There has been a study done on a South American tribe where everyone descends from one king and his three queens. It was an incestuous community for many generations. Yet DNA testing found it was no problem to uniquely identify everyone in that community." The key was using more than one test to find differences. The more tests used, the less likely the chances of confusion.

Once the jury had left the room at the start of the lunch break, Judge Dickson ordered a brief private hearing to deal with Allan Legere's outburst. Walsh, the tips of his ears blood red, accused Legere of scandalizing the court with his "scurrilous" comment about the Miramichi. Bouncing around in the prisoner's box, Legere smirked and taunted the prosecutor. They tried to shout down each other.

Walsh: "He's been warned and warned and warned and warned ..."

Legere: "He's being a jerk."

Walsh: "... in addition to that ..."

Legere: "Mr. Jerkface, so don't jerk me."

Walsh: "That comment directly relates ..."

Legere: "I went out with your cousin. You're mad now ..."

Walsh: "That comment directly relates ..."

Legere: "Cheryl Walsh, go ask her."

Walsh: "That comment directly relates to what Mr. Furlotte and the defence expert are going to attempt to try and show, that in fact there is some form of in-breeding in the Miramichi community ..."

Legere: "Well, there is!"

Walsh: "That's the reason that the *voir dire* – he's making this particular comment..."

Legere: "There's nothing considered castigating on to the Miramichi."

That was enough for Dickson. He motioned to the sheriff's deputies. "Take the accused out please and turn on the video machine."

Legere became enraged. "How can you compare the data base from the Miramichi to Camp Gagetown – when you never had a data base," he yelled as he was led away. "The goddamn people are all in-bred down there. What are you talking about? They share so many bands they look like a bunch of rubber bands."

When the trial resumed that afternoon, Legere was absent. Dickson explained he again had thrown the accused out of court. Legere would watch the trial on closed-circuit television in a room across the hall. Dickson's frequent ejections gave the prisoner a chance to lecture court clerk Gerald Pugh about good and evil while in the holding cell. "God makes it ready for people to die," Legere told him. Simultaneously repelled and fascinated by Legere, Pugh gave his charge a file folder for his notes and drawings. He also bought him high-quality art paper from a Fredericton store, for which Legere rewarded him with a drawing of Lucifer sitting on a melting block of ice, surrounded by biblical quotations.

In court, Furlotte continued to press Waye, suggesting the way scientists decide on a match is faulty. Isn't it true, he asked, that researchers depend upon their eyes, not a computer, to read the genetic-rays called autorads?

"Yes."

"So, your eyes must be pretty good then?"

"My eyes are pretty good, yeah. My eyes are a better instrument for determining a match than the computer. The human eye is more sensitive than a $400 video camera."

"More sensitive than a telescopic lens?"

"It's not better than the eye."

"I take it you don't wear glasses then?"

"I do."

"When you're reading autorads?"

"I wear them *because* I read so many of them."

The exchange at times grew testy. At one point, Furlotte questioned Waye about in-breeding and the chances it might produce a sub-group – a group of people with similar DNA.

"You don't know how to define a sub-group and you wouldn't know one if it hit you in the head," Furlotte charged.

"No," Waye replied, "I've never been hit in the head by a sub-group."

The Crown next called Dr. John Bowen. The baby-faced DNA fingerprinting expert ran the RCMP lab in Ottawa and had done more DNA tests than anyone in Canada.

Legere, allowed back in court, watched as Bowen, using a red laser light in the darkened room, pointed at X-ray slides projected on to an overhead screen. Methodically, he described his test results. Expecting the clean lines of a grocery bar code, the jurors strained to make sense of the sausage-shaped smudges called bands. The first test matched Legere's DNA to semen found on Linda Daughney. The second matched his DNA to semen from Nina Flam's vagina and Linda's body.

X-rays from the third test, using an especially sensitive procedure, prompted nods from several jurors. Gone were the fat smudges, replaced by clear lines. The jurors listened intently as Bowen announced the results: Legere's DNA matched semen taken from Nina Flam and the Daughney sisters. Additional tests matched Legere's DNA to all three women. Bowen's summary was to the point: the tests linked Legere's DNA to the three women sixteen times.

What, Walsh asked, were the chances of someone other than Legere being responsible?

Astronomical, Bowen replied. For Donna Daughney, the odds were one in 7,400; for Nina, one in 5.2 million; for Linda Daughney, one in 310 million.

Except for identical twins, had he ever seen such results before?

Never, said Bowen. "This is a rare event. Not even brothers and sisters would generate bands that similar. The possibility that this DNA came from someone other than Allan Legere is remote."

A high-pitched whistling filled the darkened courtroom as Bowen showed his slides. At first, no one could figure out where it was coming from. Reporters joked that it was Legere using mind control. It took a couple of days, but the source was located – it was the banker's lamp Jack Walsh used to read his notes. While this noise didn't bother him, the faint sound of reporters opening candies did, to the point where he would hiss at them to be quiet.

In cross-examination, Furlotte asked Bowen if he had been given enough DNA material to do the tests properly.

Yes, but just barely.

"Is that why there wasn't enough DNA left over for the defence to conduct its own tests?"

"Yes."

Legere shouted across the room from the prisoner's box. "How convenient there was not enough to make another set of tests! But the paper said in 1989 that you had done all the tests!"

Dickson tried to cut him off, but Legere ignored him. "They can alter these autorads," he yelled. "They can play with them all day and make them look like me!"

Dickson waved at the sheriff deputies to get Legere out of the room.

"There are thirty-five guys waiting for this test and I'm the perfect person to get down," Legere shouted as the guards took him out. "It's in Bowen's interests to make me look guilty and he goddamned well knows it too."

It was Friday afternoon and getting late. Weldon Furlotte made one final attempt at undercutting the credibility of Bowen's results. Wasn't it true that on one occasion the computer had failed to find a match and, he asked, Bowen had over-ruled it?

True, Bowen replied, but in another instance the computer saw a match and he didn't.


The man considered to be the world expert in population genetics was the next witness. Short, middle-aged, with a waxed handle bar moustache and goatee, Dr. Kenneth Kidd listed his credentials: professor of genetics, psychiatry and biology at Yale University; cancer researcher; co-author of hundreds of books and research papers on genetics; an architect of DNA fingerprinting; manager of a laboratory which had studied hundreds of thousands of DNA X-rays.

Kidd said he had reviewed Bowen's work and agreed with his analysis – the DNA from the murder scenes belonged to Allan Legere. He disagreed, however, with Bowen's decision to discard several DNA matches as not close enough. He thought Bowen was being too conservative. He warned the lawyers to avoid getting caught up in the numbers. Odds like one in 310 million are so remote, he said, that they're as good as one in a billion.

Walsh knew Furlotte would focus on in-breeding and the creation of substructures – groups of people with similar DNA – so he asked Kidd about it.

Very unlikely, the professor replied. Echoing Waye, he described research he had done into the DNA of an isolated tribe in the Amazon. The entire tribe had descended from a king and his three wives, yet tests still picked out individuals by their DNA.

Kidd went on to defend the mathematics used to decide if DNA samples came from the same person, saying the methods gave the benefit of the doubt to the accused. He flatly dismissed as irrelevant suggestions by American geneticist Dr. William Shields, an in-breeding expert at the State University of New York who was expected to be called by the defence, that in-breeding could distort DNA evidence. What little of it did exist, he said, didn't affect the tests.

Asked to describe the Miramichi, Kidd said, "This is not a community that is isolated. There are people moving in and out. It was settled by people of various ethnic backgrounds, including French and English. I don't see any indication of excess in-breeding, or isolation in this population."

Weldon Furlotte asked Kidd if he was familiar with blood typing and how it compared to DNA fingerprinting. Kidd said he hadn't done much of it since his graduate student days, but he knew the process and considered the chances of making a mistake greater with blood typing than DNA because there were more steps.

Furlotte wanted to know why Kidd had agreed to testify in this case if, as he had said earlier, time spent in court hurt his research?

Kidd explained that although he'd prefer to be left alone in his lab and had refused all requests to testify in the past year, his promise to help the RCMP had been made before that decision. On average, he was still receiving a couple of offers each week. "I could have tripled my income if I had accepted those offers, but I made a decision long ago that I would be a research scientist, not a wealthy man."

"So, you are paid for your professional services?" Furlotte asked.

A smile curled the corners of Kidd's moustache. "Since I'm not home to fix the leaky roof, I have to hire a workman to do it."

Dickson's eyebrows shot up. "Do you want to establish that he's a prostitute?"

Merely trying to ensure the professor is truly an independent expert and not simply a hired gun, Furlotte replied.

Kidd jumped in. "What I am charging now is more than what I am being paid for this. I agreed to testify in this trial three years ago. Today, I charge $2,000 a day."

Furlotte's lengthy cross-examination had reduced Kidd's rate to about fifty cents an answer, the judge cracked.

"That's what they're worth," Furlotte shot back, but he was unable to budge Kidd, who at one point described Shields' in-breeding ideas as "nonsense." Kidd made no attempt to hide his contempt for the long list of what he considered to be self-proclaimed experts ready to testify for a price. "There are some people who call themselves scientists who still believe the Bible creation story, in spite of overwhelming evidence to the contrary."

Dr. Ronald Fourney testified next. As the head of research and development at the RCMP's DNA lab in Ottawa, he said every precaution had been taken in testing Legere's DNA.

Furlotte challenged the assertion. "The RCMP DNA testing program is something you're proud of, it's your baby," said the defence counsel on Wednesday morning as he began his cross-examination.

"I wouldn't do it if I didn't enjoy it," Fourney responded.

"And it's under attack."

"If I was back in cancer research, the work I was doing

there would be under attack too," Fourney said. "Science is not a static environment."

"But you have a bias toward it."

"My *bias* is to do the best job I can possibly do and it's the same regardless what I'm working on."

Furlotte asked about his lab in the fall of 1989 when the first DNA testing in the Legere case was done. "Your lab was being remodelled and you had to use facilities for other types of forensic testing?"

"Sure."

"Was it crowded?"

"It's difficult to be crowded with only three people in the program," Fourney answered.

"Would you say it was hectic?"

"Any research project worth its salt is hectic. If you're trying to imply we weren't ready, you're wrong. We were satisfied with the results we got."

"Would you say you were in a state of flux?"

"I don't think we're ever *out* of a state of flux. I haven't worked anywhere where I wasn't."

"You say you were working in two facilities. You had new equipment arriving all the time?"

Fourney was unruffled. "New equipment is always coming in. I'm expecting some new equipment next month. We're constantly updating. That's not unusual."

"But things were hectic."

"I wouldn't use that word. I call it exciting."

"You must have worked long hours. What kinds of hours were you working?"

"You'd have to ask my wife that," Fourney replied, drawing laughter from the crowded courtroom.

Furlotte ignored it. "Were you working more than five days a week?"

"Yes."

"Did you work more than ten hours a day?"

"Scientists in general work long hours. They are dedicated."

"If you want to find them, call the lab," Furlotte suggested.

"We are dedicated. Regardless of where I am, I'm always thinking of new experiments that can be run."

"In your role as head of quality assurance, have you ever set any guidelines about the number of hours you should work? Tired people make mistakes."

"*Inexperienced* people make mistakes," Fourney corrected him.

On Wednesday, October 23, population genetics expert Dr. George Carmody of Carleton University in Ottawa turned the courtroom into a kind of university lecture hall with what reporters dubbed "the science lesson from hell."

Throwing around terms like linkage disequilibriums and non-parametric tests, he explained how the intricate math used to calculate odds in DNA fingerprinting required blood samples from a wide cross-section of people.

Carmody said the RCMP had tested nearly a thousand people. Their work showed the DNA of people in New Brunswick was not unusual, so the odds quoted in the Legere case were reliable. Odds based on work done in the United States would have been even more damning for Legere.

Furlotte, however, continued to plug the notion that decades of in-breeding had made the DNA of Miramichiers unique. Carmody dismissed the idea, saying he had tested nine area residents and found no signs of in-breeding.

Furlotte brought up research done by Shields, which he said raised doubts about the odds quoted in the Legere case.

"Defence counsels are getting preoccupied with the difference between odds of one in five million and one in 300 million," Carmody replied. "In the end, it doesn't really matter. When the odds are that high, both are a very rare occurrence."

At this point Legere spoke up. "May I be excused, Your Honour. I'm tired of listening to this over and over again.

They're missing the point. The Crown is parading out all these experts like a line of elephants and they're all saying the same thing. With all the money they've wasted here, they could have paid for a Miramichi data base, but then you'd have to do Nordin, Douglastown and Nelson."

Dickson motioned to the guards.

"I don't want to stay," Legere called out. "He's missing the point. He's wrong about the substructure and Dr. Shields is right. Move to the Miramichi. Take a data base. It'll come out. I'll eat my shirt if it don't."

The guards struggled to free Legere from the the chain bolted to the floor at this feet. They were unaware that the prisoner had managed to jam it with bits of paper when his guards weren't looking.

"You should go the Miramichi," Legere shouted. "You wouldn't believe it. There are fathers making love to their daughters and vice-versa. My own son was raped at five years old and the police did nothing about it. They kept it underground. Go back to the Chaplin Island Road. There are cousins marrying cousins. It's a modern day Sodom and Gomorrah."

Legere looked down at the struggling guards. "Open lock," he ordered, then started to sing "Please Release Me, Let Me Go." Nothing happened.

Angry, Dickson stood up and ordered the jury and spectators out of the room, staring at the crowd as the room emptied.

Carmody proved to be the final Crown witness. After two months, the prosecution's case was complete. They had presented 247 witnesses and more than two hundred pieces of evidence. They had done everything they could think of to convince the jury of Allan Legere's guilt. Now it was Weldon Furlotte's task to try to prove them wrong.

As expected, Furlotte called Dr. William Shields as his first defence witness. Dishevelled, looking like he would prefer a lab coat to his ill-fitting jacket and tie, Shields provided a sharp contrast to the smooth-talking, well-groomed experts called by the Crown. He described himself as an evolutionary geneticist specializing in various forms of wildlife and the practices of in-breeding. His credits included a textbook on genetics and about thirty-five scientific articles.

Furlotte had found Shields with the help of Peter Neufeld, a American critic of the use of DNA fingerprinting in the courts. Neufeld gave him a list of potential experts. A number refused, saying they were tired of spending time in court. Shields, however, agreed to testify. Furlotte had expected him to contradict previous testimony that had said Legere's semen was found at two of the murder scenes. Just before going into court, however, Shields had stunned Furlotte, telling him he couldn't do that.

Shields told the court he agreed with the RCMP's findings. In fact, he volunteered, he felt they might have been too conservative in throwing out a couple of likely matches. "I agree with their scoring," he summed up.

A dejected-looking Furlotte asked few questions. Finally, Shields felt compelled to ask Furlotte what he wanted him to talk about next.

"Go ahead. Whatever you think. You're the expert," Furlotte replied.

Using DNA information gathered from the Miramichi, Shields said, he'd come up with odds far lower than one in 310 million. It was more like one in 11 million.

So, Furlotte asked, the RCMP had misused the statistics in the Legere case?

"I don't believe they have misused the statistics," Shields said. "I believe that there were assumptions made which make the use of the formulas they have chosen "iffy." I would call it a mistake, not a misuse."

As he rose to begin his cross-examination, Jack Walsh had three tasks before him. The first was to undercut William Shields' credibility as an expert in human population genetics; the second was to show Shields knew little about the genetic make-up of the Miramichi; the third was to demonstrate that Shields' own estimate of odds of a DNA match was so high that Legere remained the only logical suspect. Both men remembered their lengthy battle in the *voir dire* that spring. Walsh was cautious, determined to limit Shields to yes and no answers. Shields was wary, unwilling to expose himself to attack.

Said Walsh: "I was looking at your C.V. and it would be fair to say that your professional experience, publications and interests primarily lies with respect to animal populations as opposed to human populations."

"That's correct," Shields nodded.

"And your empirical study, doctor, in fact is done with many kinds of animals. You deal with swallows, chipmunks, beavers. You have an expertise with respect to Mexican wolves. You deal with certain types of insects. Things of nature. Is that correct?"

"That's correct."

"And, in fact, you're the director of the Cranberry Lake Biological Station and there you do important work associated with rare species – trying to preserve the wildlife. Is that a fair assessment?"

"That's correct."

"On the other hand, doctor, if a person works exclusively, or let's say ninety-five per cent of their time on humans – particularly someone who had done post-doctoral work in human population genetics and has studied human populations worldwide – you would consider him a human population geneticist, would you not, under that definition?"

"You could, yes."

"And based on that, you would consider Doctor Kenneth Kidd to be a human population geneticist, would you not?"

"Yes, I would."

"You do not consider yourself to be a human population geneticist, do you?"

"No, I do not in the sense that you mean it, right."

When the two men started a detailed discussion of the highly technical subject of bin frequencies, Legere grew exasperated.

"Your Honour, can I be excused again, before I get sick here?"

Dickson: "What do you have to say, Mr. Furlotte? Do you concur in that?" Furlotte nodded. "Would you remove the accused, please, sheriff?"

As Legere was being taken to the holding cell, he shouted: "Don't worry, Mr. Shields, you were in Baghdad when he was still in his dad's bag."

A few minutes after Legere's departure, Walsh dropped the technical discussion and began a rapid-fire series of questions aimed at Shields' knowledge of the Miramichi: "What is the Miramichi, Doctor?"

"I've been told it's a river," Shields replied.

"What kind of populations – what kind of towns, villages, people are there, Doctor?"

"I presume mostly Canadian citizens."

"How many villages?"

"I have no idea."

"How many towns?"

"I have no idea."

"Any cities?"

"I think Newcastle."

"Is a city?"

"Yes."

"How big a county is it, doctor?"

"I have no idea."

"How many people would be in the city of Newcastle?"

"I have no idea."

"What are their emigration and migration patterns?"

"Don't know."

"What are their marriage patterns?"

"Don't know."

"Is incestual type relationships a norm in that area?"

"I would hope not."

"So, doctor, you don't know too much about that area that these people came from, do you?"

"Not about the questions you just asked, no."

Satisfied he had demonstrated Shields' lack of knowledge about the Miramichi, Walsh next attempted to dissect Shields' one in eleven million statistic. Had he considered the fact that the DNA had come from semen?

That's why it's one in eleven million, Shields replied, the other eleven million people in Canada would be women.

Wouldn't some of those men be too young or too old to be suspects?

Yes.

So, there are fewer than *ten million* men who might be a suspect?

Yes.

And the chances are one in *eleven million* of the DNA belonging to someone other than Legere?

Yes.

The implication was clear: Allan Joseph Legere was *still* the only one in the country who could have committed the murders.


The courtroom exchange between Walsh and Shields was especially fascinating for Cindy Reese, a graduate psychology student from the University of New Brunswick in Fredericton. She was watching the final weeks of the trial for a paper she was preparing on body language. She observed hand gestures, facial movements, eyes, and reactions of the jurors, court officials, lawyers, witnesses and Allan Legere.

The DNA experts were especially fascinating. She said Kidd exuded confidence. He played with his moustache all the time and tugged at his beard, signs that he was enjoying himself. In contrast, when Shields was being cross-examined, he was sweating and constantly shifting his glasses. "He seemed really nervous and uptight."

"Legere looked like he was on drugs, really gray the day of the verdict. He kept swallowing a lot." She interpreted his body language as signalling disgust, contempt and anger. The rest of the time, Legere's face was very still, which didn't surprise her. "Usually psychopaths and sociopaths don't have any type of remorse so they don't tend to show any emotion. Somehow I felt like Legere expected what he was getting, like life had always played him this hand so why should society change."

Unconsciously, the jurors tended to move together, leaning forward at the same time and mimicking each other's gestures – an indication of closeness or friendship.

On the day of the final arguments, Furlotte "drank a lot of water, kept playing with his jaw, and his papers were flying all over the place." He seemed nervous and very disorganized.

Reese noticed one RCMP officer sitting at the back of the room who chewed his fingernails for the entire time she was there.

Her paper earned an "A plus" from her professor, Fernando Poyatos, considered a leading authority on nonverbal communication.

After William Shields left the stand, Weldon Furlotte arose from behind his table and announced that that, in essence, was the case for the defence. It was Tuesday, October 29. His announcement caught the spectators – ranging from law students to RCMP officers and members of the public – by surprise. They had jammed into the courtroom expecting that this would be the day that Legere himself would testify.

Meanwhile, across the hall, unshaven and wearing a black Harley Davidson T-shirt, Legere sat in his holding cell, silent, sullen. Later, he called his former lawyer, David

Hughes, and asked him if he had done the right thing. The two men had talked often before and during the trial. Legere was looking for legal advice and, in fact, had wanted Hughes to join his defence team. Each time, Hughes had said he wasn't interested in taking on the case and didn't know enough about it to offer any advice.

## NINETEEN

# The Verdict

The summations were done on Friday, November 1, after a two-day break. The judge had asked the jury if they were willing to work through the weekend. "God won't mind if we work Sunday," replied jury foreman Letitia Lancaster.

Weldon Furlotte began his summation by noting that a real trial is nothing like a *Perry Mason* or *L.A. Law* episode. "I don't have a private investigator to find evidence the police did not. In our system of justice, we deal with reality." That reality, he suggested as he stood at a lectern placed in front of the jury, includes the very real possibility that a jury might make a mistake and send an innocent man to prison. He cited the case of Nova Scotian Indian Donald Marshall, who spent eleven years in prison for a murder he did not commit.

"The only thing that is worse than being accused of doing something you didn't do, is being punished for something you didn't do," he warned. "It's our duty to protect the criminal justice system from falling below that level of protection. If Allan Legere is wrongfully convicted today, it could be you or a loved one tomorrow. If you have any doubt whatsoever, you must acquit."

Furlotte attacked the jigsaw puzzle that Crown prosecutor Tony Allman had promised the jury at the beginning of the trial. The jigsaw, he suggested, was really a web of

circumstantial evidence shored up by a parade of forty
so-called experts. Consider that a sign of weakness, not
strength, he urged.

Piece by piece, he attempted to tear apart the puzzle.
Nina Flam said her attacker wore a chain around his waist,
yet Legere had left the body belt used to restrain him behind
when he fled the hospital. She said the man who raped her
had a slim waist, but Legere had been on the run for "only"
twenty-five days, so he could not have lost forty to forty-
five pounds in that time. Why was it that only RCMP officer
Kevin Mole mentioned Legere having light-coloured pubic
hair? Perhaps because that's what he wanted to see since it
matched Nina Flam's description.

The attacker told her "the bad guy" would be blamed. "If
Allan Legere committed the crime, would he tell the per-
son it doesn't matter; he's going to get blamed anyway?"
Furlotte asked.

The much-touted DNA evidence cited by the Crown
failed to prove that Annie Flam had been raped before she
died. The fact that her panties were rolled down in the back
could have happened while she was undressing. Her broken
jaw might have been the result of a falling timber in the
burning house.

The use of DNA fingerprinting in the Daughney case was
even more questionable, he went on, since there was evidence the DNA work had been mishandled. Some of
Legere's DNA had turned up in a test that should have been
for Donna Daughney alone. "There is no way the Crown
can prove the tests were done right. There have been mistakes made and that alone is reason not to convict only on
DNA evidence."

The testimony of Dr. Shields threw further doubt on the
DNA work, Furlotte suggested. The genetics expert had
warned that in-breeding could wreck the statistics so crucial to the Crown's case. "I ask you not to put Allan Legere
on trial, but to put DNA evidence on trial."

Turning from the DNA question, Furlotte attacked the other elements of the evidence presented in the Daughney case. Police found a set of glasses at the scene, but didn't mention that at the trial. Why not? Perhaps because it might have hurt their jigsaw puzzle? A footprint from a running shoe was found outside the sisters' home, yet Legere was wearing workboots, police experts claimed. No expert had been called to prove that the ring with the red stone used to link Legere to Donna Daughney was rare. The hotel clerk in Montreal couldn't identify Legere as the man in room 1036. The man spotted outside the Daughney house by Mark Manderson on the morning of the attack didn't match the description of Legere.

"Allan Legere might not be the common thread here. *This* man," Furlotte warned, waving at the jury a copy of a police sketch based on Manderson's description, "may be the common thread."

As for the Father Smith case, Furlotte acknowledged that the crucial evidence was the pair of boots found in Bathurst – boots which police experts said had been used by the killer, and had been worn by Legere. Furlotte pleaded with the jury to consider one thing: RCMP Sgt. Kennedy had spent almost *six months* working exclusively on those boots. "Is he going to admit failure after all that time, or is he going to interpret success? I'm not saying he lied, just that there's bias there."

The fact that Legere might be linked in some way to the theft of weapons, clothing, food, radios and other items should not be a factor in their deliberations, Furlotte suggested. "That should be put on the back burner. The fact that a person has the potential to commit a crime is not proof that they are guilty."

As he neared his conclusion, the lawyer urged the jurors to ignore Legere's previous record and his behaviour during the trial, saying no jury wants to make a mistake and convict an innocent man. "We're here to protect our interests, not to protect Mr. Legere's interest. If there is room for doubt, your common sense must prevail. It's strictly a matter of common sense."

Tony Allman looked across at the jury, then down at the approximately eighty pages of his summation. He'd spent hours polishing it and more hours rehearsing it, "previewing" it a total of eight times in front of his fellow prosecutors and RCMP officers working on the case. By the time he got up to speak November 1, some could recite entire sections from memory.

The jury had sat through ten weeks of testimony and evidence – some of it, like the photographs of the victims, brutally explicit; some, like the intricacies of DNA fingerprinting, eye-glazingly complex.

Allman reminded the jurors of his opening statement, that the Crown's case was based on a jigsaw collection of circumstantial evidence that, when put together, could only point at Allan Legere. He cited the identification papers stolen from Bouctouche-area resident Fernand Savoie while he was a guest at a Miramichi bed-and-breakfast as a piece of the puzzle with links to many others – a man carrying Savoie's ID was on the train to Montreal right after Father Smith was murdered, the maids in the Montreal hotel identified Legere as the man calling himself Savoie; the same man sold jewelry belonging to the Daughney sisters to a Montreal pawnbroker; and Legere had Savoie's papers in his pocket when he was captured.

He talked about the testimony of the Nina Flam. "There was not direct evidence from Ms. Flam identifying Allan Legere," he admitted. "She was equally unable to *exclude* Allan Legere. And there were things said and done by her attacker that could point at Allan Legere. Obviously, the basic case against Allan Legere is not her evidence, it is the DNA, plus the similarities between all four murders."

As for the Daughney murders, Allman said the key evidence linking Legere to the sisters was the DNA and the jewelry. "It's their combined, mutually supporting strength as a pattern that's so powerful."

He spent a great deal of time on the boots when discussing the Father Smith murder. He described the work of an RCMP expert who compared thirty-two characteristics of Legere's feet to nine hundred other pairs of feet to prove he was the killer.

"It's a question of common sense. What real chance is there that someone else out there in the world at large happened, in November 1989, to have identical feet to Allan Legere, including that remarkable alignment of nail to in-sole to bread bag to heel with the indentation in Allan Legere's heel?"

Jack Walsh listened closely as Allman proceeded to discuss the DNA evidence. Walsh had written that section of the summation and arranged a signal to warn Allman if he was wandering off track – he would tap his pen.

Allman urged the jurors not to worry about the details of DNA fingerprinting. They only had to decide if the experts were believable. If they were, he argued, the conclusion was inescapable – the DNA pointed at Allan Legere.

At the same time, he questioned the credibility of Dr. Shields, the lone defence witness, saying his expertise didn't stack up against people like Dr. Kenneth Kidd. "Dr. Kidd is, we submit, to human population genetics what Wayne Gretzky is to hockey."

Allman wrapped up by recalling the torture and killing of the victims. He talked about the similarity in the attacks, the slashing cuts intended to cause pain, the crushing blows to the face, the bizarre final touch in two of the attacks – tucking Nina Flam and Donna Daughney into their respective beds as their homes burned down around them.

The next morning, November 2, as part of a five-hour charge to the jury, Judge Dickson reviewed the testimony and explained the law on murder. He told the jury not to worry about having to rely upon circumstantial evidence. "If there is enough circumtantial evidence, it is as good, and sometimes better, than direct evidence."

At 3:10 p.m. that day the jurors finally filed into an adjoining room at the Burton courthouse to begin their deliberations. Some jurors poured themselves coffee before settling into the armchairs around the banquet-sized table. Others grabbed juice and muffins from a bar refigerator brought in just for the trial. The jury room was stripped of all distractions, making it simply a rectangular space with brown carpeting, blank white walls, a coffee table, and two doors soundproofed with thick leather padding. One door led to the corridor near Dickson's chambers, the other to the courtroom. There was a bell the jury could press to let the court know it was ready to deliver a verdict.

The sheriffs carted in cardboard boxes full of exhibits and and an aerial photograph of the Chatham-Newcastle area dotted with pins. They left the scientific paraphernalia behind in the courtroom, including a plastic model of DNA molecules and a special light box flown in from the Ottawa RCMP crime laboratory for use with the DNA X-rays.

Dickson held back the videotapes of the murder scenes, saying he doubted any of the jurors would want to watch them again. He'd written more than three hundred pages of notes during the trial and told the jury he could help if they had trouble remembering something. He didn't mention a series of sketches he had done of some of the witnesses.

At the opposite end of the courthouse, everyone settled in to wait for the verdict. Guards pulled tables across the hallways to block anyone from slipping past. Most of those who bet $2 on when the jury would return with a verdict thought jurors would stretch the deliberations out to the next morning so no one would doubt their fairness.

TV crews flipped over their equipment chests to use as tables and chairs for games of backgammon and chess. Some prepared background stories. CBC-TV reporter Carol Adams beaded a pair of moccasins as a Christmas present for her niece. Legere killed time doing crossword puzzles in his holding cell. Dickson sat in his chambers sipping his favourite juice, Ocean Spray Cranberry Cocktail, and flipped through the pages of a favourite travel book, *Round the World in 21 Days on $1,000.*

The first day of deliberations ended after three hours when the jurors announced they were going for supper and would return the next morning after spending the night sequestered at a hotel guarded by six sheriff's deputies.

The jurors had celebrated a few birthdays during the trial and already had plans for a reunion the following spring once one woman returned from her condominium in Florida. Until the expulsion of Moorcraft, the six-man, six-woman group was evenly split between smokers and non-smokers. The woman who served them lunch five days a week for three months at her country inn a few miles from the courthouse, learned to read their moods through their faces. "Some days, they seemed light-hearted, some days sombre. You could always tell by their faces how things were going." A telephone at the inn allowed one juror to keep tabs on his janitorial business. Messages were left there for him and he would make business calls during lunch. The jurors ate lightly and often did their own dishes to help the owner, who was studying abnormal psychology at university. No one ever mentioned Moorcraft. After his expulsion, the other jurors refused even to sit in the chair he had used at lunch each day.

Around midnight Saturday, the fire alarm at the jurors' hotel, the Fredericton Inn, went off and the building was evacuated. The guards scrambled to keep the jurors away from other guests milling around in the parking lot.

Sunday morning, the jury returned to the courthouse to begin deliberating once more. They brought with them gifts for the innkeeper and deputy sheriff Les Sears. When the innkeeper received hers at lunch, she took it as a sign that there would be a verdict that afternoon.

Allman spent the hours reading a paperback. Sleeth

stayed out of sight. Furlotte sat with his wife in the waiting area most of the time and chatted easily with reporters.

Prosecutor Jack Walsh paced through the waiting area. He was eager for the trial to end so he could return to his wife and two young daughters. During the trial, they had sent him a box of cookies containing a note saying "We love you and miss you." When the cookies disappeared, Walsh asked the RCMP to search the courthouse. The cookies turned up the next day in the jury room. They'd been mixed up with snacks intended for the jury. Waiting for the jury's verdict had him on edge. He kept running the trial through his mind. Saturday evening, he went for supper with Allman and Sleeth at a restaurant across the river from the courthouse. Walsh kept talking about the trial, wondering aloud if anything should have been done differently. When the waitress arrived with an order of french fries for Walsh, she found him staring into space. She turned to the other people at the table for help. They had to raise their voices to get his attention.

The prosecutors had become close during the long trial, despite having very different interests. Allman loved classical music, literary fiction and tennis. In fact, he played frequently at the indoor club adjacent to the Howard Johnson's where they stayed. When his tennis racquet was stolen mid-way through the trial, he borrowed one from a friend so he could keep playing. Walsh, on the other hand, preferred to go over the case in his room while sitting around in his underwear and listening to country music. Walsh and Allman had adjoining rooms and soon Walsh's interest in country music was rubbing off on his colleagues. One day a reporter heard Allman humming a country tune while walking down the corridor of the Burton courthouse.

As Sunday morning dragged on without a verdict, people began to wonder if something was wrong. There were rumours one female juror just could not believe that a man as charming as Legere had committed such brutal crimes.

Just after one o'clock on November 3, the courtroom doors
swung open and the sheriff announced the jury was returning. Most people had gone for lunch after being told the jury
would be out until two o'clock. The jurors, it seemed, were
having difficulty understanding the definition of murder –
including manslaughter. They handed Dickson a list of
questions. They wanted him to define second-degree murder and explain what category a murder would fall under if
the attacker killed someone recklessly, without thinking.
When that was done, the jury returned to their deliberations. People took it as a sign they were close to a verdict.

Legere, meanwhile, busied himself in his cell. On the
door he drew a tiny tombstone and fresh grave. The epitaph
read *Dickson 1992*. Beside it Legere scribbled, "Judge D.
Dickson died in 1992. Now he sucks dicks in hell. The
cocksucker!! Up yours Judge Dickson, you asshole." He
signed it with his trademark – a happy face.

4:15 p.m. Sunday, November 3.

An unusual coral-coloured sunset lit up the early evening sky. It was unseasonably warm with fog rising from
the river nearby into the still air, catching the colours of the
setting sun.

Inside the Burton courthouse, the jury was going over
the charges one last time. At last, after thirteen hours of
deliberations spread over two days, they had agreed on a
verdict. Deputy sheriff Les Sears informed Mr. Justice
David Dickson, who then told him to announce that the
court would be back in session in a few minutes. Reporters
and spectators had turned the courthouse lobby into an
impromptu campground, sprawling on the floors playing
cards and board games, eating cookies and candy. Some
reporters, facing a 6:00 p.m. deadline, had already written
their stories and were simply waiting to plug in the verdict.
Sears walked out the courtroom doors. "We're going back
in shortly," he shouted.

People jumped up from the lobby floor and rushed to

pack up their food and equipment. Computers, TV cameras, plastic tables, everything had to be dragged back out of the building before court reconvened. That was the deal the reporters had made with court officials who had relaxed normally strict rules during the long wait.

People lined up impatiently to go through the airport-style metal detector next to the courtroom door. The line-up formed a long "U" around the lobby. Kas Roussy, the CBC-TV reporter with *The National*, jokingly sang a few bars from "My Way" – "And so I face, the final curtain ..." The teenage daughter of Legere-supporter Lois Gaunce and two of her friends were in the line-up as well. All three looked around, seemingly disgusted at the reporters, who were laughing and joking.

By 4:45 the lobby was empty as everyone had crowded into the courtroom. Crown prosecutors Tony Allman, Jack Walsh and Graham Sleeth walked past the spectators and sat down. Walsh appeared tense. The ten weeks of trial had stripped nearly twenty pounds off his muscular frame. Furlotte rushed in, flustered after one final argument with his client. Legere was refusing to leave his holding cell, despite pleas from Furlotte and warnings from the judge that he would be carried in if he refused to come voluntarily. "All rise," Les Sears called out as Judge Dickson entered the room.

4:50. 4:55. Still no Legere. Dickson ignored the packed courtroom, staring instead at the door on his left through which Legere, hopefully, would be brought in. The room was quiet. People looked at each other, some whispered. What was taking so long?

Suddenly, the door opened. The threat of four burly officers dragging him out of his holding cell and into the courtroom had changed Allan Legere's mind. He was handcuffed for the first time in the trial, but insisted that they not force him to wear a chain around his waist locked to the cuffs. Before allowing them to put on the cuffs, he had pulled on his sports coat so he could tug the sleeves down over them.

4:58. The five-man six-woman jury entered through a door on the judge's right. They had their heads down, barely looking at the spectators and ignoring Legere entirely. Their faces gave away nothing, except exhaustion.

Four times, the court clerk asked the jury whether or not Legere was guilty of murder. Four times jury foreman Letitia Lancaster peered over her reading glasses and replied, "We, the jury, find Allan Joseph Legere guilty as charged of first-degree murder."

Across the room, Legere nodded, as if expecting the verdicts. None of the jurors looked at him. Juror number seven cried and rummaged through her purse, looking for a tissue. For many of the spectators, there was a sense of letdown. After ten grueling weeks of sometimes horrifying testimony, it was suddenly over.

Allman, Sleeth and Walsh shook hands. RCMP Sgt. Vince Poissonnier uncrossed his fingers and shook hands with fellow officer Ron Charlebois. Both men leaned forward from the front bench of the spectator's seats and whispered congratulations to the three prosecutors. Kevin Mole wasn't there. He had decided not to spend the weekend hanging around the courthouse.

Furlotte looked deflated. He didn't bother to ask each juror to rise and confirm his or her verdict as is sometimes done. Instead, he rubbed his chin and resumed scribbling the rest of the appeal Legere would file from prison the next morning. He glanced over at his client, who ignored him.

After thanking the jury, Dickson ordered Allan Legere to stand. Following tradition, the judge ordered the shackled prisoner to surrender any explosives or firearms he might possess, which drew a nervous titter from the crowd. "In respect to your convictions," Dickson said, "on each I sentence you to life imprisonment without eligibility of parole for twenty-five years. Sheriffs, please remove Mr. Legere from the court."

"The trial's not done yet, Your Honour, we'll have round number two," Legere vowed as he was taken away.

Dickson turned to the jury. The law prevented him from saying anything in a case such as this where the sentence is automatic, he explained. "But I will say this, don't lose too much sleep over your verdict."

He then slammed the amount of violence on television and in movies, saying it helps create criminals. Citing his experience as a soldier wounded in Normandy during the Second World War, he attacked those who opposed gun control saying, "I can't understand people who argue there is a need for handguns and automatic weapons in our society."

Dickson predicted a bright future for DNA fingerprinting and credited the jury for helping make that happen. "I read a story recently in *The New York Times* about a man who was convicted of rape several years ago. The authorities were able to pull evidence from that case out of cold storage and subject it to DNA analysis. It proved the man who was convicted was not the man who committed the crime and he has since been released. So you see, DNA is a two-way street."

He complimented the prosecutors for "a most meticulous job in as very difficult case." He singled out Furlotte for praise, saying he had shown ingenuity in the face of extremely difficult odds and an uncooperative client.

When court was dismissed, the prosecutors made the rounds, shaking hands with Furlotte, the guards, just about everyone in sight. Reporters dashed up looking for a comment. There were loud groans when Tony Allman refused. Twenty minutes later, after reconsidering behind closed doors, the prosecutors relented.

"It's the belief of everybody involved in this case that it's finished, including the people of the Miramichi," Allman said outside the courthouse, blinking into the glare of the dozens of television lights.

Furlotte, in the meantime, announced Legere would appeal. "The verdict was basically what I expected before Mr. Legere was ever charged," the lawyer said. "Mr. Legere is no more surprised than the rest of you. You don't have to ask me if it was a fair trial. You were there."

Asked if he was going anywhere for a vacation, Furlotte replied, "Towards sanity, I hope."

RCMP Sgt. Vince Poissonnier was beaming. He'd been debating what to say the entire day. When approached by a reporter, he said simply, "I hope now that it's over, the people of the Miramchi can put it behind them."

Back inside the courthouse, Legere ignored the chicken dinner served him in the holding cell. (Chicken had been his favourite meal during the trial, although one day he had requested escargots – snails – and a guard was dispatched to buy a can of them from a local store.) Legere spent his time completing a four-page letter he hoped to slip to *Telegraph Journal* reporter Shaun Waters on his way out. His belongings, including the colour drawings done during the trial, had been jammed into two green garbage bags. When a guard rapped on the door and told him it was time to go, Legere carefully folded the letter over and over until it was a compact ball in his hand, then slipped it into a newspaper.

"Good luck in the future," said clerk Pugh, who carried the two garbage bags to a pair of waiting police vans. "Stick with your art," Pugh advised him. "I think you really have something going for you there."

"Why is it you only meet nice people in jail?" Legere replied, prompting laughter from guards circled around him.

Police hustled Legere through a gauntlet of reporters and television cameras. Clutching his newspaper, Legere looked from side to side, seeking out Waters.

"Let him speak," Pugh yelled at the guard trying to push Legere into the back of the van. "Allow the man to speak." The guard shot Pugh an angry glance, but even the judge had suggested the guards move Legere slowly so he could talk to reporters.

Reporters shouted out questions. Everyone wanted to know why he hadn't testified.

"They didn't want me to," Legere shouted from inside the van as the guard held the door open. "There was a lot of obstruction. They kept a lot of evidence back. I needed two good lawyers. Weldon couldn't do much on his own."

Legere managed to slide open a side window and shouted at the reporter he'd been looking for. He dropped the crumpled letter into Waters' hands, then the van rumbled down the driveway and into the foggy night.

"I wanted to testify at the conclusion of this trial," Legere wrote at the beginning of the letter. "But, since the judge had (earlier in the trial) refused to sever the murder counts, it's very difficult to divulge any possible knowledge about the comings and goings in 1989, when I would be cross-examined on all counts."

He accused the judge, police and prosecutors of conspiring to convict him. Judge Dickson blocked his attempts to get help for Furlotte. The police lied when they said he'd admitted being on the train to Montreal. The DNA experts faked the lab results to implicate him.

He'd added a quick note at 5:15 p.m.

"Well, just found guilty of 4 first-degree murders. It is no surprise with a panel of 12, where 6 formed opinions prior to being selected. That, coupled with a lawyer who wasn't able to do the trial by himself, as well as he was capable of doing. Take 3 crown prosecutors against a lawyer with 6 years experience. He didn't have ample time to do DNA witnesses, because of inability to interview each potential defence witness."

He went on to describe how he'd wanted to defend himself.

"I know that if I had had 2 good lawyers. One for DNA, and one for 240 plus witness & to seek out defence witnesses, I would have done better. And say, 12 jurors with no formed opinion, would help. Smith case, for example? How many people involved? Death & robbery occur might prior to being found? Two parties to that house? Whose blood on door frame? Whose hair on Mr. Smith's legs? It matters not who trodden through blood stained floor, because so did the police & curiosity seekers.

"There are many things not put forward by the crown, since it could help my case. You never hear of such things. (Another word for obstruction)

"The judge? Biased against me and anybody who represented me. It showed.

"As I say, there's so much more!"

# TWENTY

## An Interview with Allan Legere

THURSDAY, *December 12, 1991. Atlantic Institution in Renous.*

*The high-ceilinged security room was split down the middle by a wall of plexiglass so thick it was clouded and yellow in spots. On both sides of the glass were stalls resembling phone booths. They were painted bright red and each had a narrow stainless steel counter, a plastic chair, a black telephone receiver, and a roll of toilet paper. On the prisoners' side of the room, there was a dark window on the wall. Behind the window was a control room where a guard hovered over a bank of recording equipment, TV monitors and radios.*

*Allan Legere entered wearing glasses, a dark blue velour V-neck sweater with short sleeves, green pants and running shoes. He walked to the booth quickly, reaching for the phone as he sat down. His hands were cuffed together with a short thick chain and a rectangular black box was braced between his wrists to prevent him from picking the lock. The box had rubbed his wrists raw. To keep the phone at his ear, Legere had to hold his hands to his chest as though he was praying.*

*On the other side of the glass was Shaun Waters, a reporter with* The Telegraph Journal. *For the first time ever, Legere had agreed to an interview.*

The first thing I noticed was the size of his arms and hands. Legere's biceps bulged beneath the short sleeves and his hands seemed to be too large for a man who was about five foot nine. I couldn't help thinking of the battered murder victims and shifted a little, back from the window. There was a large diamond ring on Legere's right hand and an expensive-looking wristwatch up on his forearm, above the handcuffs.

Legere leaned forward until his face almost touched the glass. His eyes were pale blue and expressionless.

"What's the use talking?" he said into the phone angrily. "I mean like, you guys ain't really doing much to help me. You could have did a lot to help. What I can't understand, Shaun, is why they won't print anything that's good, that's factual. That's pretty low because my name is ..."

Struck once again by the voice, which is pitched higher than one would expect, I interrupted to ask what he was talking about. Prison officials had decided to transfer him to the super-maximum security Ste. Anne des Plaines prison in the Montreal area, he replied, eyes flashing. He said he hadn't done anything wrong at the Atlantic Institution and his lawyer, Weldon Furlotte knew it, but wouldn't say anything to the media. (Police later said they had received a reliable tip that Legere was planning to take a female guard hostage at Renous. Hence, the transfer.)

"You saw the papers didn't you? I called Furlotte and I said the way the public sees it now is as if it's something that's being concocted now and they're probably saying, 'Oh Jesus, he's trying to escape, get rid of the guy,'" Legere said.

"The thing is a lot of people are telling me – why isn't Furlotte doing something? It's like when I was a kid and you go to a rich person's place and they let you play with them, but they don't want you in their house.

"In other words, he [Furlotte] takes Legal Aid money, but he doesn't want to do nothing for you. You almost got to prod that guy. Either he's awful shy or he just can't be bothered. I think it's a bit of both really.

"If they were going to do this, now that I'm suddenly dangerous, they should have done that from day one. If I was a suspect in four murders – whether I did it or part of it or whatever – they should have taken control and kept a strict watch on me immediately. But they didn't ... I was allowed closed room visits with case workers. I had open visits without any hassles at all. Nobody was bothered as usual.

"And like the papers often said, 'He has a way to manipulate.' Well the thing is, I don't manipulate. I'm the same way all the time. And as one guard said and Weldon Furlotte knows it, cause he's got the tape ... anybody could have run away here in '89.

"The thing is, I also know the policy in these places. You could have a gun, you could have ten hostages and they would not let you out the gate. Why would I give up a guy in a truck with a gun in my hand and then try it from the inside out? I'm too smart for that shit."

He switched topics.

"When I came back, I was more or less resigned to just doing my time and say, 'The hell with it.' I figured I really screwed myself up by running away because I would have got a new trial. I'm sure of it now, so like I kick my ass. I tell you something Shaun, like people think I liked to run away out there, but the fact remains I was out and there's nowhere to go. In fact, an honest free man today has a hard time to make a living and survive. What would Allan Legere do out there with no money, nowhere to go and with a $100,000 reward on his head? Where would you go?"

"Couldn't you have just gone to the States or something?" I asked.

"What would you do there?" Legere retorted.

"Paint?" I replied.

"How long would you last? How many times have you

seen this happening where guys like me stay out a year or two, but eventually it catches up to you?"

"Don't you have a trades licence?"

"I'm a machinist. The thing is you almost need a phony ID or something. It's hard to get a proper one with your right height and everything. I don't have the contacts. I've never been much of a traveller. Like, I've been around but never any farther than like Ontario. I've never been out West. So like, I was lost and actually I gave up. That's why they caught me there. I gave up. They didn't catch me. I knew where I was going. I was going into the hornet's nest, it's obvious."

Legere claimed to have one hundred pages of transcript from the police interview the day he was captured.

"I denied being chased by dogs, I denied being on the train, but yet, they went ahead and put every bit of information they could glean into that fifteen minutes around 7:30 in the morning on November 24, 1989."

So what did he do that summer?

"Well, the thing is…," Legere said, squinting behind his glasses. "Well, for one thing like, I can't really delve too far into it 'cause I still got appeals out there. But I can tell you this much right now, when they were chasing Tom, Dick and Harry, it wasn't me. They don't know really where I was. They don't know how many times I was gone or back. Later on that stuff will come out."

I asked him about the murders, but Legere waved off the question and started talking about Furlotte and the trial. He said Weldon Furlotte practically chased after lawyer David Hughes to get the case.

"Once he got it, he backed off a lot. He was under too much pressure, he bit off more than he could chew. Do you realize I has to do every one of these 240 witnesses? I had to write out notes every night and give it to [Furlotte] in the morning to photocopy. I did them and he was embarrassed because I was passing him notes. He may have had some of his own, but in the morning – and you can check with the court clerk Les Sears, he did the photocopying — I would write out everything 'cause he wasn't prepared. So I got a severe screwing and I never even got a kiss.

"So the thing is, he got a free DNA course. So the fact is, I got to stick with him because it would cost them money to get a new one. Yet if I asked him to do anything, he's not doing it for me, I got to fight with him to do something and he won't say nothing to the press on my behalf."

Why didn't Legere testify?

"I was planning on taking the stand from day one and Weldon knows that. But a few days before the trial ended he told me, 'If you take the stand, I won't do your appeal.' First of all, since August, he told me I'm gonna be found guilty because he's not prepared for the case. Very, very flattering to hear."

"Which murder did you want to testify about – the Smith case?"

"Well, first of all, I could have explained a lot of that stuff. It's not hard to explain that. They don't know what happened to Smith. They don't know when he was killed. He could have been dead for twenty-four hours. Shaun, look it, it wouldn't matter who was in the boots. You could have walked through that house the next day. Follow me? That's one example. I won't be specific on which charge but the thing is it was just too much for the jury to hear – three different cases at once."

What about the DNA?

"Don't forget, we're relying on the one RCMP – the blond fella – Dr. Bowen. You must remember that all the other fellas mimicked him. All they did was read his test results, so they're probably telling the truth. But how do we know about Bowen? He made the tests over a period of a year. There wasn't any great hurry for such an important case. He sure took his time. I mean, how many more samples did he play with?"

Legere complained, too, about the way police treated him when he was captured. He said they took the bloody

Kleenex from him illegally and lied at the trial about what he told them. "I was exhausted. I asked for a lawyer at least twelve times and that's on the tape transcript, a hundred pages. I have it. They erased the first hour and a half on the tape. It suddenly, mysteriously erased. They searched me quick. They jumped back out of the cell again and left me there naked, no mattress, no nothing. It was cold. Nobody was in the cell asking me questions and Allan Legere was not motormouthing around. That was a great ploy. (RCMP Sgt.) Mason Johnston did the same thing at the '87 Glendenning trial in January. He kept on saying that I said this and that. There was no evidence at all – no tape recording, no statement and they got me convicted."

"Do you think the police are trying to get you?"

"The RCMP and the Chatham police used to always try to get me to turn my friends in from Chatham Head. And whenever I stopped talking to them at all, they started stopping my car every time I went for a drive. They would search my car. They pulled in my driveway as my ex-wife, Marilyn, could tell you and used to say, 'How ya doing, Al?' I'd have to kick them out of the driveway. Just intimidate and try to ridicule me. They'd see me walking down to Chatham and I'd have a book in my pocket and they'd say, 'What do you got in your pocket, Al? A dirty book?' They used to harass me all the time. That's the main reason I broke up with my wife in '77."

"Do you miss her?"

"Oh ya, but I figured my name would have dragged her and the kids around here and they would never live a normal life. It wasn't that I wanted to go out and party all the time. I just thought it was the best thing. Around June before school got out in '77, my young fella, Dean – I just got out of jail for three months for fighting – said the kids were saying, 'My father said your father is in jail.' I thought, 'Oh, now this is gonna start.' I told my wife to go on up to my sister's in Ottawa and live there. I'll move up after."

"What about your daughter?"

"Yes, I spoke to my mother-in-law in Chatham in '85 when I got out of prison. She said my daughter, Natasha, had been home that summer and asking about me. The thing is, I didn't think it was wise to keep going back to the kids. I figured once they got old enough, if they wanted to talk to me, they could talk to me."

"Have they talked to you?"

"No, I think my wife got it into their heads a bit."

"Do you miss them?"

"Oh yes, I miss them. Actually what I'm really sorry about is that Glendenning thing. It went right haywire. That was not meant to happen."

"What do you mean?"

"I was there for money. Oh Jesus Christ, I regret that. People think I must be some hard son of a whore, must be a bad nut. When I got there the door was being crashed open and Curtis and Matchett were in the middle of a fight with two people. But they didn't know [the Glendennings] were home. Apparently the man was lying down and the woman was in the kitchen. I've had people say to me, 'Why didn't you stop the beating or something?' The only thing I seen is the old man ran towards the road and Curtis tripped him. I said 'Take him in the house.' I stopped Curtis and picked up the man off the ground. Matchett had the woman in the kitchen. All I did was stay in the porch and when Matchett came up to me once – I didn't see the woman anymore. I found out later he shoved a chair into her. But he come out and said the numbers are such and such. I ran up the stairs. I tried the safe. I said it's not working, I'm going to go get the car. I didn't have no mask on. I wasn't even in the house when the man died."

"Why didn't you go to the police?"

"I thought my life was over. Yeah, at that time I figured at the most it was going to be was armed robbery or violence. Christine [Searle] said she found out from her mother. I sat down in a chair. I didn't want nothing to do with nothing. She said, 'What are you looking so sad for?

You didn't do it.' I said, 'Yeah, but I'm going for it because they wanted me, eh."

Legere blamed his criminal career on the people he associated with in the 1970s. He said his friends included a man who worshipped black magic, another who used to poke out cows' eyes with a knife, and the man who cut the head off a corpse and left it on a Chatham Head doorstep (mentioned earlier in the book). "I saw [him] with the head. He just came down the road one day and he had it in a bag. He was tossing it around like a football. He didn't know who the person was. It was just random. Actually, I felt bad about it. He put it on somebody's steps as a joke."

"What were you like back then?"

"I always had a car and had money. I didn't think I was going to end up in prison."

He said in the early seventies people at the local paper mill were jealous of him being a well-paid machinist.

"How about your days as a student?"

"That was the biggest thing – to go to school and not have enough money for the right books and clothes. Oh Jesus, even today, if you say you're from Chatham Head, you get looks. If your name is French, it's even worse, even if you don't speak it. I remember when I was a kid – 15 or so, and you go to town to see a show, people would say, 'Watch out for him, he's from Chatham Head.' And if you were poor, you were really screwed.

"Me and my buddies, like, they would say, 'Keep your eyes on them guys.' When I was 16, I was still going to confession every week and everything. I came home from Ontario in November of '71 and I had a '69 Cobra Jet [car] and I remember going into a Pizza Delight here in Newcastle. I remember two guys standing at the counter and the car was rumbling eh, I heard a guy saying, 'That belongs to Allan Legere, you know, the guy from Chatham Head.'

"And I had not been there since 1967 – I couldn't fuckin' believe it. Here I come back, went away and took a trade and everything, and they still won't forget me. What happens to a guy is he should move away and stay away, because I had a chip on my shoulder where I said you're not going to fuckin' well move me. That's what happens. You stay for spite and this area is spiteful ... if you're not in, you're out."

"What were you like as a kid?"

"I used to be on the river skating and that stuff. I know a lot of rich people, too, a lot of their daughters. I get along with all of them. We had a poor childhood, single parent stuff. Like, you know, there's nothing there. You see other people with fathers and you don't have any. You miss out on an awful lot of things. There was lots of times when we were hungry. We never used to have running water when we were kids. We never even had a well one time back in the fifties. We used to have to carry [water] back from neighbours. I think it was '59 before we had our own running water. I was about 11 years old.

"When you were from Chatham Head, you were screwed, that was it, right from the beginning. Teachers hated to go there except for one, who was real nice."

Legere reeled off the names of more than one dozen classmates from Chatham Head. He hadn't seen most of them in years, but knew who they were married to, where they lived, what they did for a living – even the criminal records of some of their children.

He remembered the first girl he "played doctor" with and a girl he used to throw stones at. He spoke fondly of a time in the seventies when he felt people looked up to him. "I always had a car, always had money. People figured I was smart. They used to blow their money. I was always kind of a wheeler dealer. I didn't spend much. I wasted more on other people than I did on myself. I liked the women."

"Do you have a bad side?"

"Well, I think if you put a guy in the right position, I think any man is capable of probably hitting his wife a slap in the face. I must admit, nowadays, I'm probably more apt to ignore it than I would back when I was say, 20."

"So you have a quick temper?"

"Well, it wasn't that quick. I used to take an awful lot of shit before I'd finally say something back. I've seen a lot of guys who are worse. I was never cut out to be married. I always wanted to be on the road."

"What bothered you about being from Chatham Head?"

"There was always wars going, real fighting and with chains. When we went to town, we stuck together. Nobody helped me. If you were rich and you had good names, you could get a good summer job or something. They were reluctant to hire you if you were from Chatham Head.

"My dad apparently was a bastard. My sisters say he wasn't very nice. My mother had to raise us the best way she could. She had to be a man and a woman. Wasn't much time for anything in between. That's where you lose out. You gotta be strict. There's no room for love, that there shit. She did the best she could with what she had. She never had the education or the means.

"I used to get an awful lot of beatings in Chatham Head. I couldn't go to the store without getting a kick in the face. Then I began weight-lifting in 1964. I took second place in Moncton in 1967 at the YMCA. I put over 205 pounds, clean and jerk, and I think I only weighed 160 pounds."

He still remembers the day his older brother, Freddy, was struck and killed by a taxi in 1956, on a road not far from his family's home. Legere was eight.

"I was looking out the window early in the morning. I heard the car screeching and going off the road. Freddy was well-liked. I remember all the people going up to the corner, then I found out he was killed. He was just like a father to me. I knew the guy that killed him. He did it on purpose. He steered for them, to scare them. He was showing off and it got too far. I never liked that son of a whore. One day I seen (the driver) when I got older. I always thought when I'd seen the son of a whore, I'd beat his face in. But when I seen him, I looked at him and said time really took care of him. He looked down, looked miserable."

In 1966 Legere was arrested for shoplifting – his first criminal offence – and sentenced to eighteen months, later reduced to six months. It still bothers him. "Why did everybody else get probation [for shoplifting] and I got jail? There were guys in their twenties and thirties at the old Newcastle jail. First time I was in, there were two guys forcing this Indian to have oral sex with them – 'Do it.' First thing I seen. It left an imprint on me."

He talked about living in North Bay, Ontario, calling that period the best time in his life. Between 1967 and 1972, he took a machinist course at Cambrian College of Applied Arts and Technology there and worked. His sister Kay also lived in North Bay at the time with her husband in a military neighbourhood.

"I used to race my car and go to the Y there. I was going out with a French bilingue, used to model for Kresges."

"Why did you move back?"

"We were in a big strike up there. The police started charging us for having rocks in our pockets. They were going to be hard on us. We were working for the strike leaders. They had us lawyers and everything. But I said fuck it and came back home. That was mistake number one."

He said he'd been in North Bay only three or four months in 1967 when his girlfriend, Marilyn, called from the Miramichi to say she was pregnant. They married the next year and settled in North Bay. "Around December 1968, I was screwing [a woman] on the couch while my wife was sleeping. That's how much love I had. I didn't like fatherhood. I didn't appreciate it. I loved North Bay. If I was out there now, I'd still be there. The only thing I ever got up there is a speeding ticket – because I was married and always working. I never did drugs till I came back to Chatham Head – marijuana in 1972."

He hasn't seen his two children since 1978. He said they're living in Ontario with Marilyn and their stepfather. His son is 24 this year, his daughter 17.

According to Legere, he drifted back into crime after

being laid off from a job at the pulp mill. The bills were piling up and he was arrested for possession of stolen goods. While serving his sentence, he was given medication that blurred his vision. He couldn't see straight when he got his job back at the mill and they transferred him to manual labour, so he quit. In 1979, he returned to Ontario for a few months, taking a job as a car salesman in Winchester, about thirty miles from Ottawa. He boasted he sold three cars a day there.

I interrupted to ask him if the stories he told police about how he lived before his capture were true, things like taming squirrels.

"Nah. First of all, I wasn't even down to earth for three or four days like when I was arrested. I was exhausted, like a person out in the desert. You're almost incoherent. In fact, [lawyer] David Hughes read a statement that the Moncton cops took from me here before they took me to court a couple of days after I was arrested and I said, 'Jeez, that doesn't even sound like me.'"

"Even if I was around here at any time, they wouldn't want to find the person anyway. If they think a guy's apt to hurt them or something, they're not to anxious to find ya. It's only common sense. I've talked to those guys [the RCMP officers] during the trial and I said, 'If they would have just told me on the radio, Allan, you're getting your appeal.' That's all I would have needed. So I got all panicky and impatient."

"Would you have given up?"

"Yes, really," Legere replied, his eyes narrowing, a slight grin on his face.

"You know, your mother asked you to turn yourself in?"

"They were using my mother and at the same time they were going out with SWAT teams and rifles. They weren't out to talk, they were out to kill. It doesn't jive with the way they were talking."

"You never denied living in the woods in the Miramichi area during the trial."

Legere ignored the comment and talked about how difficult it was after he escaped. He said he didn't know how to
get out of the country.

"If I was out there on the street right now even, I
wouldn't know where to go. No matter where you went,
you'd have to sleep some time. The first place you look is
your YMCAS and shelters, especially for a guy like me. I
have to laugh when they say he might escape again and do
this, do that. I've had it. I've given up on the running part,
Shaun. Freedom is nice, but there's no freedom when
you've got people looking for you with guns. It's not like the
movies."

"You're going to be an old man if you ever get out."

"You accept it. The thing is, if I'd kept my cool and not
run away, I'd have a better result today. I blame myself for
that and the administration here. If I was so dangerous,
what was I doing being a cleaner in the segregation area?
Why would it matter being here till my appeal's over? I
can't escape. If I had a gun right here, I couldn't go nowhere.
If I was out in the yard, they'd do me in, shoot me."

He said he didn't mean to leave behind the letter found
in the Saint John bar the night before he was captured in
1989. The letter was his "last will and testament," he said.

"How did you survive for eight months?"

"I'll tell you about that sometime," Legere said, wink-
ing. "You know something, Shaun. People think I'm right
bonkers and everything else. I could leave right today and
go and live and never bother anybody. All they have to do is
leave me alone. There are more guys getting out of these
places that are more apt to kill you than I am."

"What would you do?"

"I've learned a lot in the last five years. I've seen a lot of
things. I feel like I'm different inside, you know. I'll live till
I die and if I die tomorrow, I don't give a goddamn. But the
thing is, I try to live each day as I can and I always try to
make myself a little better each day. Like I say, there were
ways to get me back to prison in 1989. If they wanted to get

a guy back, you use sugar … you don't use machine guns. They were like a dog chasing a car – when he catches it, he doesn't know what to do with it."

He said he used to listen to the radio during his seven-month escape and laugh at the reports on him.

"Who do you think killed those people?"

"Well, I've got my ideas. I do."

"Why don't you tell the police?"

"Well, on October 13 for example [the night the Daughney sisters were murdered] if you checked in the police files, you would see there are more break-and-enters that happened that same night. One woman had her place broken into, another guy had his cable wire cut."

Legere said one of the other suspects in the Daughney murders failed the polygraph. "They asked him. 'Did you kill those women?' Flunked. 'Did you know who did it?' Flunked. 'Were you in the area?' Flunked. They went and searched his house in Chatham Head and found sperm all over his bed and his walls. He hung around the Fitness Warehouse the same time as the Daughney girls. He knows me real well. He lifts weights, he's real strong. He hates women." Legere stared at me.

"So you can honestly say you didn't kill any of those people?"

"Let's put it this way. I know what's going on pretty well in a lot of those cases, you know."

"What do you mean?"

"I can't be specific. That's not the first thing. Police don't care who else was involved. In the John Glendenning thing, they said I was the ring leader but I didn't have to tell them guys to do anything." Legere lowered his voice to a whisper. "Hey, Shaun, maybe Lois [Gaunce] told you, the cops are positive, well maybe not positive, that Curtis and Matchett killed another man in Saint John three months before the Glendennings."

"Are you trying to tell me you didn't kill any of the people, but you know who did?"

"I didn't kill the people, but I have an idea. I know more than what I have been saying. Like I say, Weldon doesn't want me taking the stand."

"If you had taken the stand, could you have explained everything?"

"Well, I wanted to explain one thing real good. The thing is it would have shed a lot of light on several issues and it would have cast doubt on a lot of other issues."

"What issues?"

"Well, if they would have been so wrong about one thing, it would have also said, well, Jesus Christ, what about the other things."

"Are you religious?"

"I'm no fanatic. You can't use the Bible for fighting because it's supposed to be a peaceful Bible."

"Do you believe in good and evil?"

"Oh definitely. They're a force to be reckoned with, they're there. They are there, whenever. For example, you have the Archangel that never would have rebuked the Devil because he was too powerful for him. Just like in Second Corinthians 4:4, the evil god of this world is Satan."

"What does Satan do?"

"He influences mankind in wars and things. He can probably be more predominant depending on how you live your life, I suppose. you don't have to be evil in deed, you can be just evil in thoughts. That's why it says in the Bible: 'Do it in your heart, consider it done.' Like whenever I see people hating me and despising me, then in the next breath wishing people a merry Christmas, it's hypocritical. Because it says if you can't forgive the least among you, you're not forgiven yourself. See, the thing they forget, the more they hate a person and make him the least is the more they're kicking themselves in the groin."

"Is it fate you ended up the way you are?"

"Probably. I wouldn't wish this on anybody – it's not a very attractive lifestyle. I'd certainly know how to go about it this time. First of all, there'd never, never be any crime at all. If I had a second chance and knew about it, I'd be able to do some good. It would certainly be a lot different, I can guarantee that. I could tell every young fellow from the time they make their first error, it's going to escalate. You're going to end up doing the same kind of thing. Once you hit the pen, you're ruined. Who wants to hire you? Who's going to take the risk? Nobody'll touch you after that.

"Everybody goes to the pen and they have mental problems when they get out. They get depressed and try drugs to elevate themselves. That just leads to more depression. I bypassed that level altogether.

"I could leave here today without hatred. One time I could've left prison, even a couple of years ago, and be full of it. I don't know what God is saying. Like I say, the local media around here have thrown more shit in the fan than ten Allan Legeres could have caused. They've cast a pall around this area, worse harm than ten Allan Legeres could do. There's a lot of shitheads on the Miramichi but there's also a lot of nice people."

"Why did you yell out during the trial when the Crown said that the female Mountie you kidnapped was going to testify that you said you killed a priest?"

"That's not what I said. I told her I knew a priest. In 1982, I went into a house in Moncton down by the RCMP station on MacBeath Road. There was a pulpit in the middle of the floor. I said, 'Oh no, I'm in the wrong house. This guy's got nothing.' So I said let's see how the other half lives. I opened this drawer. It was full of pornographic material. I took them and laid them out on the sidewalk in front of his home. I thought he'll get a good laugh. At least people will know what he's like."

"What about your reputation for other crimes?"

"They've created me. They want me to be like this here. They want to see no nice guys. In the book [*Terror: Murder and Panic in New Brunswick*], they have Allan Legere breaking into motels and taking clothes off women. I've never been picked up, never asked about that. I've never done that. If I wanted to do a B-and-E, I could do it. You wouldn't even know I was there. But the things they're saying is strictly fantasy. I got charged once for B-and-E in April 1982. It was the first time."

"What support do you get from Caroline Norwood and Lois Gaunce?"

"Caroline and Lois have been real good to me. Two of the nicest people I've ever met in my life, better than both my wives. If I would've had people like that on the street, I'd still be married. They don't curse and swear. They don't lie to my knowledge. They're the most honest people I've ever met. I certainly wouldn't ask them to do anything illegal. I don't think they would anyway. I would never lower them to even suggest it. That would be using them.

"Whenever I hear I'm manipulating or hypnotizing people, that's horseshit. I'm the same way all the time. Come here next week, next month, I'll treat you the same way I do today. People think because some women write to me now that I'm always hypnotizing people, but I was the same way on the street. You treat them the same way on the street. They get to know me through the mail, then they get to meet me and they like me. They're not looking at the old Allan ways, the things they're saying about the monster. They're not looking at that part. They know I have a bad name and it will probably never change any."

"Do you realize you're still a prime suspect in the murder of Beatrice Redmond [she was murdered in March 1974]?"

"I agreed to meet the police and take a polygraph test back then. All my friends took it. I thought I'll get them off my back too. I said [to the police]: 'Don't ask me about any criminal activity other than this here murder.' But whenever they put the wires on me they started asking about the criminal activity. So, of course, I knew I was going to be guilty about that because I was involved with all the boys – they would say it probably had to do with the murder. So I got up, took the wires off, and said, 'I have nothing more to do with this here.'

"I don't even know myself who did it. I have my suspicions. She was the nicest person in Chatham Head. In fact, I can think of people down there who'd get hurt before she would ever get hurt. She was not a gossiper and she wouldn't bother anybody. I've often meant to talk to her daughter and say, 'I know you have been hearing a lot of things but I had nothing to do with it.'"

It was 2:30 p.m. and Legere seemed tired. He said he used his pillow cases stuffed with up to fifty pounds of transcripts from his trials as weights to stay in shape. He prided himself on being able to solve all the crosswords in the daily newspapers in less than a half-hour without resorting to a dictionary. He said he also liked to read books about the lives of famous painters.

Suddenly he asked: "Don't you ever eat lunch, Waters?"

At that, I collected my notes. Legere suggested I visit again, then motioned to the guard in the control room to let me out. As I started to leave, Legere shouted through the window. He gestured for me to return to the booth. Instead of picking up the phone, he leaned close to the window.

"Do I wish I could take back 1989?" There was a long pause.

"Yes, I do," he said, answering his own question.

"Do I wish all those little kids weren't scared to sleep when all that terror stuff happened?"

"Yes."

# TWENTY-ONE

# Postscripts

BERNARD and Mary Geikie still live next to the former Daughney home. It has taken two years, but they can now remember the sisters and laugh about the good times they shared.

Frances Pilcher, the oldest of the three Daughney sisters, still lives in Anchorage, Alaska. A few days after Legere was convicted, her husband wrote an open letter to the killer: "Now that you have been found guilty of the murders of my wife's two sisters, I can publicly say that I consider you a gutless piece of slime," he said. "Your victims have been women and old men and it is obvious you are too yellow to stand up to someone who could defend themselves. I hope your time in prison is a living hell for you and that you die there. Rot in hell, Legere."

Nina Flam lives with relatives in the Miramichi. She is often visited by Kevin Mole, the RCMP officer who helped her throughout the period after the attack and was with her the day she testified.

Mary Glendenning lives in the Black River area with her daughter.

Father Smith's rectory is home to another priest who serves the parish.

Tony Allman remains the senior Crown prosecutor in Moncton, where he plays tennis and listens to Mozart in his spare time. He is preparing for Legere's appeal of his four murder convictions.

Jack Walsh is still a prosecutor in Newcastle. He is handling another murder DNA case, this one in the Fredericton area. He is preparing for publication a number of scholarly papers on the use of DNA in the courts. By coincidence, the number of his license is BIN 092. It's not a reference to the use of binning in DNA fingerprinting, he says.

Graham Sleeth has been named a Queen's Counsel by the provincial government. Intended to recognize his outstanding contributions to New Brunswick law, it allows him to put the initials Q.C. after his name.

David Dickson continues to sit as a judge and bicycles to work in Fredericton. A few weeks after the Legere trial, he was handling a civil case involving missing jewelry. Three days after the trial, he joined court officials and the RCMP in the Burton courthouse while the Legere exhibits were packed and removed. Dickson took photographs. Court Clerk Gerald Pugh posed with one of Legere's sawed-off rifles. A transcript of the Legere trial has been prepared for the appeal. It's nearly ten thousand pages long.

The trial sparked at least two romances. Court Clerk Pugh began dating CBC-TV national reporter Kas Roussy, and CBC-TV provincial reporter Carol Adams started going out with prosecutor Sleeth.

Weldon Furlotte is handling Legere's appeal. "I'm still burned out from the trial. I'm handling the appeal because I did the trial. I feel I'm in a better position than any lawyer who'd step into it cold." Asked about Legere's criticism of his handling of the case, Furlotte said, "My client can sit back and talk about me all he wants, but I can't say harsh things about my client. The rules of the game aren't the same for both us." If he had it to do over, would he? "No. I would never touch it. It was just too much work. It's not fair to ask any man to do what had to be done in that case. There's no one man can do that case. Not if you're going to do it right."

An appeal court decision blocking the hearing of a case involving thirteen sex offences allegedly committed by Bill Kearney while a prosecutor has been appealed to the Supreme Court of Canada by the provincial government.

Fred Ferguson is still a prosecutor in Newcastle. He was to deliver a paper related to the taking of bodily substances from suspects in Saskatchewan in the summer of 1992. He is working on a lighthouse he bought a few years ago and installed on the corner of his waterfront property.

David Hughes continues to practise criminal law in Fredericton. Asked if he would consider taking Legere's case to the Supreme Court of Canada, he said, "I have always believed that lawyers should not turn down a case because it is tough or unpopular. Everyone is entitled to adequate legal counsel in our criminal justice system. Once you do accept a case, you must do your utmost to advance your side of it within the bounds of legal propriety. Because I firmly believe this, it can truly be said of me that I would defend the Devil and prosecute God. In light of this, circumstances permitting, there is always a possibility that I might represent Allan Legere in his future battles with the legal system. Allan Legere is a very complicated troubled individual who is perhaps a little too smart for his own good. He perceives the whole legal system is in a conspiracy against him for whatever reasons. The conspiracy includes policemen, prosecutors, judges and defence lawyers who he feels are all intent in putting him behind bars for the rest of his life. He has a craving for publicity and the worst thing you can do is to ignore him. He will, however, fight all cases to the last degree. If, after all appeals have been exhausted, it is still determined that he must spend the rest of his days in prison, he will still be convinced that it was the conspiracy of those in the legal system that put him there and not the evidence that has been proffered against him in his trials."

RCMP Sgt. Vince Poissonnier is still the head of the general investigation section of the RCMP in Moncton. Two days after the trial, New Brunswick Premier Frank McKenna called Poissonnier at his office, but he was still in Burton cleaning up some paperwork. McKenna left a message congratulating Poissonnier and all the officers involved in the case. In April 1992 Poissonnier delivered a lecture on the Legere investigation at an advanced homicide symposium in Toronto. He is investigating another Miramichi murder, also using DNA fingerprinting as an identification tool. He, along with Const. Ron Charlebois and Cpl. Kevin Mole, were awarded special commendations for their work in the Legere case.

Mole works in the finance section of RCMP headquarters in Fredericton. Mason Johnston has been promoted to a staff sergeant in the RCMP and is based in Moncton. Charlebois has been placed in charge of the continuing investigation into the unsolved 1974 murder of Beatrice Redmond.

Caroline Norwood was re-elected by acclamation in October 1991 to a seat on the municipal council in Digby council. She remains in contact with Legere and is still convinced of his innocence. His conviction was a difficult blow, but no surprise given the attitude of the New Brunswick legal system, she said just after he was found guilty. "It seemed to me that they never wanted anything that would benefit Allan to be in the public, but anything against him was fair game." Her husband, Laforest, sent a letter to the *Miramichi Leader* in November 1991: "Since Allan J. Legere has been convicted of committing horrible crimes, and since Canada does not have capital punishment, Corrections Canada should punish Mr. Legere by making him serve his twenty-five-year sentence in a prison cell with Caroline."

Lois Gaunce and Pamela Kellar have picketed the New Brunswick legislature protesting Legere's treatment. Gaunce's sign said "Legere's involuntary transfer bases on lie." Kellar's said "Federal court will bring out all."

Louise Legere continues to live in Newcastle and does not give interviews.

The Atlantic Institution made a number of changes as a result of Legere's escape. Among them: there is now a list of inmates deemed most likely to try to escape; and there are refresher courses for guards escorting prisoners to ensure they follow regulations.

Long after the fact, the New Brunswick and federal governments were still bickering over who should pay the costs associated with catching and convicting Allan Legere. In 1990, the province sent Ottawa a bill for $700,000 for the 1989 manhunt. In November 1991, the province said extra security associated with Legere's trial cost another $1.2 million, not including the costs of doing the DNA fingerprinting work, which had not yet been calculated. The province argues that because Legere was being escorted by federal prison guards at the time he escaped, the federal government should pay the bulk of the bills.

The use of DNA fingerprinting in the courts remains controversial. In April 1992, the National Research Council in the United States, a federal research panel, endorsed the use of genetic evidence in criminal trials. But it warned that unless nationwide standards are set for laboratories doing the testing, errors could occur.

The Legere case has affected people throughout New Brunswick. Duncan Matheson, who covered the trial for CBC Radio, discovered one day that his son, Quentin, and Grade 8 classmate Stephen Smith had composed a poem about Legere set to the tune of "Santa Claus is Coming to Town" for a class assignment:

> You better watch out, you better not cry
> You better not shout, I'm telling you why
> Allan Legere is prowling in town.
> He's making a list and checking it twice,
> He's living in the woods, eating rotten old
>     mice
> Allan Legere is prowling in town.
> He knows when you are sleeping,

*He knows when you're awake,*
*He knows if you have testified,*
*So run for goodness sake.*

They received a mark of 92 per cent.

The people of the Miramichi continue to struggle with the aftermath of the Legere case and an unrelated series of other murders which have happened since his capture. CAUSE – the Committee Against an Unsafe Social Environment founded as a result of the Legere case – has folded, saying it feels its work is done. It published a list of services for people caught in violent relationships. A 911 system for the Miramichi, promised in 1989, is still not in place.

A paperback book by Prince Edward Island author Sandra Mitchell, *The Miramichi Axe Murder: Was Robbie Cunningham the Scapegoat for Allan Legere?* was published in the spring of 1992 by Nimbus Publishers of Halifax. Mitchell suggests Legere, not Chatham Head teenager Robbie Cunningham, used an axe to murder Nicholas Duguay in his Chatham Head home in 1979. Legere has denied the charge.

Scott Curtis, 24, is trying to raise money for an appeal. He claims he, not Legere, was the "big man" standing in the porch of the Glendenning home the night of the murder. He says Legere went back in the house after he and Todd Matchett left and beat up the elderly couple. He is serving a life term in the Atlantic Institution in Renous. He is eligible for parole in 2003.

Todd Matchett, 24, is in segregation at the same prison after a rumour spread through the prison that he had sexually assaulted Mary Glendenning. He is trying to find someone to help him write a book about his life. He too is eligible for parole in 2003.

On April 13, 1992 Matchett was scheduled to hold a news conference at the Atlantic Institution in Renous to tell his version of what happened at the home of John Glendenning on June 21, 1986. More than twenty journalists asked for permission to cover it. The session was cancelled at the last minute, however, following an intensive telephone campaign by provincial justice department officials. They argued Matchett's appeal of his sentence of life with no chance of parole for sixteen years was still before the courts. Matchett's decision to "tell all" was seen by the province as an attempt to win a new trial based on the same defence Legere has used in his appeal: that he had been convicted of murder just because he took part in a robbery where a killing took place. In other words, Matchett wants a new trial because he says the Crown used the ill-fated section 213(d) of the Criminal Code of Canada struck down by the Supreme Court just months after his conviction.

Here is what Matchett had planned to say:

"I want the truth to be finally be known as to what really happened and who's responsible for all that happened at the Glendenings (sic) on the night of John Glendening's murder.

"You see there is too much misconceptions out there and most certainly in here as to who did what. For the last 6 years, Scott Curtis and myself let people believe what they had heard and were told. We never said anything against Allan Legere at the trial or at any other point in time even thought he tried to put everything on Scott Curtis and myself and he did a pretty good job of it. He had a great many people believing that he was innocent and that Scott and myself were the bad guys.

"But now with everything that has taken place with Allan Legere over the years, well I feel not that I can't hurt anyone by coming forth with the truth. But before I go on, I'd like to apologize to the Glendening family for bringing this matter up again. I'm not doing it to hurt them. I don't want to hurt anyone anymore. I met Allan Legere at my father's house in the early month of 1986. I really grew to like him in the months that follow, we became good friends or so I thought.

"I was approached by Allan Legere at my father's place

sometime in May of 1986. He knew I was trying to put some money together to move to Toronto, Ontario. He asked me if I would be interested in doing a job with him if one came along. I stated I would be. He then told me to keep our conversation to myself and not to let my father know what we were up to.

"A few weeks later, Allan Legere approached me at my father's place and said he had a job lined up. He asked me to meet him late that night so we could go and check it out. So we did, just Allan and myself.

"During this trip he explained to me that he had inside information on this job. He told me that he was told that there was a few thousand dollars in cash in this safe which was in this house.

"The second time we went to check out this place there was Scott Curtis, Allan Legere and myself.

"The third time we went up to do the job. Allan Legere had picked up Donnie Langan and myself and we had to go pick up Scott Curtis. He was at a private party with a few girls. We got there and I went in to get him and he was all high on some pills and he told me that he didn't want to go through with it on that night.

"I then told Scott that he should go out and tell this to Allan himself, so he did. I'll never forget how upset Allan Legere got. He told Scott off pretty good and he told Scott not to ever fuck with him or he'd punch his fuckin head in and he'd better not fuck up this deal. Allan told him: 'You knew we were suppose to do this trip tonight and I suggest you get in this fucking car right now and lets go.' So Scott went back in to get his coat and we all left. Scott never said a word all the way up.

"We got there and Allan dropped us off and parked the car down the road a bit and Donnie Langan, Scott Curtis and myself moved in from behind the house.

"I remember this very well, we'd all be laying on the ground behind the house trying to decide what to do, you see we didn't want to go through with it so we came up with a plan and we went back to the car where Legere was waiting and we lied to him by telling him that there was about 5 people in the house when there was only two and then he lost it again. He started going on and on telling all of us off and how stupid we were and how much of a fuck up we were.

"About a week later, Legere arranged to meet Scott Curtis and myself and so he picked us up and were off again. The plan this time was we were to steal a car, break into Glendenings' home and tie them up and get them to open the safe. If they refused we were to just leave with the safe, so that was the plan.

"I knew things were going wrong when Legere said we'll use my mother's car rather than steal one as agreed upon.

"So we get there and parked the car on a side road and walked into the porch area of the house at which time Allan tried to open the door. It was locked so he began to boot it in. By the second boot, John Glendening was at the door. By the third boot Allan's foot went through the door and by the forth boot Allan managed to kick the door in. A piece of the door broke off in the size of a 2″ x 4″ and fell alongside John Glendening.

"John Glendening had picked this piece up and I was the first to go in through the door with Scott Curtis right behind me. I had a sawed off shot gun in my hand with no bullets. You see, I left the bullets home so I wouldn't be responsible for hurting anyone.

"I was then beat over the head with this piece of door by John Glendening and he hit me about 3 to 4 time and I did nothing. I then turned around and Scott did the same and we both ran back out through the doorway. As soon as we got a couple of feet outside the door, Allan Legere then grabbed both of us and threw us into the house to face Mr. Glendenning again.

"Mr. Glendening started to hit me again so I hit him back in return with the butt of the shotgun on top of the head.

"Scott and myself got everything under control by tying up John and Mary Glendening and Allan would keep calling me to the door to tell me what to do next.

"I remember John Glendening managed to get up and ran out the door. Scott and Allan ran after him and caught up with him in the driveway and I looked out to see Allan Legere haul off and boot John Glendening about 5 times in the ribs. I remember thinking to myself that this is getting way out of control, Allan is getting out of control.

"They then brought John Glendening back into the house. Allan tried to stay hid out on the porch for a while longer.

"Next Allan called to me from the porch to tell me to turn Mary Glendening's head so he couldn't Allan enter the house from the porch. Allan then worked his way behind me and Mary Glendening.

"I then got back to asking Mary Glendening where the safe was and I was asking her where's the safe? and then I'll never forget this, she started to say to me: "tell him to stop, tell him to stop." I had no idea what she was talking about so I asked her what. She stated again to me: 'tell him to leave me alone.' so I then looked behind me to see Allan Legere with his hand up under the dress.

"I had no idea what to do. I wasn't into that trip, so I told Allan to leave her alone man and he told me to fuck off. And then I told him to come on man and leave her alone so then he finally did.

"John Glendening then told us where the safe was so we all went upstairs and I kneeled down on my knees beside John Glendening in front of the safe and Scott Curtis stodd off to the side of the room and Allan was directly behind John Glendening. Allan was sitting on the bed.

"John Glendening was trying his hardest to open the safe and I was helping him out as best I could but every time he went to turn the dial of the safe Allan would hit him very hard with an open hand in the back of the head. John's head would smash off the safe and come back and I'd be telling

Allan to leave him alone he's trying to open the safe give a chance will you. Allan wouldn't listen to me, he just kep doing this and I asked him to stop again and he then told me to fuck off and then John Glendening was unconscious. Allan told me to get Mary Glendening so I did and we sat down in front of the safe where it all began once again. Allan was off. I tried to help Mary as much as I could. I remember her telling me that she couldn't see out of her glasses because there was too much blood on them. So I took them off and gave them back to her and Allan wouldn't stop. It's as if he wanted to beat them and he did just that. Mary then fell unconscous also.

"So Allan then told Scott and myself to take the safe out of the room. But before we did so Allan stood over John Glendenning and booted him in the head several times before stomping on his face also. And Allan wasn't holding anything back in the way of power.

"I couldn't understand why he had to do all of this stuff. I told him once again to calm down and he then told me to fuck off once again and he pushed me into a wall quite hard.

"Allan then left and got the car and parked it in front of the house and he told Scott and me to take the safe downstairs and put it in the trunk of the car.

"I remember leaving the room with John Glendening on the floor still breathing quite well and normal. So then Scott and myself left to put the safe in the car leaving Allan upstairs with John and Mary Glendening alone. Three to five minutes later he came down the stairs to help Scott and me lift the safe up into the trunk and he told me to tie the trunk down and he said he'd be right back and he went upstairs and within a couple of minutes he returned to the car.

"But I want this point to be known that when Scott Curtis and myself left John and Mary Glendening they were both still very much alive. I can't say what kind of shape they were in Legere last seen them.

"After we got the money divided up, Allan told me and

Scott that we had better leave town tonight and he didn't want to see us around tomorrow. That was the plan anyway. But it's the way he said it to us like if we didn't he'd be coming after us.

"I remember Scott and myself talking as we were leaving town about how sick Allan was and why he did all that he did. We'll never understand that. I'll never understand Allan Legere."

Legere responded quickly with a two-page hand-written letter dated April and sent to a number of journalists around New Brunswick:

"Today, I notified my lawyer, Weldon J. Furlotte of Moncton, that due to recent remarks that my co-accused Todd Matchett (also includes Scott Curtis) was trying to 'weasle out' of his present life sentence(s), by casting the blame on me about the June 21, 1986 Glendenning case, and that I did the actual deed, ... that I would "willingly' undergo a 'polygraph' examination to these facts, which were echoed by Mrs. Glendenning during her Jan. 9, 1987 testimony at the Newcastle courtroom, shortly after both co-accused (Matchett in the morning, Curtis minutes before she testified) had "plead guilty"! Mr. Furlotte is to notice Newcastle Pros. Fred Ferguson that I will also take a polygraph for '74 Redmond case and 1979 Cunningham case.

Facts:

(A) Both co-accused were first in that house and Matchett beat the lady and Curtis kicked and punched the man. (And I left first.)

(B) I tried to open an upstairs 'safe,' and as I came down the stair case, both had Mrs. Glendenning (The Mr. was tied up) on the hallway floor. Matchett had his hands under her bra, and Curtis was poking a sawed off shotgun by her thighs. (She had untied herself after Matchett tied her.)

(C) After trying to open the safe, & failing, I told both fellows to stop slapping each victim, and I would get the

car, which was 1/4 mile away. I stopped both, from burning
(house) with victims.

(D) Upon return with the car, the safe was outside, & so
were they. All lights were smashed. Curtis said – "the old
guy ain't breathing" – I said – "impossible, he was just holl-
ering not to take his safe!" Upon looking, Matchett had
thrown Mrs. Glendenning in a room, all beat! And Mr. G
had a rag on his face & he couldn't breath. I took it off (off to
one side), but Curtis had already did his deed, which I
learned about only next day ie: – that he had died."

The Legere letter goes on to accuse Matchett of other
crimes allegedly committed before the murder – including
murder, arson and theft. "Basically, these two creeps are
just dying to get a reduced charge by blaming me. And I dare
them to pass a polygraph test on any of 8 items mentioned."
He ends his letter by saying: "Let them free and they'll do it
again! Lay down and do your time, 'Maggots' – you've got
lots of it."


On Friday, December 13, 1991 Allan Legere was transferred
from the Atlantic Institution in Renous to the supermax-
imum security Ste. Anne des Plaines prison near Montreal.
A tip that he was plotting to grab a female guard in Renous
as a hostage and try to escape was cited as a reason.

Legere's attempt to have a New Brunswick court ban
this book was rejected on March 18, 1992. No date has been
set for the appeal of his murder convictions. He has, in the
meantime, set in motion a $20,000 libel suit against the
authors and publishers of *Terror: Murder and Panic in New
Brunswick*. He has also signed a deal with a Hollywood pro-
ducer for "exclusive motion picture, TV and publication
rights" to his story. Legere already has had one hearing
aimed at having his security level dropped from super-maximum to maximum. Those who know him say he will try
to escape again.

**WOMEN WHO KILLED**
**Stories of Canadian Female Murderers**
by Lisa Priest
Eleven stories of murders committed between 1975 and
1990, by the award-winning author of *Conspiracy of
Silence*.
"Lisa Priest at her best." – *The Globe and Mail*
"This collection has rewards on every page." – *The
Toronto Star*
0-7710-7153-1  $6.99  8 pages b&w photos

**FATAL CRUISE**
**The Trial of Robert Frisbee**
by William Deverell
The critically acclaimed inside story of the 1985
shipboard murder of a wealthy widow by her seemingly
passive manservant. Written by the killer's lawyer — and
the author of *The Dance of Shiva* and *Needles*!
"The real goods from an ultimate insider ... Gorgeously
written. " – Jack Batten, *Books in Canada*
0-7710-2668-4  $6.99  16 pages b&w photos

**UNKINDEST CUT**
**The Torso Murder of Selina Shen and the Sensational
Trials that Followed**
by Doug Clark
Four years after the body parts of beautiful Selina Shen
were found scattered throughout south-eastern Ontario,
her former lover was convicted of her murder. By the co-
author of *Billion-Dollar High*.
0-7710-2117-8  $7.99  16 pages b&w photos

## True Crime from M&S Paperbacks

---

### TERROR'S END
**Allan Legere on Trial**
by Rick MacLean, André Veniot and Shaun Waters
Through much of 1989 New Brunswick was gripped by a
reign of terror. Four people were brutally murdered during
that period, and in 1991 Allan Legere, already convicted of
an earlier murder, was found guilty in those deaths. The
complete, definitive story by the authors of the best-
selling *Terror*.
0-7710-5595-1   $6.99   16 pages b&w photos

### THE DEATHS OF CINDY JAMES
by Neal Hall
Was it suicide — or murder? That's the mystery police
faced when the decomposing body of a Vancouver nurse
was found beside an abandoned house in 1989.
"Well-documented and well-written ... Intriguing." – *The
Ottawa Citizen*
0-7710-3784-8   $2.99   8 pages b&w photos

### CONSPIRACY OF SILENCE
by Lisa Priest
The powerful, award-winning best-seller about racism,
murder, and apathy in a Manitoba community. Basis of
the acclaimed CBC-TV movie. From the author of *Women
Who Killed: Stories of Canadian Female Murderers*.
0-7710-7152-3   $5.99   Photos